JUST – RICHMAL

Richmal Crompton.

JUST – RICHMAL

The Life and Work
of
Richmal Crompton Lamburn

by

Kay Williams

Genesis Publications Limited
Guildford

First published in Great Britain 1986

ISBN 0 904351 35 1

Published in 1986 by Genesis Publications Limited
Lynwood House, 51 Lynwood, Guildford, Surrey, England GU2 5NY

Distribution in Australia and New Zealand by

Hedley Australia (ISBN 0 949104 02 7)
4 Farm Road, Alphington, Victoria 3078, Australia

and

Hedleys Bookshop
150 Queen Street, Masterton, New Zealand

Printed and bound in Great Britain

Contents

This book is dedicated to William fans everywhere, especially

Roy, Gareth, Simon, Megan, Toby and

my mother

Catherine Merriman

Foreword

When I was a mere slip of a lad, waiting to discover a new William book was like waiting for a new Beatles LP was to be ten years later. William brought much the same sort of pleasure: a warm glow of identification with something cheeky and irreverent, without ever being malicious, inventive without ever needing magic or high technology, and naturally funny. William's world was a world behind adults' backs, on the other side of garden walls; a world of misplaced ingenuity, of great schemes doomed to glorious failure, of enormous ambitions thwarted. Not necessarily irrelevant and childish for all this; in fact, I find the William stories convey much of what adult life is really all about. The course of the affairs of great men and institutions in the world today is all mapped out in the William books.

But for a child it was also a hugely liberating world; a world of grubby nonconformity, of grazed knees, bad spelling and dams made out of sticks. It was a rebellion against the 'Put your coat on', and 'Don't go near there!', 'Are you wearing a vest?' and 'Be in by five' philosophy of the grown-ups. Richmal Crompton created one of the unforgettable originals of English literature. Though the apparently comfortable society in which William moved has now changed, his restless anarchic spirit should still be an inspiration to us all. I will be one who will read and reread Kay Williams' book.

Michael Palin

Acknowledgements

I am greatly indebted to Richmal Ashbee, literary executor, for her generous assistance and for permission to quote from her aunt's writings and to reproduce photographs from the family collection. Others of Richmal Crompton's family who contributed to this book include her sister, the late Gwen Disher; Margaret Disher and the late Thomas Disher; Paul, Edward and Kate Ashbee; David Lamburn and Sarah Welbourn. The prodigious memory of the late Sir John Wrigley, Richmal's cousin, was invaluable in illuminating her early years in Bury; a period on which the recollections of Ethel Crompton, Jane Golding and Mary Wild shed further light.

I am grateful to John Murray (Publishers) Ltd. for permission to quote from Dorothy Whipple's novel *Greenbanks*; to Anthony Sheil Associates for permission to quote from Fay Weldon's novel *Female Friends*, published by William Heinemann Ltd.

I am beholden to David Schutte, whose research brought to light two very early non-William stories by Richmal Crompton and who permitted us to photograph items from his own extensive collection of her works; to Terry and Erica Morris, who supplied valuable information concerning William's early appearances in *Home* and *Happy Mag*; and to Nancy Bowden and Bryan Blades, who nobly lent their complete collections of letters from Richmal. The debt owed to Constance Hall, literary *accoucheuse* to William, is not mine alone; though for her vivid account of his genesis, I offer my own thanks here.

Much helpful material came from the following staff and former students of Bury Grammar School: H. Asquith, B. Howarth, S. C. Jackson, T. Eatough, F. Stott, R. Calrow, R. Mace-Barlow, T. A. Whittam, T. Oldroyd and R. Taylor; of St Elphins School: Miss P. M. Robinson, Winifred Birch-Jones, Sybil Osmond, Gladys Thomas and Margaret

Morphew; of Royal Holloway College: Miss J. L. Hurn, Bridget Birts, Miss P. Comrie, Mrs W. Stiff, Miss K. E. Light, Miss K. Sampson, Anna Wilson and Lucy Shrubb; and of Bromley High School: the late Miss K. D. B. Littlewood, Miss P. M. Reid, Audrey Carr, Gwen Payne, Miriam Place, Joan Bramhurst, Shirley Baylis and Joan Young.

I owe thanks also to Philip Zatland of Broadway Communications Group (Holdings) Ltd., Ray Juson of Focus Photoset Ltd. and David A. Rego of Doubleday; to Mrs H. C. Barrett and Mrs J. Hirst, former and present Bury Reference Librarian; to F. Hilson and the Chief Executive's Department in Bury; to Peter Lowe of *Reader's Digest* and Robin Lloyd of the Taunton *Evening Post*; to K. R. R. Wilson, formerly of King's College, Taunton, and Old Aluredian Mr Trythall; to Robert Dunning, Editor, Victoria History of Somerset; to Rosemary Green, Wiltshire County Reference Librarian; to Ken Murrell, former editor of the *Bromley Times*; to Anne Fisher, widow of Thomas Henry; to Darrell Swift, originator and co-organizer of the annual gathering of William fans; to E. H. Burton, D. J. Venn, J. Young and Mr Wiseman of the London Brick Company; to the Balderson family, Jean and Simon Bannister, Jill Anne Bowden, the late Rev. S. Gordon Budgett, Dorothy Cleary, Mary Crawshaw, Peggy Davies, Joyce Evans, Paul Futcher, Francesca Hall, Gerry Haylock, Barbara Healey, Catherine Jay, Louise Leatherland, Derek Lord, Mrs B. Marke, Lynn Mirrey, Suzie Moss, Peter Openshaw, James Pargiter, Eileen Phelps, Nancy and John Rhodes, Miss A. M. Richardson, Dym and Arthur Roberts, Vera Shaw; to those contributors who requested anonymity; to Brian Roylance and Anne Simmons of Genesis; to all at Mid-County Press, especially Paul Howell; to Roy Williams for his illustrations and layout and much else; and to Simon, Toby, Megan and Gareth Williams for reading the proofs.

Who's Who

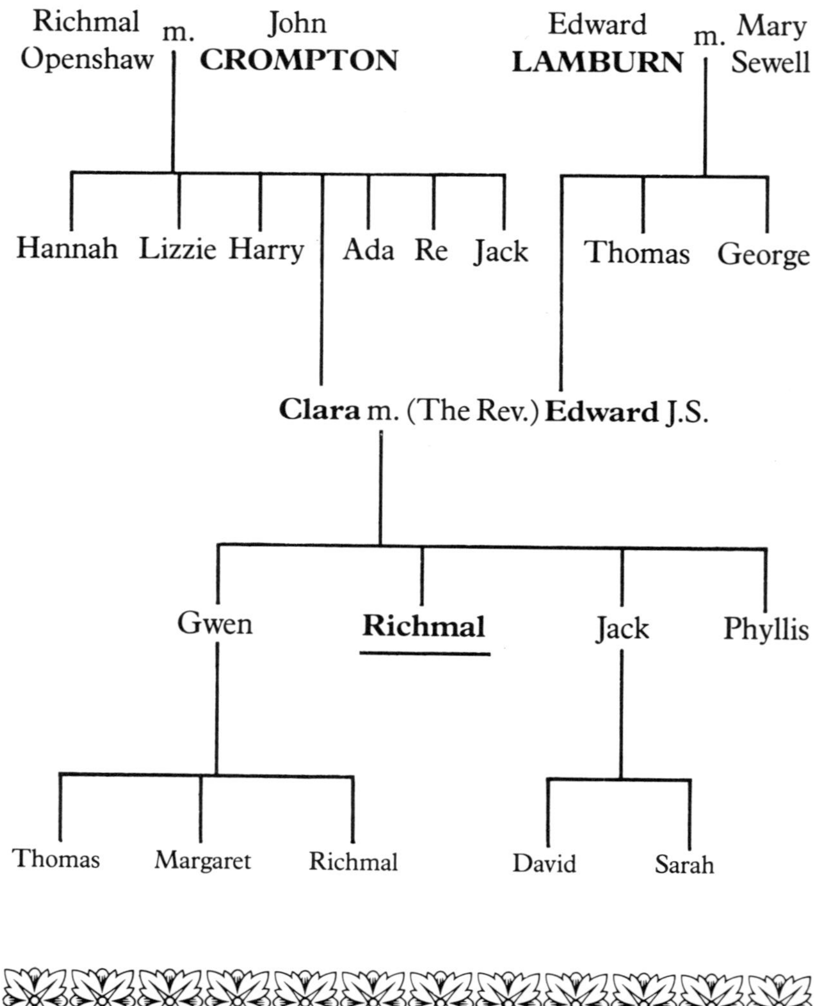
Richmal Openshaw m. John CROMPTON
Edward LAMBURN m. Mary Sewell
Hannah
Lizzie
Harry
Ada
Re
Jack
Thomas
George
Clara m. (The Rev.) Edward J.S.
Gwen
Richmal
Jack
Phyllis
Thomas
Margaret
Richmal
David
Sarah

Richmal

I

Nestled snugly between converging rivers, beneath the rising glory of the Pennines, the Lancashire town of Bury had once held many claims to beauty. By the end of the nineteenth century, she held none. Gross and grumbling, she lay under the tangible culmination of six centuries of exploitation: a sooty haze that hovered day and night above black mill chimneys, above mill-owner's folly and labourer's slum. Grimy tendrils reached out to the blue-green moors behind her, cutting off the last refuge from industrial clamour and ugliness. Bury, in her youth both pretty and tranquil, was now a belching harridan; a Gorgon the more hideous for being couched in so perfect a setting.

Virgin Bury had offered much – moorland forests, confluent rivers, nearby seaport and canal – and her suitors, importunate and often unprincipled, had been many. First had come the woollen manufacturers; then miners of coal and iron ore, tanners, paper-makers and hat-makers; and finally the omnipotent King Cotton. His demands were on the grand scale: more factories, more labour, more slums to house his workers. In less than a century the population grew fifteen-fold, from 2,000 to 30,000; and by 1890, the year of Richmal Crompton's birth, the rape of Bury was complete.

Small wonder that the principal element of Richmal's regard for her birthplace was to be indignation. Contemplation of Bury's Pennine backcloth would merely fuel her youthful resentment, for the hills that might once have framed scenes of pastoral charm now served only to enhance the desecration. The imagined, unnamed horrors of the slum area – not so far from the comforting safety of home – might be avoided; but to 'forget the snorting steam and piston stroke' was impossible. Though the young Richmal contained her sense of outrage, as she contained every painful emotion, within the confines of a deep inner reserve, her resentment on Bury's behalf would ultimately find expression. It was to surface in print in 1925, ten years after she left the area; in her third novel, *Anne Morrison*, whose heroine reflects with passion on her mill-town birthplace: 'She had bitterly hated those chimneys, hated the ugliness of them, hated the dirt and sunlessness and noise they brought with them . . . If right up on the hills you took a blade of grass in your hands and drew it through your fingers, it left a black smudge . . . '

Richmal's acute sensibility – a quality not widely esteemed in industrial South Lancashire – is unlikely to have been an inheritance from the distaff side. Her mother's family, the Cromptons, had inhabited the area for centuries; since Norman times, they believed. And her maternal grandmother's family, the Openshaws, could point with pride to documentary evidence of an ancestor born locally in 1295. The Openshaw pedigree, published privately in 1893 complete with coat of arms and motto (Just and Tenacious), gives prominence to Openshaws of middle-class occupation, such as clergyman and army officer; those of humbler pursuit (for instance, hat-maker and inn-keeper) reached its pages in name only. The two professors of music, father and son, who grace an early-

Victorian branch of the family tree constitute the only representation of the arts; though if little inclined to follow the Muses, the Openshaws indisputably excelled in another area of creativity. The wife of one nineteenth-century Openshaw, a clergyman, produced sixteen babies in as many years, and a seventeenth before quite understandably expiring.

Also recorded is the harrowing experience of an earlier Openshaw wife, who in 1800 roamed an Irish battlefield with her infant in her arms in search of her husband and finally stumbled across his dead body. This incident apart, however, the pedigree's only truly dramatic feature is the mortality rate of young Openshaws. With its air and rivers polluted, not only by industrial effluvium but also by the town's sewage, Victorian Bury was not the healthiest of birthplaces. Encouraged by powerful local reactionary influences, the town lagged behind its neighbours in all areas of social reform. By the year of Richmal's birth, local landowners led by Lord Derby were still able to ignore Health Committee warnings that the town's old-fashioned middens were injurious to the health of the millworking families living near them; and thirty years on, Bury aldermen were continuing to ridicule the notion that the middens might be responsible for the area's high infant-death rate. 'Babies under twelve months,' said one alderman in 1923, 'do not play around middens.' As the historian Geoffrey Best concluded, in *Mid-Victorian Britain*: 'Bury Improvement Commissioners were not a prestigious body and one must presume that their generally sluggish record was largely due to their inability to make way against the opposition of local property interests.'

The town's favourite son is Sir Robert Peel, twice Tory prime minister and founder of the modern police force. Though indeed born in Bury, where his father was a mill-owner, Sir Robert was raised in Staffordshire and educated at Eton; which makes his monument in Market Place seem disproportionately large. If length of residence were the criterion, Richmal Crompton would have a stronger claim than Sir Robert to remembrance by the town of their birth. She might also be said to qualify on nobler grounds, for in William she created a source of material wealth for this nation and lasting enjoyment for many another. The time is surely come for official local recognition of her contribution to children's literature: and what better moment for commemoration than 15 November

1990, the hundredth anniversary of her birth.

The grandmother after whom Richmal was named was born in 1833, the last of nine children of a local woollen manufacturer. Richmal Openshaw was the third member of the family to bear that unusual Christian name, which originated in the equally long-established Kay family. First bestowed by Richard and Mary Kay in October 1705 on their infant daughter, 'Richmal' was almost certainly created by the couple from their own Christian names ('Mal' and 'Mally' being then common diminutives of Mary). By the 1740s, several baby girls in the area had been baptized in the name, though its popularity does not appear to have spread beyond Bury. It came into the Openshaw family in 1782, with the baptism of a daughter of Thomas Openshaw (Richmal Crompton's great-great-great-grandfather), three of whose many nieces had married into the Kay family.

In 1852, Richmal Openshaw married John Battersby Crompton, fourth of seven children of a Bury chemist. John Crompton followed his father's profession, in a chemist's shop in Stanley Street, one of the four short streets in the town centre that now comprise The Rock. In the ensuing nineteen years, the Cromptons produced eleven children, eight of whom survived infancy: Hannah, Lizzie, Harry, Clara (mother of Richmal Crompton), Ada, Re (christened Richmal Ellen), Arthur, who lived only two or three years, and Jack. The Crompton parents must have counted themselves fortunate to raise seven of their children to adulthood; a cousin of Mrs Crompton saw seven of his nine children die before the age of twelve. Child mortality in Bury in the 1850s and 1860s was appallingly high, particularly during the summer months, when diarrhoea killed many who had escaped the regular scourges of typhoid and scarlet fever.

By the time Mr and Mrs Crompton had produced half their brood, Bury was in the grip of a serious depression. From 1861, the year of Clara Crompton's birth, the southern United States had little time or resources to devote to the growth and export of raw cotton; and by 1862, Lancashire mills stood grimly silent while the American Civil War raged. Despite the administration of a relief fund and the distributions of charity, hundreds of Bury families were starving; and the poverty of the millworkers soon had its effect on local trade. Clara and her brothers and sisters were all born above the chemist's shop; probably owing to the recession, it was not until 1871 that the family left Stanley Street and moved to a larger residence. Their new house, 210 Walmersley Road, still stands in its respectable terraced row: a three-storied villa with a long, narrow front garden and a small backyard. The move represented a definite step up from living over the shop. Walmersley Road led north from the town, towards the area in which the mill-owners chose to build their residences, well away from the offensive sight and sound of their livelihood.

The Cromptons were Anglican churchgoers, 'rather anti-Catholic', and much involved in the parish work of the church they attended, St John's. John Crompton had been educated locally, at the endowed Bury Grammar School; but the academic standards of the school had declined since his day and he decided that his older son, Harry, would be better educated at Manchester Grammar School. The Bury school's standards were soon restored, however, by a new headmaster; and Mr Crompton evidently felt quite safe in committing the education of his younger son to its care.

The Crompton daughters, however intelligent, could not expect equal deliberation on the matter of their education. For them, formal education would begin and end in the local Dame school. Hannah, the oldest child, is said to have been very bright. After leaving school, she expressed a desire to qualify as a chemist and eventually to take over the running of the family shop; and Mr Crompton was at first willing to consider this suggestion. But then Harry, for whom a Cambridge scholarship was confidently prophesied, announced that he also wished to become a chemist and take over the shop. It made no difference that Hannah had asked first; or that she was not only older but also much more capable and businesslike than her brother. As expected, Harry qualified easily; and proved, to the surprise of no one, a poor businessman. According to Hannah's son, Sir John Wrigley, Uncle Harry regarded the arrival of a customer as an unwarranted intrusion of his reading time.

Clara, too, is thought to have been quite clever. Her children were often surprised by the range of her 'snippets of information', though she modestly claimed to be merely a 'snapper up of unconsidered trifles'. The Crompton girls' Dame school based its teaching on that mainstay of the Victorian schoolroom, Mangnall's *Historical and Miscellaneous Questions.* (Its author, Richmal Mangnall, was thought to have been a distant connection; possibly a first cousin to Thomas

Openshaw, Clara's great-great-grandfather.) First printed privately in 1800, Mangnall's *Questions* was originally intended for the use of private governesses, who responded with an enthusiasm born, perhaps, of desperation; at any rate, it sold well enough to attract Longmans, who took over publication in 1808, and soon was being widely used in schools for young ladies. The questions, their author sternly warned in her Preface, had been compiled 'not as substitutes for, but as guides to, History':

> They are intended to awaken a spirit of laudable curiosity in young minds; and as they may again be divided and subdivided at pleasure, they will serve as Exercises for the ingenuity both of pupil and instructor.

Clara and her sisters, however, were required to learn by heart the answers to the questions; which suggests that curiosity and ingenuity were not much encouraged in their place of learning.

Miss Mangnall herself, however worthy her declared aim, can hardly be credited with having encouraged a spirit of 'laudable curiosity'. In conveying her own high-minded prejudices, she scorned equivocation:

> Why are the fine arts neglected in Italy, which once was famous for encouraging them? Because the modern Italians are sunk in ecclesiastical slavery, and weakened by luxury and sensual pleasures.

Proper but never prim, stern but never harsh, she set down her judgments with admirable clarity and a breathtaking assumption of infallibility. Of Rabelais, she declared:

> . . . his humour and wit were his chief recommendations; but they were greatly deficient in that delicacy, without which genius may sparkle for the moment, but can never shine with pure undiminished lustre.

Could any young lady have dared to challenge such a judgment? In the biography sections, men of letters, painters, sculptors, even actors were quite as well represented as statesmen and soldiers. On music, however, Miss Mangnall was weak: of the 700 biographical sketches she provided, only three related to composers. She disposed of Corelli ('an Italian musician') in four lines, of Mozart ('a good composer') in five. Handel fared better ('The greatest musician and composer of his time') with thirteen lines. J. S. Bach, of course, was neglected by all in 1800; but Miss Mangnall cannot be excused for ignoring two hundred years of British musical genius.

The early editions of Mangnall's *Questions* were nonetheless superior to the more comprehensive, extensively revised editions available to Clara and her Dame-school contemporaries. A succession of male editors over four decades had introduced a strong flavour of paternalism. Who but a male Victorian, in listing important social developments of the late-sixteenth century, would have ranked 'the invention of the art of knitting' above the revival of the study of anatomy and the compilation of the Book of Common Prayer? The editor of the 1876 edition informed the fifteen-year-old Clara, as dogmatically as his predecessors had informed her mother's generation of young ladies, that the world was created in 4004 BC (a 17th-century 'fact' regarded by Miss Mangnall herself, perhaps, with a degree of scepticism: it is not to be found in pre-Victorian editions of the *Questions*); and almost

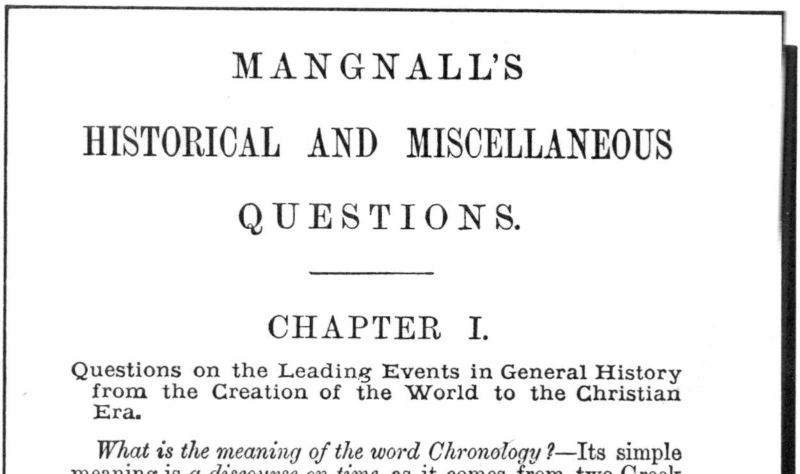

MANGNALL'S

HISTORICAL AND MISCELLANEOUS

QUESTIONS.

CHAPTER I.

Questions on the Leading Events in General History from the Creation of the World to the Christian Era.

What is the meaning of the word Chronology?—Its simple meaning is *a discourse on time*, as it comes from two Greek words, one of which (χρονος, *kron'-os*,) means *time*, and the other (λογος, *log'-os*,) a discourse.

To what science do we apply the term Chronology?—The science of computing the dates of past events.

With what event does our system of Chronology commence?—The Creation of the World.

At what date is this event supposed to have occurred?—In the year 4004 before the birth of Christ.

How are dates of events happening before the birth of Christ distinguished from those happening after the birth of Christ?—Those that happened before the birth of Christ or the twenty years after publication of *On the Origin of Species by Means of Natural Selection*, the biography section continued to ignore Charles Darwin. Clara was to tell her children that Mangnall's *Questions* had been her academic Bible; and certainly she and her sisters, if they retained only half its encyclopaedic contents, emerged from the schoolroom stuffed thoroughly with facts if not with education.

Four of the Crompton girls – Hannah, Lizzie, Clara and Ada – had inherited their mother's features and short but solid build, though all were spared her apparent grimness of aspect. Clara, indeed, was both pretty and handsome; a Juno in miniature. The youngest daughter, Re, was built on more slender lines and took after her father. Photographs show John Crompton to have been a handsome man; and the benevolent twinkle in his eye suggests that he was much more approachable than his wife, who was remembered by her last surviving grandson, Sir John Wrigley, as a 'splendid matriarch'. The youngest Crompton child, Jack, was to retain much fonder memories of his father than of his mother.

The Crompton parents were once approached to allow Clara to enter for an examination (probably in music). It is easier to imagine the final decision, that it 'would not be proper' for her to sit an examination, coming from Mrs Crompton's lips than from her husband's. Clara's reaction is not recorded; though it seems likely that she accepted the decision with equanimity. The journal she kept throughout the early 1880s contains no hint of resentment, no gleam of rebellion; nor are its pages much enlivened by the spirit she is said to have possessed. She recorded a life of busy contentment: helping with church societies, serving occasionally in the family shop, sewing ribbons onto hats, visiting the many aunts and great-aunts with her mother and sisters. She had a fine contralto voice and used to sing with Ada at 'suitable' gatherings. 'The new curate begged me to continue', she recorded after one such occasion.

Clara's journal is a closely written, meticulous daily record of the years before her marriage. Page after page recounts in minute detail the domestic routine and limited social intercourse of Clara Crompton, young lady; but of her ideas, feelings, aspirations, nothing was recorded that might give posterity a rounded portrait of Clara Crompton, human being. Temporarily immersed in those days when the earnest suitor is supposed to have declared his love with the most restrained ardour and frequent avowals of his unworthiness to aspire to the beloved, one is again disappointed. Deprived of a rebellious spirit in our heroine, surely we might expect a little romance in compensation? But no: Clara hardly mentioned in her diary the curate, who, after three and a half years of patient courtship and a two-and-a-half-year engagement, was to become her husband. She merely recorded, matter-of-factly, in the back cover of her 1886 journal:

Introduced to E. J. S. Lamburn	August 13th, 1882
Engaged to him	January 9th, 1886

The background of the Reverend Edward John Sewell Lamburn was virtually unknown to his surviving family. Those born before 1900 could recall having met his two brothers but knew little of his parents and nothing of their origins, beyond a mistaken belief (fostered by his obituary notice, which referred to him as 'a native of Taunton') that he came of a West Country family. In fact, he was born in North Buckinghamshire, where his parents also had been born and where, at the time he met Clara Crompton, his grandmother and many of his aunts, uncles and cousins were still living. The paucity of information available to the younger generation no doubt owed much to a fact that must have shocked the very respectable Cromptons: the Rev. Mr Lamburn's father was a drunkard.

Edward Lamburn senior, future father-in-law of Clara Crompton, was the sole black sheep of a numerous farming family resident in Charndon, a hamlet just east of the North Bucks/Oxfordshire border. The Lamburns had farmed in Charndon since the early 1600s; and before that rather more prosperously in the nearby parish of Waddesdon, six miles from the market town of Aylesbury. They had briefly owned, in Tudor times, a part of the 3,000-acre Waddesdon Manor estate; but thereafter suffered a sharp decline in fortune and status. Charndon is in the parish of Twyford, whose parish registers contain an abundance of Lamburns, Lamburnes, Lamborns, Lambourns and Lambournes; but in fact the area contained just two prolific families of similar name. Richmal's ancestors continued doggedly to sign themselves 'Lamburn'; the other family, illiterate, could only put their cross to whatever version of their name the current parish clerk devised. Though there had probably once been a connection between the two families, by the early nineteenth century there was a considerable difference in station: Richmal's Lamburn forefathers had become yeoman farmers, while the other family remained agricultural labourers.

The first of Richmal's forebears to inhabit Dunsty Hill Farm, birthplace of her paternal grandfather, was an eighteenth-century tenant farmer, John Lamburn. In 1819, his son William – the first Charndon Lamburn to describe himself as 'yeoman' – bought a share in the 230-acre farm; and in 1826, William's oldest son John took over Dunsty Hill. John Lamburn and his wife Susan, a local farmer's daughter, had already been blessed with five children in their nine years of marriage. (The survival of their first child, born six and a half months after the wedding, hints at the gulf then existing between urban and rural respectability.) In July 1826, when they took over the running of the farm, they were daily expecting the arrival of a sixth child.

Dunsty Hill, now owned by the London Brick Company and farmed by a tenant, has shrunk to about half its original size; but the farmhouse itself has changed hardly at all in 150 years. It is reputed to be haunted by the spirit of a male Lamburn, murdered in the country road – known locally as Lamburn's Lane – that bisects the Dunsty Hill acreage. He is, however, a disappointingly ill-documented ghost. His full identity and the period and method of his murder are unknown; and the present tenant, Mr Balderson, has never witnessed any spectral manifestation. He admits to having heard the inexplicable rattles and rumblings from above that inspired his more credulous predecessors with fears of a supernatural presence; but claims that the noises ceased as soon as the roof was repaired.

Haunted or not, Dunsty Hill cannot have been the most comfortable of places to be during a hard nineteenth-century winter. Set halfway up a lonely hillside, a good mile and a half from the few farms and cottages that comprise Charndon's main street, the farmhouse surveys rural North Buckinghamshire from a point of chilly isolation. With six large living rooms, a vast kitchen, washhouse, dairy and cellars, the house was no doubt a great deal roomier than many farmhouses of the period; but Susan Lamburn's efficient production average of a new baby every eighteen months ensured that every inch of the space was filled. The birth in April 1831 of Richmal's grandfather, Edward, brought the total of Dunsty Hill residents to twelve: eight children, parents, grandmother and a general servant. In

Dunsty Hill farmhouse, Charndon, Buckinghamshire

the decade following Edward's birth, six more children were born; but only two of them survived, and the Lamburns also lost a teenage daughter during this period.

Of the nine children they raised to adulthood, only Edward and an older brother, Henry (who by the 1880s was living in Brighton and designating himself 'gentleman'), seem to have envisaged horizons other than agricultural. The other seven stayed in the area and settled to life as either farmer or farmer's wife. Yet after John Lamburn's death (from 'natural decay' at the age of sixty-nine) in 1860, the family soon disappeared from the village it had inhabited for nearly three centuries. His widow moved out to Charlbury, Oxfordshire, where two of her children were by then farming; and in 1883, the surviving Lamburns sold their interest in Dunsty Hill farm. Susan Lamburn was nearly ninety when she died in November 1888 – three months after her grandson's marriage to Clara Crompton. Those of Susan's children who had stayed in farming rapidly followed her to the grave (one ended his days grimly as a pauper in Buckingham Union Workhouse); and by 1900, only the gravestones in Twyford's parish churchyard bore witness to the Lamburn family's long connection with the Charndon area.

Edward Lamburn, Richmal's grandfather, seems to have left Dunsty Hill at the earliest opportunity. He alone of the nine children was absent at the time of the 1851 census, which was taken just before his twentieth birthday. (Gentleman Henry, then twenty-seven, had not yet set out for Brighton.) At the time of his marriage, two years later, Edward was a schoolmaster at the National school in nearby Waddesdon. He was just twenty-two when he travelled to Guildford to marry 27-year-old Mary Sewell. The Sewells, a farming family, had only recently moved to Surrey; Mary was born and raised within three miles of Dunsty Hill, in Stiffland House, in the village of Steeple Claydon. Her family being as firmly rooted as Edward's in the area, it is almost certain that the couple had known each other from childhood.

Waddesdon, on the main Aylesbury-to-Bicester road, was large enough to boast a British School as well as the National, of whose 100 pupils Edward seems to have had sole charge. And with Edward's large family and her older sister (who had not joined the family exodus to Surrey) only eight miles distant, Mary cannot have felt herself too isolated when her first child, named Edward John Sewell, was born on 15 February 1854, nine months after her marriage. By 1857, however, when a second son was born, the Lamburns were living in Derbyshire, in the tiny village of Ockbrook, where a third son was born in 1859; and here, Mary may well have felt the absence of familiar faces. Ockbrook consisted of only church, rectory, small National school, two or three 'gentlemen's houses', a few pretty cottages and, next to the school, a less picturesque terraced row into one of which schoolmaster Lamburn had to squeeze his family.

Neither existing National Society records nor surviving family letters or diaries throw any light on the trail the Lamburns subsequently pursued across mid-Victorian England. But it is probable that these were turbulent years for Mary and her children. A photograph taken in Liverpool in 1868 presents us with a complacent Edward senior, a nervous Mary and a grave Edward junior, at fourteen already seeming to hover protectively about his mother and younger brothers. Two years later, a Shipley photographer captured Mary alone: a study in melancholy. By 1883, the year of her death at the age of 57, her husband was the National schoolmaster in a small village east of Macclesfield; in 1886, he was teaching in a village on the outskirts of Leeds; and just before his death in the 1890s, he was teaching in a Wiltshire village.

The regular movement of staff was not a policy of the National Society, although their teachers could apply to be transferred. Requested moves, however, were generally made in the course of furthering career ambitions; it was not usual for a teacher to move, as Edward did, from one small school to another. It is not unreasonable to assume that, in his case, each departure was made just ahead of scandal. Certainly, the National Society – founded 'for the Education of the Poor according to the Principles of the Church of England' by a body that almost equalled the Noncomformists in disapproval of the demon drink – would not have been inclined to treat leniently any member of their staff who was known to drink heavily. Edward was an alcoholic; and his grand-daughter's largely autobiographical third novel, *Anne Morrison*, suggests that his addiction had begun early. Of the early years of Timothy Morrison, Anne's father (and clearly identifiable as her own father), Richmal was to write:

> His father had been . . . a drunkard even before he married. His mother had been warned against him. But he was a handsome

> man with a tall figure and flowing side whiskers, and between his drinking bouts charming. 'I'll please my eyes if I plague my heart,' she had said lightly, and had married him. She had 'plagued her heart', poor woman, plagued it into the grave...

One wonders, in the light of that passage, if the Sewells' abrupt removal from their Buckinghamshire setting to unfamiliar Surrey had been a final, desperate effort to avert a marriage they sensed would spell just such tragedy for their daughter Mary.

There is little doubt that childhood was for Richmal's father, Edward J. S. Lamburn, a miserable time. The stress under which he lived induced nervous habits that would endure into his adult life: his speech, in public, was at first slow and deliberate and then gathered speed 'like a train going down a slope'; and in moments of tension, he would bite the little finger of his right hand and shake his head from side to side. He was to impart to his own children few details of the privations of his early years; but the little that Richmal did glean, in adolescence, inspired her with a horrified pity that found expression twenty years later in *Anne Morrison*:

> To Timothy childhood had meant a ceaseless fear of his father's blind drunken rages, and an almost greater fear of the fits of maudlin sentiment into which his old charm had degenerated, a heart-rending pity for his mother and ineffectual attempts to protect her.

The fictional Timothy Morrison leaves home after his mother's death, to become a student teacher in a boys' school. Edward Lamburn also left home, a good decade before his mother's death but evidently with the same purpose. By 1874, he was resident at Fullands School, Taunton, where he passed the London University matriculation examination. Little is known of this private boarding school, beyond the fact that it numbered General Gordon among its more distinguished alumni; for the past forty years it has been a part of King's College. But private education was not a tradition in either the Lamburn or the Sewell family; Edward's own father had almost certainly been educated in the Waddesdon village school in which he later taught. There would, in any case, have been little money to spare for his sons' education if Edward senior regularly drank away the salary that, even carefully managed, would have been barely adequate. His oldest son, therefore, was probably not a fee-paying pupil at Fullands but a pupil-teacher, earning his educational way.

In 1876 Edward junior took up his first full-time teaching post, at Bury Grammar School. His initial aim on leaving home had been to earn enough to enable him to follow an external degree course; his ultimate aim, to devote his life to the service of God. As a young assistant master at Bury Grammar, he led a spartan existence of work, study and stringent self-denial. He made it his duty to provide for the education of his young brothers (Tom, who also became a teacher, and George, who eventually owned a drapery), in whose protection he had left his mother. During this period he had also to endure the humiliation of visits from his father, asking for money to pay his debts. In 1882 Edward was awarded an external B.A. (London) pass degree. Two years later, he was ordained deacon and granted the curacy of Radcliffe parish church, about three miles south of Bury town centre; and in 1886, he was ordained priest by the Bishop of Manchester. Ambition, secular and sacred, was at last fulfilled. The newly reverend Mr Lamburn would sooner have been a full-time clergyman; being without money or influential connections, however, he was obliged to settle for the role of schoolmaster-priest.

The portrait of her father Richmal Crompton fashioned in *Anne Morrison*, ten years after his death in 1915, has preserved the image of a quietly remarkable man. Evangelist in spirit if not in name, Christian Socialist by instinct if not by profession, the Rev. Edward J. S. Lamburn exercised a profound influence, not only on his family, pupils and parishioners but on many others in all walks of life. There was much in him of Trollope's Josiah Crawley: the lack of desire for worldly pleasures; the total commitment to bringing others to faith; the joy of a burning love of God, and the attendant agony of a heavy spirit. 'Worn and stooping and overworked, but upheld by a strong will and a passionate, simple, childlike love for God', Edward was, perhaps, Mr Crawley on a smaller scale and yet distilled: the sin of pride, at least, could not be laid to the charge of the Reverend Mr Lamburn.

He first met Clara Crompton in 1882, three months before her twenty-first birthday. Their early encounters arose from the fact that Edward taught her younger brother, Jack, at Bury Grammar School. The Rev. Mr Lamburn had been calling at the Walmersley Road house for some time before it dawned on the Cromptons that this slightly built, shy young man was concerned less deeply with Jack's academic progress than with his sister's grey-blue eyes. But the courtship was to proceed slowly; Edward, not yet ordained, felt he must establish himself before venturing to ask Clara to share his future. After Mary Lamburn's death, in 1883, his father became an increasing burden; and by the end of 1885, Edward was spending much of his very limited spare time in Leeds, where his father now lived. Nevertheless, on 8 January 1886, a month before his thirty-second birthday, the schoolmaster-curate summoned his courage and wrote, from Leeds, a letter of proposal to Clara Crompton. He said all that mattered in the first sentence: 'Miss Clara, I love you & have loved you since the first time we met.'

He proceeded, painfully, to enlighten her about his father's drinking habits, expressing the hope (inordinately optimistic, but who could blame him?) that he was 'now cured'. Miss Clara's letter of acceptance has not survived; but her new fiancé's next letter provoked a pert reply: she 'didn't expect a travel guide' (he had gone into considerable detail over the complications of his journey back to Leeds) and while of course she did not expect 'a public display of affection', she had hoped that his 'private letters would have been more loving!'

Clara was the second to leave the Crompton nest. By the time she married her curate, two and a half years later, Hannah had been Mrs George Wrigley for five years and had a small daughter and infant son. Lizzie was well established in spinsterhood; Harry was not to marry for another twelve years. Ada would marry five years after Clara; and would lose both her sons in the Great War. Clara's youngest sister, Re, never married; her life, early centred on the church of St John, where all the Cromptons were faithful in attendance, later revolved around the Bury Charity Services Organization. ('Richmal Crompton House', which existed until recently in St Mary's Place, was named not after the creator of William but after her Aunt Re, in memory of her work there on behalf of the local CSO; and though half a century has passed since her death, many older Bury residents still think of Clara's sister rather than Clara's daughter when Richmal Crompton is mentioned.) Jack, the youngest child, was only seventeen when Clara married.

The wedding took place at St John's Church on the first day of August 1888. The 26-year-old bride wore, the *Bury Guardian* reported, 'a dress of cream-coloured embroidered

Richmal's birthplace in Manchester Road, Bury

Indian silk with a tulle veil and carried a beautiful nosegay'. The bridesmaids were Clara's best friend, Mary Roberts, and Ada and Re. Tom and George Lamburn, Edward's brothers, were there, the elder performing the solemn duties of best man; but their father was neither present at the ceremony nor mentioned in the list of wedding-present donors. After a honeymoon in Devonshire, Edward and his bride settled to married life in a terraced villa in Manchester Road, the main road running south of the town. No. 519 (renumbered in 1936 and bought by the council) was a corner house with four bedrooms, two living rooms, attic and cellar space; and conveniently sited for both Radcliffe, where Edward had his curacy, and Bury Grammar School.

The Lamburn's first child, Gwen (Mary Gwendolen), arrived in June 1889. Seventeen months later, on 15 November* 1890, a second daughter was born. She was named, after Clara's mother and sister, Richmal Crompton.

* Fittingly, the birthdate of three famous Williams: Pitt the Elder, Cowper and Herschel.

II

In May 1892, when Richmal (by now known to all as 'Ray') was eighteen months old and Gwen not yet three, tragedy cast its first shadow across Clara Lamburn's domestic contentment. One morning, after opening the family shop as usual with his son Harry, Mr Crompton went upstairs to the former living quarters, now used as storerooms. A little later Joshua Openshaw called at the shop, and Harry sent the apprentice upstairs to tell Mr Crompton that his brother-in-law had arrived. The apprentice rushed down again in seconds: Mr Crompton was ill. Joshua Openshaw ran to summon the nearest doctor as Harry tore upstairs. But the doctor, though he arrived within minutes, could do nothing for John Crompton: the small blue bottle lying empty beside his body had contained prussic acid.

The family's physician for more than twenty years, a Dr Nuttall, said at the inquest that his 65-year-old patient, 'troubled by nervous exhaustion, and anxiety on account of his wife's illness', had 'suffered acutely' in the weeks before his death. It was concluded that Mrs Crompton's ill-health had been a significant factor in the tragic affair and, after a brief summing-up by the deputy coroner, the jury returned a verdict of temporary insanity; thus ensuring burial in consecrated ground. One family source claims that John Crompton killed himself for a reason unconnected with his wife's illness (in fact, she survived him by thirteen years) but maintains that the rest of the family, even ninety years on, is better left in ignorance. Whatever his motivation for choosing so horrible an end, the fact of John Crompton's *felo de se* was assiduously kept from his grandchildren. The few who did learn of it heard the story in adult life, from sources outside the family.

Eleven months later, in April 1893, the Lamburns' only son, Jack (christened John Battersby Crompton after Clara's father), was born; and the family was completed in September 1894 with the birth of a third daughter, named Phyllis Crompton. There had been little improvement in the local rate of child mortality since the time of Clara's own birth: in 1894, more than 45% of Bury-born infants failed to survive their first year. In the autumn of 1895, a severe attack of whooping-cough left the two younger Lamburn children very ill with bronchitis: Jack recovered but fourteen-month-old Phyllis died, five days after Richmal's fifth birthday.

Malvern Villas, Chesham Road, Bury

Early in 1896, perhaps to escape constant painful reminders of their loss, the Lamburns left the Manchester Road house and moved north of the town centre to Chesham Road, just around the corner from Clara's widowed mother. The new house, the fourth of a terraced row named Malvern Villas, faced open fields, across which Edward was to walk each morning on his way to Chesham Reservoir for an early swim. Further up the winding Chesham Road, his splendid residence screened by trees from the common stare, lived the widowed Colonel Oliver Ormerod Walker, 'the only gentleman Bury possessed', whose four unmarried daughters were to prove a rich source of inspiration for the maiden ladies of impoverished gentility who people the fringes of so many of Richmal's novels.

Two temporary curacies, at Salford and Newchurch, followed the removal to Malvern Villas; and in February 1897, Edward was licensed as stipendiary curate to the new district of

Thornham-with-Gravel-Hole, between Rochdale and Oldham. He walked to Thornham and back – about twenty miles in all – every Sunday to take a service at one of the district's two schools. This duty, which he was to retain for ten years, might seem to have been onerous for one who already put in hours of coaching on top of a full week's teaching, and who gave as much time as he could spare to the parish work of his own church of St John and to the old and sick in the neighbourhood; but Edward Lamburn, inspired, was indefatigable.

He seems to have been, too, despite the demands on his time, an unusually helpful husband. Bert Howarth, a pupil of Edward's who lived next door to the Lamburns in the Malvern Villas terrace, used to hear Edward call up the stairs of No. 4: 'Clara, breakfast's ready!' (The opinion that Clara 'took advantage' of her husband's goodness is not exclusive to Mr Howarth; most of the very few people now living who remember the couple recall Edward much more warmly than Clara.) Every Monday morning Edward would stoke up the old boiler for the household wash before leaving the house for his daily swim, which he followed with attendance at the early service at St John's en route to his day's teaching at Bury Grammar School. He followed this austere pattern to the end of his life. On dark winter mornings, he used matches to light his way to the reservoir; if the water was frozen over, he broke the ice.

Since his limited teaching salary was not much augmented by the income from his curacy, a living-in servant was beyond Edward's means; though Clara did enjoy the services of a daily 'skivvy' and the occasional 'holiday governess'. To stretch the family purse, the Lamburns undertook to provide lunch for two of Edward's pupils who lived at Heywood, too far from the grammar school to allow a return home for lunch. These boys were to make an appearance in Richmal's third novel, *Anne Morrison*: 'Jeremy', clever, charming (to adults) and adept in the art of subtle cruelty; and poor 'Colin', kindly, slow-witted and the inevitable butt of the other's malicious humour.

The bathroom wall of No. 4 displayed a large map of Europe, and Edward, who never missed an opportunity to inculcate knowledge, used to conduct a short geography lesson in the bathroom immediately after lunch, for the benefit of his own children as well as the two visiting pupils. As the children perched themselves around the edge of the bath, 'Jeremy' always took care to position himself near the taps: a little surreptitious splashing generally ensured that one of the others, usually 'Colin', would end the lesson in Mr Lamburn's bad books. Much admired, even held up as an example by other children's mothers, 'Jeremy' derived much enjoyment from hiding Richmal's dolls and books; 'Colin', bigger than the bully but scared to challenge him, used to tell her in a frightened whisper where her possessions were hidden. According to those who remember him – with a dislike unmitigated by the passage of three-quarters of a century – 'Jeremy' became either a surgeon or a dentist. Either career would doubtless have afforded ample scope for his sadistic tendencies.

Edward Lamburn, though invariably courteous, lacked the ready affability that conduces to social ease; his small talk was laboured, and his 'terrible clerical jokes' were legendary for their length rather than their humour. In the pulpit, however, he lost his customary diffidence and reserve. His sermons, 'marked by sound knowledge and profound thought', were delivered with a force and fluency that belied his hesitant social demeanour. This was the work God had called him to do, and Edward never doubted that He would supply the courage needed to do it. Eloquence was a feature also of the stories he told at home, as his younger daughter was to record in *Anne Morrison*:

> It was as a wonderful story-teller that she first remembered Daddy – as someone who only appeared at very rare intervals for a breathless hour or so, and peopled her baby world with a wonderful assemblage – with Odysseus, Perseus, Psyche and countless others. He was impatient of all fairy-tales except those of Ancient Greece. Hours with him had been golden hours . . . She did not see him often in those days. He had frequently gone out when she got up and had not come home when she went to bed. Yet he lived in her mind almost as a hero of fable himself . . . Odysseus, Jason, Perseus . . . Then he took more definite form. He became teacher now as well as story-teller . . . And the Story-teller gradually disappeared when the Teacher came . . . except the stories in lessons . . . William Rufus and Henry V and Joan of Arc . . . he spun his web of golden magic over those, not because he wished, but because he could not help it . . .

To the extent that he stimulated imagination and encouraged questions, the Rev. Mr Lamburn was the ideal parent for an academically inclined child such as Richmal. But even stronger than his desire to transmit his own love of learning was his conviction of personal responsibility for ensuring that the love of God was instilled into the three small vessels in his especial care. He took very seriously Proverbs 22, 6: Train up a child in the way he should go: and when he is old, he will not depart from it.

Gwen and Jack, both of whom possessed a healthy tendency to occasional rebellion, were well equipped to cope with consistently high parental expectations. Richmal, however, was a highly imaginative, sensitive child, and it is plain that her father's 'stern love' had a profound effect on her. Like the heroine of *Anne Morrison*, she stood slightly in awe of her father; she was 'not quite at her ease with him, conscious chiefly of a wondering admiration for him and a haunting fear of disappointing him'. There were times when she basked happily in the glow of his loving approval; but there were times also when she became fearfully aware of his capacity for anger. Like the Rev. Timothy Morrison, his fictional counterpart, Edward Lamburn achieved a gentle manner only by forcible suppression of his natural impatience and fervour: 'His gentleness held that suggestion of strength that natural gentleness lacks. Sometimes he came home weary to exhaustion, and the children's noise or inopportune questions or naughtiness was treated by him with a shortness of manner that frightened them by its suggested fierce impatience, barely held in check . . . She would never be good enough for Daddy. She would never be worthy of him – never, never, never . . . ' A cry from the heart, indeed.

Years later, Richmal told a friend that she had only once heard her parents quarrel. Lying in bed one night, the child heard their voices 'raised against each other' in the next room; greatly shocked, she 'lay trembling'. Edward and Clara do indeed seem to have been devoted to each other, and to their children; in this respect, the security of Richmal's early background is beyond dispute. Yet several of her novels (*Naomi Godstone*, *Blue Flames* and *The Ridleys*, for example) were to delineate with remarkable insight the sufferings of the child who strives unsuccessfully to win a deeper maternal affection. One suspects that Clara, herself confident and lively, was sometimes irritated by her younger daughter's shyness and general reluctance to assert herself. In adult life Richmal mentioned to a friend that Clara used to refer to her daughter's 'spineless amiability'; not a malicious observation, perhaps, but certainly not one calculated to enhance a child's self-esteem. Richmal related the comment with depreciatory humour, seemingly untinged by resentment; but that it was remembered at all after so many years suggests that it found a mark. It found its way also into a novel she wrote in her sixties:

> 'Don't be ridiculous,' said Honoria impatiently. 'One must *learn* to snub people who waste one's time, if one's to make anything of life. Spineless amiability gets one nowhere.'[1]

The Lamburn sisters' formal education began under the benevolent supervision of 'Miss Annie', at a tiny local school, and continued at a larger Dame school in Mount Terrace, situated just behind their first home in Manchester Road. Jack, being younger, attended a small school within easy walking distance of Malvern Villas. Early examples of Richmal's handwriting suggest that her first teachers were zealous in their efforts to eradicate any sinistral tendency in their pupils. In later years she ruefully recalled the emphasis on penmanship in her early schooldays: 'I learned to write in double lines with the constant admonition, "Now, keep inside the lines!" I never could manage it.'

Gwen, who had inherited Clara's self-confidence, found no difficulty in making friends in the neighbourhood, particularly among those of her father's pupils who lived nearby, and their sisters. She took seriously her responsibilities as older sister: on one occasion, she avenged the family honour by routing a local bully who had persecuted little Jack to the point of dislocating his arm. The Rev. Mr Lamburn would no doubt have been shocked (and Clara even more so) to learn that his older daughter had engaged in physical combat, and further horrified to learn that his own pupils had formed a partisan ring around the adversaries. But all was well: Gwen triumphed, Jack was avenged, the bully was shamed for ever and Authority, parental or otherwise, remained happily unaware of the incident.

Richmal, a slender, pale child with blue eyes and curly light-brown hair, spent most of her spare time in these early days in the company of Jack and her beloved dolls, and with pencil and paper. Gwen recalled her sister's frequent escapes to the attic, for 'scribbling sessions' (during which she composed stories and poems 'she would have died in torture rather than show to anyone') and for bringing her 'very private' diary up to date. The attic of the Malvern Villas house witnessed also the birth of *The Rainbow* (a title inspired by the facility of cover design), a magazine whose circulation was limited to two: little Jack and Lena, Richmal's favourite rag doll. This privileged assembly sat on 'doll-sized chairs' while the budding author paced the attic boards reading aloud the magazine's contents.

The demonstrative affection Richmal bestowed on her dolls – and particularly on Lena, the only 'character' in *Anne Morrison* to retain her given name – indicates clearly the child's capacity for tender devotion. Nor had she forgotten this aspect of her early emotional life by the time, in her thirties, she came to write the book:

> It was Lena that she loved most of all . . . Lena with her battered 'unbreakable' face and wobbly limbs and utter absence of hair. She had had Lena since she was three. She had spent a lot of time comforting Lena when people said unkind things about her. Lena was very sensitive and required much affection and many comfortings . . .
>
> She took them all out of the chest and dressed them and sang the long-clothes baby to sleep, then put her in the pram and walked round and round the attic with her, and gave them dinner and then put them all on little chairs and recited to them . . . Then she read them a poem she had made up herself. Before she did this she went to the door and listened to be sure that no one was coming upstairs. It was a sad poem about a fish that fell in love with a mermaid and died of a broken heart.

Retiring by nature, Richmal shrank from boisterous play and her company was rarely sought by the local children of her own age, many of whom regarded her as 'queer'. Bridget, the heroine of her first novel, *The Innermost Room*, was to suffer similarly in childhood under the careless judgment of her contemporaries: 'She'd been called "queer" so often that "queer" didn't hurt.' Richmal's 'queerness' included providing terminal care for dying flowers; throughout her life she kept a special vase in the kitchen for wilting blooms broken from their parent plant. This botanical benevolence was duly shared by her *Innermost Room* heroine: after her sister has expressed contempt for anyone fool enough to bother with rescuing trampled bluebells from the roadside, Bridget, 'with that dull feeling of misery that the disapproval of anyone she loved always brought her', nevertheless goes 'doggedly, silently on, picking up each dead flower' as she comes to it.

The 'queerness' attributed to the young Richmal by many of her peers doubtless owed much to the sense of isolation that so often accompanies superior intellect in childhood. Richmal's greatest asset in these early years was surely her fast-developing, beautifully proportioned sense of the ridiculous, which later would bring forth William. Her vivid sense of romance, too, must have leavened the tendency to self-torturing introspection; though her fascination (apparent in several of the novels) with the more romantic aspects of gipsy life evidently countered a nervous distaste for the reality of poverty in the form of Bury's mill-workers:

> The midday siren had just sounded, and crowds of mill girls were flooding the main streets, in shawls and clogs, with little bits of white fluff clinging to their clothes and hair. They besieged the trams or walked off in little groups. All of them seemed to be shouting to each other at the tops of their voices and uttering shrill screams of laughter. The screams frightened (her), the whiff of humanity as they pushed her sickened her. She hated them. They were part of the system of smoke and dirt and chimneys that spoilt her beautiful country and killed her flowers . . .[2]

Threats to the precarious peace of mind of the over-sensitive child being legion, one suspects that Richmal retreated quite as often as her heroine Bridget was to retreat into her 'innermost room', last refuge from 'the enemy'. The construction of this asylum was evidently simple but rigid: 'She had a curious mental picture of herself as a series of rooms, beginning with an outer room and ending with a small innermost room. Some people did not go into any of her rooms . . . Some people came into some of the outer rooms . . . No one came into the innermost room. (Her) little soul dwelt there – impregnable, aloof and remote.'[3]

The passage in *The Innermost Room* that describes the first encounter with 'the enemy' is graphic and entirely convincing. As Bridget and her sister witness the passing of a hand-cart bearing a drowned corpse ('They could see the hand – white and wet – and part of the shirt-sleeve, dripping, dripping, as it went along.'), the younger girl is stricken with 'a sudden horror – a sickening realisation of nightmare depths beneath the clear calm surface of life, beneath the violets and primroses and woods and games and people who laughed and talked'. Following this grisly experience, Bridget finds herself constantly on the defensive, 'always ready for the enemy to pounce out upon her'. It could happen in all sorts of ways, 'from the newspapers, from books, from things people said'; life would suddenly be dark 'and there couldn't be any God and sheer terror came and even the flowers and woods weren't the same'. With the Irwell, the Roch and Chesham Reservoir so conveniently situated, death by drowning – accidental, suicidal and even homicidal – was so common in Bury that only the most eminent victims received more than a passing mention in the local paper. It cannot therefore be proved that the fictional corpse came from Richmal's own experience; but it is surely significant that her description of the incident is far more chilling than anything she wrote later for her collection of mystery/horror stories (*Mist and other Stories*, 1928).

Another incident in Richmal's first novel that clearly reflects the terrors of her childhood introspection is indisputably factual. Bridget is struck with a 'dull, creeping horror' on hearing of a double suicide by poisoning at a local hotel. One day in January 1899, when Richmal was eight years old, a man and woman registered as a married couple at the superior Derby Hotel in Bury. The following morning they were found dead in bed, clasped in a final illicit embrace. Police investigation into the 'mutual self-murder' revealed facts that further shocked Victorian Bury: the young woman had been a foreigner – a Mlle. Rousseau – and her British lover not only wealthy and 'of an aristocratic family' but also the British Consul to Turkey and Belgium. His pathetic suicide letter, addressed to the coroner, enclosed money 'to cover the funeral expenses' and a request that the pair should be buried together; but his mother refused the request and poor Mlle. Rousseau lies alone in Bury cemetery. In the fictional version, Bridget's older sister, pleasurably scandalized, acquaints her with the details of the tragedy: 'No one knows why they came to Galton. But, Bridget, she was a *wicked* woman; they could tell she was wicked, Gladys said. Gladys didn't know how . . . ' Another face of 'the enemy', instinctively recognized:

> Oh, the nightmare things beneath the fair surface of life . . .

> something linking up with a thousand dark whispers to which she had shut her ears . . . something heavy with black mystery . . . something more sinister than death . . . And there she was now in the Mortuary . . . her beauty and wickedness exposed to all the world . . . Her wickedness . . . That was the crowning horror. It spoilt everything . . .[3]

Ever sensitive to the inner conflicts of others, Richmal must early have been aware of her father's efforts to subdue his natural propensity to passionate feeling. Her own deep need to give affection was fufilled without reserve only in the direction of little Jack and her dolls, none of whom was likely to reject her overtures. The moral had been powerfully if involuntarily transmitted: restraint is nobler than passion. So many of Richmal's fictional heroines were to yearn for an impossibly romantic love that one can hardly escape the conclusion that she was unable in adult life to reshape her idealistic childhood conception of the emotion. True love in her novels is a communion of souls, a mutually rapturous exaltation of the spirit, asexual ecstasy. Her first heroine, Bridget, recalling the tentative approaches of an easily discouraged admirer, remembers 'the feeling of his arm around her, his body pressed close to hers for just that second . . . and the quivering horror returned . . . There came with it a bitterness. "All men are beasts, really," Gloria had said . . .'

In a letter written in 1951, Richmal drew a friend's attention to the distinction drawn by Berdyayev, in *Dream and Reality*, between love and sex: 'So far from increasing, real love can weaken sexual passion . . . When love is strong it has a depth which reaches out to infinity; sex, on the contrary, carries within it the sting of finitude . . .' That she was in adult life familiar to some degree with the psychology of sex is plain from the behaviour of many of the characters in her novels; and certainly she could never justly have been described as conventionally narrow-minded. But the 'thousand dark whispers', the 'something heavy with black mystery, more sinister than death' had evidently formed a knot of personal apprehension that was not to be unravelled.

In 1898, Edward Lamburn's troublesome father died in the Wiltshire village of Urchfont. His second son, Thomas, had travelled from London to be with him at the end. It is doubtful whether Clara Lamburn had ever met her father-in-law; and certain that Gwen, Richmal and Jack had never met him. Gwen's vague recollections on the matter – she thought that 'both sides were probably too hard up' to afford the necessary travelling expenses and remarked that she had 'never even met Father's mother, of whom he was very fond' (in fact, Mary Lamburn died six years before Gwen was born) – suggest that Edward's father had not been much discussed in the Malvern Villas house, at least in front of the children.

The family income being fully stretched to cover the necessities of life, holidays were generally taken wherever and whenever Edward could find a suitable parish requiring a locum priest during Bury Grammar School holidays. Gwen remembered one unscheduled Christmas holiday in the late 1890s: the chaplain of the Lancaster lunatic asylum had died suddenly and Edward was summoned to take over the chaplaincy until the new appointee arrived. The family stayed in lodgings in Lancaster and Edward went alone daily to the asylum. The entire family, however, attended the asylum's Christmas party, at which the inmates wore white gloves to ensure identification. One white-gloved old lady, having informed the visitors that she was not a patient but the mother of one of the doctors, spent the rest of the evening busily knitting socks for her 'son'. But there was not much to gladden the spirit in a Victorian institution for the mentally ill; and when his brief chaplaincy ended, the humane Edward departed from Lancaster considerably depressed.

Though remembered with deep affection by his former pupils, Edward is not generally reckoned to have been blessed with a great sense of humour; the clerical jokes he told were thought to be ample proof of his deficiency in this respect. But Bert Howarth, the Bury Grammar School pupil who lived next door to the Lamburns, remembered an incident that suggests that Edward was not lacking in humour. 'Lammy', as the Rev. Mr Lamburn was early rechristened by his pupils, used to walk slowly up and down between the desks in his classroom, giving his pupils' homework a brief inspection en route. On one such occasion, he paused behind a boy who regularly copied Bert's homework and who had, on this particular morning, only just finished doing so. Lammy gazed down on the boy's book. 'When did you do this, boy?' Last night, sir . . . 'You forgot to blot it.' And Lammy blotted the final sentence with his finger before resuming his patrol.

But such moments were rare. Edward Lamburn took life very seriously; Clara was the partner with high spirits and a ready wit. In *Anne Morrison*, Timothy's wife Aineen, a thinly disguised Clara, was often able to lighten her husband's heavy mood; and many years later Richmal expressed to a friend her belief that wit in a woman is 'a preservative of married happiness'.

Mr Howarth recalled also an incident that illustrates Edward's more typical seriousness of purpose. Whenever a Bury Grammar pupil won a scholarship to Oxford or Cambridge, the entire school was granted a half-holiday. On one such occasion, the half-holiday had not been announced in advance and Edward therefore commissioned Bert Howarth to leave school early and call at No. 4, to warn Clara that the two Heywood boys who normally lunched with the Lamburns would instead be going straight home at the end of the morning. Bert, delighted to be released from school earlier than the rest of his form, delivered the message willingly and then escaped to his own house to devise his programme for the afternoon. By the time lunch was over, however, sheets of rain lashed the windows of No. 5, which ruled out any prospect of open-air activities. Bert consoled himself with the thought that he still had half a day off school – nearly three-quarters of a day, really, if one counted the fact that he'd escaped that morning's English lesson... But anticipation of the potential delights of an unexpectedly free afternoon was rudely interrupted by a knock at the door.

'As you missed your English lesson this morning, Howarth...' said Lammy, smiling gravely through the rain. And since the torrential downpour precluded his pleading with any conviction a prior engagement, poor Bert succumbed to the inevitable. (He felt, justifiably, hard done by at times. Not only did he live next door to his form-master; the Malvern Villas terrace also contained two more Bury Grammar School teachers and another priest. One can imagine the aggrieved monologue in which William would have railed at the unfairness of such a situation...) On another occasion, Lammy was called away while supervising a detention. As the minutes passed and he did not return, the boy's hope became conviction: Lammy, notoriously vague, had forgotten all about him. It would be quite safe now to run for his train and go home to tea. History does not record the boy's feelings as he looked up from the tea-table and saw Lammy – who had caught the next train –

marching up the front path in pursuit of his defaulting detainee.

Clara Lamburn's nephew, John Wrigley, who was also taught by Edward, recalled that he had enjoyed an early reputation as a strict disciplinarian. By the late 1890s, however, when Sir John began to attend Bury Grammar School, that reputation was 'no longer justified' and Edward no longer held the rank of Third Master. 'Lammy' is nevertheless remembered as a learned teacher, with a passion for sharing his knowledge and an infinite fund of patience. He gave additional coaching to students preparing for scholarships (among his successes was a future Lord Chief Justice, Gordon Hewart), but the less able pupil received just as much encouragement as the one who learned easily. Edward never belittled or ridiculed his students, and despite frequent provocation – one former BGS boy declares that Lammy's own form in the 1890s, Lower Vb, held over the years 'most of the school's potential criminals' – he rarely resorted to corporal punishment. According to his obituary notice, the Rev. Mr Lamburn never punished a boy 'save with a single eye to the boy's good'.

His self-discipline was impressive, his discipline of Lower Vb less so. His small eccentricities were a source of great mirth to his pupils. One recalls Lammy's genius for wounding himself with his cut-throat razor: 'On some mornings, he looked as if he had been on the losing side in a gang battle.' On wet days, he would arrive at school with his trouser legs stuffed with newspapers, the removal of which always caused great hilarity in the classroom. He used to place his umbrella in the waste-paper basket; an irresistible temptation to Lower Vb, who looked forward all day to the moment when Lammy would open the umbrella and receive a shower of screwed-up paper and other rubbish.

In a lesson on Australia, mention was made of the fecundity of rabbits, and the necessity of controlling their progeny. The class wit asked whether just two rabbits could produce an enormous family; and when told that they could, asked, 'What if they were two bucks?' This brought forth the 'typical Lammy reply': 'Boy, boy, you are provoking beyond a degree!' When his class became near-riotous, Lammy would abandon the classroom and move them into the hall, where the remainder of the lesson would be taken standing. Lower Vb regarded this occasional punishment as a rare treat. Once in the hall, they would rush to the far end of the room, where bentwood chairs were stacked high; each boy would seize a chair and push it at top speed along the highly polished floor. Upon Lammy's stern reminder that the class was to stand, the chairs were returned with equal speed and noise. When Lammy at last had the class properly assembled around him and resumed his teaching, the circle of miscreants, innocent eyes fixed respectfully on their mentor, would very gradually diminish until reduced to a tight knot of humanity in the centre of the large hall. Lammy's subsequent order to widen the circle was, of course, instantly obeyed: the circle would spread right to the perimeter of the hall...

One former pupil confesses that, in devising different ways of enlivening Lammy's classes, many of the boys expended more time and energy than they would have used in doing what had actually been demanded of them. One pupil, having written 'witty versions of the more serious bits of the Lay of the Last Minstrel', went so far as to paste them over the book text in order to justify what he would read out in class. Such thoroughness and ingenuity remind one irresistibly of William's lesson-avoiding techniques; and indeed, Richmal must have heard of many of these escapades, from Bert-next-door, from her cousin John, from Gwen through her Bury Grammar School acquaintances, and later from her brother Jack, even if she did not hear of them from Edward himself. William's especial skill in maintaining a look expressive of an earnest desire to understand, while leading the unfortunate teacher through labyrinthine explanations, seems to have been a particular favourite with the students of Lower Vb.

At school reunions, Edward was invariably given a riotous welcome: 'Old Boys would get this little man to stand on a chair at their functions and then cheer him to the echo.'[4] The teacher who fails to control the unruly element in his or her class is usually remembered, if at all, with contempt. The Rev. Edward Lamburn is remembered by his surviving pupils – the youngest of whom is now eighty – with an affection and esteem undiminished by the passage of time.

Richmal's Happy Days

III

In September 1902, two months before her twelfth birthday, Richmal left Malvern Villas to become a boarder at the Clergy Daughters School in Warrington, 23 miles away. Bury had by now its own well-regarded girls' school – sister to Bury Grammar School, where Edward taught – but expense was of necessity a major consideration, and the Warrington school offered bursaries for the daughters of clergymen within the archdeaconry of Chester. Gwen had already been a year at Warrington; Jack, to his chagrin, was to remain at home and attend Bury Grammar under the watchful eye of his father. Edward was deeply concerned that his only son, for whom he had envisaged a university degree and subsequent entry into the Church (the dream, so long in its fulfilment, of Edward's own youth), was showing little aptitude and even less enthusiasm for study. Jack's popularity with his peers, his success on the games field, his love of natural history, did nothing to assuage his father's fears: the boy's good looks and easy charm were dangerously reminiscent of his grandfather, and the Rev. Mr Lamburn continually sought the least sign of an inherited tendency to irresolution and self-indulgence.

The Lamburn daughters, however, learned quickly and with enjoyment; and Richmal arrived at the Clergy Daughters School with the advantage of a rich appreciation of classical literature and a good grounding in Latin, to which her father had introduced her nearly four years earlier. Headmistress of the school in 1902 was the formidable Catherine Kennedy, a niece of the Victorian classical scholar, Benjamin Hall Kennedy. Herself profoundly religious, Miss Kennedy regarded academic achievement and moral virtue equally highly. Discipline in her school was rigid and punishments excessive, even by the standards of the day; the very mildest form of naughtiness or disobedience was deemed a serious moral lapse and so entailed a shaming entry in the school's Black Book.

The school building, large and rambling, had once been a convent. Steps led up or down into nearly every room, the walls were so thick that 'half a dozen girls could curl up comfortably on the window seats' and there were legends of 'secret passages that we tried in vain to discover'. The more imaginative of the Clergy Daughters would claim to have glimpsed, in dim-lit corridor or darkened dormitory, the flitting form of the spectral nun who was said to haunt the building. Ghosts began to figure in Richmal's stories soon after her arrival at the school; though her own fearful enjoyment of the nun legend, to be faithfully recorded two decades later in *Anne Morrison*, was evidently underlain by a healthy scepticism:

> That night when Anne turned out the last light and turned to grope her way out of the dark schoolroom down the dark corridor to the friendly lighted staircase her heart beat so loudly with terror that the noise of it seemed to fill the house. She was firmly convinced that something stood beside her in the darkness. She ran blindly, trembling, towards the glimmer of light that showed that staircase where friendly faces were waiting for her. As the days went on she found that she enjoyed the sensation. She would have been bitterly disappointed if she had not felt as if 'something else was in the room' when the last light was turned out, if she had not felt that delicious thrill of terror . . .

The fact that belief in the ghost was strictly forbidden no doubt strengthened its appeal for the Clergy Daughters.

Austerity was the keynote of life at Warrington. The food, barely adequate in quantity, lacked variety and nutritional quality, and often was poorly cooked. No fresh fruit was provided in the standard diet, though Richmal might, as a Lower School pupil, squander up to threepence of her own money each week on fruit. Morning chapel service at eight was followed by the first of the day's lessons, which, for Lower School pupils, must have been something of an ordeal. The school hall was divided into four 'class squares' for the Lower School; in each square, a mistress struggled to concentrate on imparting knowledge to her own class in competition with three other mistresses, classes and subjects. Miss Kennedy presided majestically at a large desk on the platform, ostensibly occupied with pen and paper but in fact, as everyone in the hall was uncomfortably aware, closely observing progress and behaviour:

> It did not conduce to the easiness of either mistress or girls. There were thrilling moments when her terrible voice boomed forth suddenly:
>
> "Miss Butler, who was that girl speaking to you in that tone of voice?"
>
> Or: "Miss Harris, who is that girl stumbling so over her lesson? Stand up. Haven't you *learnt* your lesson, child? Bring your book to me."
>
> And the other three classes would turn round to gaze with morbid interest at the culprit, and the other three mistresses would make half-hearted attempts to continue their lessons as if nothing had happened.[2]

A short break at mid-morning, for bread and water (or milk, if one's father forked out for such 'extras'), was followed by lessons till 'dinner', after which games were played or a walk was taken. Walks usually ended in a sedate tour of the nearby cemetery, an appropriately depressing destination for those in the throes of digesting lumpy, undercooked milk pudding. The ensuing three-hour prep. period was not much enlivened by a minuscule tea at five; and the Clergy Daughters' day ended as it had begun, with chapel.

Games periods, it seems, were largely spent in wild, if enjoyable, confusion. Provided with hockey sticks, goalposts and balls but no games mistress, the girls were obliged to make what they could of the rules of the game. Two teams of eleven players were assigned to the correct positions; others wishing to play were admitted as 'fishes', to dart about the field and hit the ball 'as best they could in the right direction when they got the chance'. The older girls wore beneath their ankle-length skirts voluminous cambric petticoats, which frequently escaped their moorings and descended to the ground; players and 'fishes' would then enjoy a brief respite while the offending garment was more securely fastened. Other hazards included a shallow, sluggish stream known as 'the moat', which ran alongside the playground. Whenever a particularly vigorous swipe sent the ball into the moat, all the players would gather on the bank and stir up the mud with their hockey sticks, 'releasing a most unwholesome stench but seldom managing to retrieve the ball'.

The freedom of the hockey field may well have compensated

to some degree for the rigours of the classroom. Learning by rote was the teaching method employed: the aim was 'to get even the dimmest through their examinations'. One struggled, unaided, until the Latin Unseen was correctly translated; as a former pupil ruefully recalls, 'one could be sent back time and again with just "No!"'. Health care, too, at the time of Richmal's arrival, was decidedly primitive; no preventive measures were taken, even when epidemics threatened. (It was chiefly owing to pressure from concerned parents, after an outbreak of scarlet fever at the school in the following year, that the decision was at last made to remove from industrial Warrington's ambient grime to more salubrious surroundings.)

The Second Mistress, Mrs Flood, had overall responsibility for the Lower School; except when a particularly heinous offence had been committed, juniors rarely came into contact with their awe-inspiring headmistress, and were relieved that it should be so. Yet, hard though she undoubtedly was in many ways, Miss Kennedy had her human side. She gave financial help in several cases where a pupil's family had fallen into straitened circumstances; and the Second Mistress herself was deeply indebted to her. Deserted by her husband, without means, and totally unfitted to become provider for her children, Mrs Flood had been in a desperate plight until Miss Kennedy took her in hand, coaching her first for the Cambridge Higher locals and then for a teaching qualification. On accepting the Warrington headship in 1896, Miss Kennedy had brought with her Mrs Flood, and also her 18-year-old daughter Margaret as a student-mistress.

For Richmal, the shock of contrast between the familiar comforts of 4 Malvern Villas and the spartan rigours of the Clergy Daughters School must have been cushioned to some degree by Gwen's protective concern. A few days after the beginning of her sister's first term, Gwen noted in her diary: 'Ray not at all homesick. She keeps one from being so; she's a darling.' But that brave front was soon to crumple. Gwen recorded, somewhat incoherently, on the following day that her sister 'went up to hall in outdoor things & looked for me & Mrs Flood scolded her & then she tried to go out at front door & Mrs Flood scolded again'; Richmal was 'awfully upset & upset me too'. Later in the day, however, Gwen observed with relief that Richmal was 'now reading & seems quite happy'.

The two sisters lived for the weekly letters from home, which arrived from Clara regularly and without fail. Edward, his time as always filled with teaching, ministering and – his only indulgence – improving his knowledge of Hebrew (he considered the language a *sine qua non* for a clergyman; poor Jack was to spend many an unrewarding hour grappling with its mysteries), wrote (occasionally in Latin) less often; but his influence was no less strong for being at a remove. Gwen, in a letter home, once misguidedly referred to a fellow pupil as 'stuck up'. In his reply, the conscientious Edward did his best to combine reproof with affection:

> My darling little Gwen,
>
> Thank you very much for the kind birthday wishes that I received yesterday...
>
> It would be much nicer if you did not pass such severe strictures upon others especially those who are older than yourself. She may be stuck up; or it may be that you do not understand her. But Our Lord's command Matth. VII 1 is "Judge not, that ye be not judged"... The habit of evil-speaking grows on one unless it be effectually checked, and leads to much misery & unhappiness in the world... If we all knew how much our words affected others, I think we should become changed beings...
>
> I am afraid you will think I have been scolding you, my darling; but I have really no intention of doing anything of the sort. I only wish to warn you against habits which may do mischief & which will certainly tend to make your own school days miserable. Society is like a looking-glass; if you smile at it, a smile is returned to you; if you look crossly at it, it returns an unkind look to you.
>
> I love you intensely & wish for your happiness in every way, so I give you my best advice. Please regard all I have said as very kind words of love not as rebuke...
>
> With a heart full of love
> Try on dearie
> I remain
> Your ever loving father
> E. Lamburn

His strong sense of duty in relation to the children's moral development was undiminished. He still disapproved of their reading fiction on a Sunday; he was grieved by any manifestation of a fall from the standards he had set, by precept

Clergy Daughters School, Warrington

and by example. Gwen, evidently the only one of the three to have inherited Clara's musical ability, took piano lessons at boarding school. She enjoyed playing but found the examinations so unnerving that eventually she pleaded to be allowed to stop taking lessons. Edward himself was not at all musical; indeed, he was tone-deaf (which says much for the eloquence of his sermons – it was clearly not his intoning that attracted the capacity congregations). But he disapproved of his daughter's reason for wishing to abandon her piano lessons; her aversion to the exams surely was 'all the more reason for keeping on'. Moral victory was to be Gwen's, whether or not she sought it.

After the outbreak of scarlet fever in the autumn of 1903, plans were made to transfer the school from Warrington to Darley Dale, in Derbyshire. During the move, at the beginning of the following school year, Richmal and others were put up at Darley Dale Hydro until the new school's dormitories were ready for occupation; and from this period comes her earliest recorded literary effort. A friend had poked a small piece of plum cake under her door; Richmal's thanks, delivered in the same way, came scrawled on a laundry list:

Although from this sad world of pain
Your piece of cake has gone,
Yet in my heart the thought of thee
Will ever more live on.
(I will do your laundry at cut prices.)

Once settled in Darley Dale, the Clergy Daughters School amended its name to St. Elphins (after the parish church at Warrington), and began to accept the daughters of laymen as fee-paying pupils. The new site was a delightful contrast to the old. At Darley Dale, the afternoon walk took on new dimensions: glorious adventure beckoned 'up the hills and over the moors' and the older girls enjoyed much greater freedom, to 'break line' and wander more or less at will from the tiny village. The new freedom was not, however, to revolutionize school life: one titled mother, anxious lest her daughters' white hands be scratched or roughened, could still insist – and thereby earn the undying resentment of St. Elphins girls – that the wearing of gloves in the school grounds be made compulsory.

Sundays also were more enjoyable than they had been at Warrington: at Darley Dale, the school attended services in the local parish church, where Richmal looked forward particularly to 'the prayer for the king and Royal Family'. A romantic reverence for monarchy was to be characteristic also of the adolescent heroine of *Anne Morrison*:

> King Edward had now ascended the throne and Anne had conceived a passionate admiration of Queen Alexandra. Someone had given her a Commemoration Prayer Book at the coronation and it had a photograph of King Edward and Queen Alexandra in front of the Coronation service and Anne loved to glance at the photograph surreptitiously during the dragging minutes of the Litany.

Anne's youthful idealism was confined largely to the maintenance or restoration of privilege: the historical injustices to be remedied in imagination clearly were not those suffered by history's oppressed masses. Escaping the ordeal of introductions and social chatter at a garden party, she

St. Elphins School, Darley Dale

daydreams with grandeur: sword in hand, she convinces the Paris mob of their 'wrong judgment' and leads Marie Antoinette and Louis back in triumph to Versailles; as General Lee, she 'beats the North to their knees', then pardons them 'freely and graciously'.

Though the move to Derbyshire had deprived Richmal of one source of inspiration ('we missed our ghost!'), she continued to write, 'chiefly because I couldn't stop!' A star contributor to the school magazine, she also kept a 'somewhat satirical semi-public' diary of school events, in which pupils and staff were represented as different kinds of animal. Gwen (the horse) and the few others for whose amusement the diary was produced enjoyed it hugely. At Warrington, Richmal and a few friends had formed a secret society, whose aims were 'mildly literary'; at Darley Dale, members continued to meet weekly, 'in a secluded part of the garden', to dissect the fruits of the week's creative labours. Votes were cast and the winner was solemnly decorated with a bow of purple ribbon on a safety pin. The society's exclusiveness was evidently quite as important as its aims: 'We imagined that the rest of the school was consumed by envious curiosity about our activities; but probably they never even noticed them.'

The aspiring writer's academic progress was rapid: she eagerly absorbed Latin, history, English (though her spelling was always to leave something to be desired), geography and later, and even more eagerly, Greek; mathematics, however, failed to catch her imagination and brought her bad marks for inattention and lack of application. It was surely after a maths lesson that she wrote home, despairingly: 'Sometimes I do get so mad & sick of the same things day after day & week after week with nothing but bad mark (sic) in the least exciting . . . ' Fellow sufferers will no doubt identify with the basic sentiment of the following passage from *Anne Morrison*:

> It was so difficult to be interested in lines and angles and triangles. Triangles always seemed to have such ugly little faces.
>
> 'Required to prove that the triangle ABC equals DEF,' said Miss Vaughan.
>
> 'Who cares if it does and who cares if it doesn't?' thought Anne rebelliously.
>
> Miss Vaughan's voice, clear and musical and soothing, went on . . .
>
> Anne was crossing a road in London and was knocked down by

> a carriage. She was not very badly hurt but her ankle was sprained and she could not walk. The lady in the carriage got out to see what was the matter. It was Queen Alexandra. She took Anne into the carriage, and Anne sat on her knee and they drove to Buckingham Palace. The doctor said that Anne must on no account be moved. Anne lay in a golden bed in a bedroom which was suggestive of the Transformation Scene of last year's Pantomime, and Queen Alexandra sat by her bedside and Anne told her how she'd always loved her...
>
> 'Now is that *quite* clear to everyone before we go on to the next set? Anne, do you understand?'
>
> Anne started.
>
> 'Y-yes, thank you,' she said guiltily.
>
> She really *must* attend, she *would* attend. The next one... oh, dear, ABC and DEF again with their stupid ugly faces, and this time you'd got to prove that they *weren't* equal. How silly, and you began by pretending that they were equal... sillier still!

Richmal disliked sewing, battled conscientiously with a natural tendency to untidiness; and was occasionally seized by a spirit of mischief that overrode caution and prompted her to instigate the ever more daring 'ragging' of ineffectual mistress or monitress. As Gwen remonstrated with her young sister over the demerits for inattention, untidiness and 'silliness', so was older sister Laura to take Anne Morrison to task:

> 'I know you're the youngest in your form, but you ought to do better. You're clever.'
>
> 'Oh... not clever,' said Anne, deprecatingly.
>
> 'It makes it all the worse being clever and doing so badly,' said Lorna sternly.
>
> Anne meekly accepted the additional crime of cleverness.

But these 'giant crimes' were tamed with the coming of sobering Responsibility. Richmal was made first a 'downstairs monitress' (a position involving 'a lot of trouble and little honour') and then a dormitory monitress. One former St. Elphins pupil recalls her arrival as a very apprehensive eight-year-old: Richmal's 'motherly care and help in her capacity as dormitory monitress' ensured that the younger girl settled down quickly to school life and was soon able to pen with truth the opening sentence obligatory in letters to home from St. Elphins: 'I am very well and happy.'

During holidays at home, Richmal was growing gradually

closer to her father. Her intellectual ability was increasingly apparent to him; and his pleasure in her dawning appreciation of all that he himself found absorbing was balm to the pain of his disappointment in Jack. Father and daughter walked miles together over the moorland, refreshing eyes and soul with its melancholy beauty: soft blue and green hills, split here and there by crags and small ravines; so near to the grimy pall that overhung the town yet so clean, the landscape so vastly empty. Their silences were comfortable, their conversations animated; they discussed many things, not least Edward's favourite books – Dickens, Trollope, Thackeray – which Richmal was now devouring, and the poetry they both loved. The grave, encouraging interest he showed in her own ideas and opinions dissolved much of the awe in which she had previously held him.

But with each return from school, Richmal became more acutely conscious of the worsening relationship between Edward and her brother. Jack had long resented his father's setting him extra school work, in holidays as well as in termtime; and matters came painfully to a head with the advent of one Bury Grammar School sports day. Jack, the great athletic hope of his school house, had demonstrated in his training for the big day all the vigour and enthusiastic ambition so clearly lacking in his pursuit of knowledge. But there was only a slim chance of his passing a coming examination and any distraction from his studies would, said Edward, be fatal: Jack must not take part in the sports. Mr Rowland, Edward's colleague at the school and a frequent visitor to the Lamburn house, interceded via Clara on Jack's behalf; and the boy's housemaster, unwilling to contemplate the loss of his star athlete, approached Edward direct. But the Rev. Mr Lamburn proved immoveable. Clara, seeing both points of view, did her best to reconcile the unhappy pair when the bleak day was past; but the strain on the relationship was not eased when it was learned that Jack had, despite a genuine effort, failed the examination for which so much had been sacrificed. Edward Lamburn was not a harsh father; simply, he could never forget that his first duty was not to enjoy his children but to watch for and eradicate any tendency to weakness of character.

Eminently satisfactory school reports ensured Gwen's and Richmal's freedom from the holiday study periods that so irked Jack. For the girls, there was little time for boredom in those precious days between departure from and return to Darley Dale. In the Christmas holidays, the Lamburns gathered with their Crompton aunts, uncles and cousins at Grandmother Crompton's 'smashing family Christmas parties'. In return for the matriarchal munificence, the grandchildren were expected to show their paces; though the only one who evinced 'the slightest enjoyment or histrionic ability' in the entertainments they put on for their elders was Richmal, who, as soon as she was old enough to remember her lines, 'showed a marked predilection for playing witches'. Richmal's love of the drama clearly was sufficiently strong to transcend her shyness; during holidays, she and Gwen produced and acted in several plays in Church of England school buildings in Bury, in aid of the Waifs and Strays Society, one of their Aunt Re's major concerns before the founding of the local Charity Services Organisation.

After Richmal's grandmother's death in 1905, Aunts Re and Lizzie moved round the corner from Walmersley Road to a smaller house, a few hundred yards from Malvern Villas, in Chasham Road. Despite their proximity, however, there does not appear to have existed between Clara Lamburn and her two unmarried sisters that tender devotion so frequently recorded by novelists of the period. Clara was not above noting, from her elevated status of wife and mother, and indeed remarking upon her younger sister's constant if unsuccessful pursuit of successive curates (a pursuit, it must be said, believed by a friend of Re to have taken place only in Clara's imagination); and Lizzie was to appear in more than one of her niece's novels as the envious, fault-finding spinster aunt. Aunt Re, no doubt with the intention of insuring against any unfortunate inheritance from the Lamburn side, had enrolled Clara's children in the Band of Hope almost as soon as they were able to articulate; their drink, sang the three in unison with fellow Band of Hopers, was 'water bright from a crystal stream'. This early moral fervour notwithstanding, at least three local members of the 300,000-strong movement were to backslide: in spite of Aunt Re's efforts, 'we all inherited a strong head for drink!'

Richmal's third novel, *Anne Morrison*, in its detailed account of life at 'The Priory', gives a largely accurate picture of life at St. Elphins in her own days there. At 'The Priory', 'sentimentalism' flourishes: a highly strung new girl, Miriam (reminiscent of Louise in Clemence Dane's *Regiment of Women*, published eight years before *Anne Morrison*), is rapidly enslaved by the beautiful ('so bewilderingly sweet... so bewilderingly cruel') head girl; and when faced with humiliating rejection, Miriam tumbles over the heights of ecstasy into dark despair. Her suicide attempt fails; but the near-tragedy brings the unhealthily simmering situation to boiling point and thus to the scandalized attention of the authorities. The head girl is expelled, a new mistress with whom the head girl herself has formed a 'violent sentimental friendship' is dismissed, and Miriam is restored to the calm of her home environment.

In this particular incident, the influence of Clemence Dane's book is very much apparent. But the 'sentimentalism' that flourished at 'The Priory' was based also on Richmal's own awareness of the murkier side of boarding-school life. A portion of her sister Gwen's 1904 diary describes, with innocent scorn, an expectant queue of 'smuts' awaiting 'their innings in the Chem. room', where a young mistress embraced and whispered to the favoured first of their number. Whether the St. Elphins mistress concerned was ultimately exposed and dismissed, as was her counterpart in *Anne Morrison*, is not known; relevant records are said to have been destroyed in a fire. In any event, Richmal, in her guise of Anne Morrison, observed it all with a certain detachment, her own brief emotional attachment subsiding as abruptly as it had flared.

The sensational revelation of 'secret goodnight visits' and meetings in 'shadowy corners' being followed pretty smartly in *Anne Morrison* by the arrival of The Priory's first games mistress – a brisk, no-nonsense type – one is inclined to regard as equally significant the arrival of a games mistress of similar temperament at St. Elphins. The decision to create such a post had been taken, it seems, at some cost to the sensibilities of the headmistress. Miss Masters, Miss Kennedy's counterpart in *Anne Morrison*, was to suffer much in the sacrifice of propriety to 'the onward march of progress':

> The sight of the games mistress in her very abbreviated tunic was a source of continual horror to Miss Masters (who) considered the 'gymnastic tunic' to be a most unwomanly garment. She only allowed the girls to wear it for games and the actual gymnastic class. They changed immediately before and immediately afterward. It seemed to Miss Masters that Miss Monks, the games mistress, need not have worn the offensive garment so continually... Miss Monks was the vanguard of a

class of schoolmistress who would turn Miss Masters' world upside down... she revelled in the shocked horror of Miss Masters' face as she passed her in the passage with an impudent swing of her kilted tunic.

Miss Masters had once had a vague but horrible suspicion that Miss Monks' nose was powdered. If she could really have proved that against the nose, she would have dismissed its owner at once. But Miss Monks as a games mistress was an asset. She was very competent. The games at the Priory improved beyond recognition under her tuition. The girls liked her, and even Miss Masters approved of the way she snubbed any display of sentiment...

These were, on the whole, happy days for Richmal: the scholar's passion satisfied; the bustle of school life no longer intimidating; the comforting bulwark of home watched over by Clara and Edward. The latter's daily regimen, though he was now fifty-three, was no less demanding than it had been twenty years earlier; he still rose at five every morning, took a dip in the reservoir and attended the early service at St. John's before starting his teaching day. One weekend in 1907, John Wrigley, on vacation from Cambridge, joined Edward, Gwen, Richmal and a school friend on an excursion down a Barnsley coal mine. (The girls wore white dresses for the occasion 'because they would be easier to wash'.) At the end of their weekend, Edward suggested that he and John might walk the thirty miles back to Bury. Clara remonstrated vigorously: Edward had walked from Bury to Barnsley at the beginning of the weekend; he must be exhausted. 'Not exhausted, my dear,' Edward protested, mildly; 'just a little tired.'

Richmal had been writing – stories, plays, verse and the 'animal diary' for the entertainment of schoolfriends and family; poetry, more stories and her private diary for no eyes but her own – since she had first learned to write. Years later she said that she had 'given up hope of ever reaching print' long before she had anything published (she had regarded the time and expense involved 'as one would regard golf or tennis club subscriptions'); so it is certain that she had been submitting work for some time before her first acceptance, which came in 1908 or 1909. Still at St. Elphins, now working hard toward university entrance, she acquainted only the immediate family with her success. Her cousin John, again down from

Cambridge, heard it from Clara. Richmal, she told him proudly, was now 'an authoress', with a magazine article to her credit.

Two months before her 19th birthday, Richmal became a pupil-teacher. She taught in the Lower School and received tuition from the headmistress in preparation for an open scholarship in Classics. This close personal contact proved Miss Kennedy to be much less austere than she appeared. The incident in which her unsuspected humanity first revealed itself to Richmal was duly recorded in *Anne Morrison*:

> Just at first the old fear was there – the nervousness, the dread of making a mistake and so drawing upon her the terrible wrath. That dread began to disappear during a coaching, when Miss Masters looked up from her book with a far-away, anxious expression and said:
>
> 'Oh, dear! I don't know what to do. One of my stay bones is broken and is running into me, and I can't make up my mind whether to go and change now or wait till after.'
>
> A stay bone . . . Why, she was human, human . . . It was like the withdrawing of a curtain . . . Miss Masters, no longer magisterial and terrible, was friendly, actually friendly. Anne was working harder than she had ever worked in her life, and was enjoying her work more than she had dreamed that work could be enjoyed . . . It was Miss Masters's asking her opinion about the girls in the Lower School that touched Anne most deeply . . . It inspired her with a grim determination to do credit to Miss Masters and The Priory.

Miss Kennedy proved an 'inspiring and stimulating' coach; and her premature death, following a bout of pneumonia early in 1910, very much upset Richmal. Margaret Flood, the Second Mistress's daughter, had recently come down from Girton and now returned to St. Elphins to take over the headship. Under her rule, conditions became marginally less spartan: a fire was permitted in Hall and staff-room, and staff were allowed to take afternoon tea in their rooms instead of in the staff dining-room. She instituted lectures on a wide range of subjects, from astronomy to zoology; sex education, however, was not to be introduced until after World War I – too late to be of any use to Richmal's generation of St Elphins girls.

Uncharacteristically, Richmal was, for most of her adult life, at odds with Miss Flood. The quarrel, which seems to have been entirely one-sided, stemmed from the publication in 1925 of

Anne Morrison; Miss Flood was 'much displeased' with the book (doubtless because of its description of 'sentimentalism' at the school, which Miss Flood evidently felt to have been too accurately recounted) and forbade St. Elphins pupils to read it (One might expect such a ban to have ensured that every girl would read the book at the earliest opportunity. Miss Flood, however, seems to have carried as much authority as her predecessor; many of the girls obeyed her injunction and refrained from reading the book until after they had left the school.) Richmal and Miss Flood were certainly on excellent terms prior to the publication; in 1917, the latter expressed in a testimonial 'a very high opinion' of Richmal's classical ability 'and of her character'. The rift nevertheless spanned forty years, until the two – Richmal in her seventies, Miss Flood nearly 90 – met at the home of a St. Elphins Old Girl and 'willingly buried the hatchet'.

By the time Miss Flood took over as headmistress, Gwen had left St. Elphins to attend a secretarial college and study for an external London University degree. Jack was to go up to Manchester University, where he would enjoy his first release from his father's close supervision. The university's sporting opportunities and social life were to prove much more to Jack's taste than sober study. Edward had gradually become reconciled to the fact that there would be no Oxbridge scholarship for his son, and was now able to accept that Jack had done his best; though he still expected that Jack would take Holy Orders after coming down. Jack, however, found himself increasingly attracted to the idea of farming or some other outdoor work, preferably abroad. After not much more than a year at Manchester, he took his future into his own hands: he applied to join the Rhodesian Mounted Police and told his father only after the job was assured.

Richmal, after two years as a pupil-teacher, sat her university-entrance examinations. She had hoped for a Cambridge scholarship, but heard nothing; and so accepted the entrance scholarship – £60 a year for three years – offered by Royal Holloway College, University of London. She went up on October 5, 1911; having learned, too late, that her Cambridge Higher Local results had brought the offer of a place at Newnham.

IV

Royal Holloway College had been in existence a respectable quarter of a century by the time Richmal went up. Outside academics, however, were still inclined to 'look down their noses' at this 'latest experiment in women's education about which the strangest rumours were circulated'. Fewer than 150 students inhabited the vast, elaborately ornamented college building, situated just outside Egham on the Surrey/Berkshire border; and they were relatively isolated, by 'sheer lack of transport', from the rest of the university and from London itself. The college lifestyle, however, was enviable: student and staff-member alike enjoyed a near-sybaritic comfort in her well-furnished, centrally heated bedroom and sitting-room; and the very good food, most of it the college's own produce, was expertly prepared and ceremoniously served. The college bequest provided for a four-course dinner; and though by 1911 the final course had come to consist of just a biscuit apiece, it was appetite rather than resources that had diminished.

Holloway, with its startling appearance (inspired by the founder's passion for French châteaux) and its curious blend of formality, freedom and paternalism, can hardly have failed to make an impression on Richmal. Her sister had been with her at boarding school, where the majority of their companions had been the daughters of clergymen; and the atmosphere at St. Elphins had been, like that of Malvern Villas, strongly religious. Now, for the first time in her life entirely separated from home and family, Richmal could find her place among intellectual equals, many of them from backgrounds more moneyed and sophisticated than her own. It was a relief to discover that, at college, being 'different' didn't seem to matter so much: 'People took you just as you were.' The Holloway custom of college 'families' eased the settling-in period: congenial students of the same year formed their own 'family' of around eight members,

Royal Holloway College, University of London

who 'met daily for tea and generally clung together'. Richmal joined a 'family'; she joined also the Classical Club, the Christian Union and the hockey, tennis and boating clubs.

Still pale and slight, she was nevertheless active and strong. There was clearly nothing of the torpid bookworm about Miss Lamburn. Christian names were used only between close friends: one Holloway contemporary was amazed to learn, at the age of 84, that the 'quiet, modest' Miss Lamburn she remembered had become 'Richmal Crompton of William fame'. Another recalls Richmal's going habitually 'at a little run' down the very long college corridors, her long grey skirt 'swishing round her ankles'. She continued to play hockey into her early thirties; and her membership of the college boating club suggests she was a reasonably competent swimmer, 'three lengths of the Swimming Baths, comfortably' being then the minimum standard for aspirant members.

Her facility in producing rhymes at short notice proved a definite social asset; her 'gorgeous capacity for writing ribald verse' is recalled with particular appreciation. Occasional reading parties during vacations added a pleasurable dimension to learning: a few friends, usually under the leadership of one of the younger lecturers, would take a cottage in the country and divide their time between study and outings. Though the local train service was inadequate, Holloway students made frequent use of the regular bus service to and from London. Among Richmal's companions on outings to theatre matinée performances were two sisters, the daughters of strict clerical parents in whose eyes The Stage was synonymous with Depravity. But rebellion was tempered with caution: the dissidents would prudently take to the floor as the open-topped bus approached the family vicarage en route to London.

Richmal was 'not a surprising choice' as 1911/12 Senior First-Year Student: according to one fellow student, she showed 'sound common sense, a gentle approach and a ready response, and great modesty – but also real firmness'. And the testimonials to be provided by her lecturers after Finals would describe her as 'always cheerful, good-tempered, and very ready to be useful in any way'; possessed of 'plenty of spirit and enterprise, of a sociable disposition and . . . generally liked by her companions'. Richmal was, indisputably, popular at college; even those whose contact with her was slight recall with patent enjoyment her innate sense of fun. But not one of her

Holloway contemporaries can remember her having any very close friends at college. Everyone liked her; none, it seems, came to know her intimately. Indeed, the more perceptive of those to whom she was closest throughout her life would be aware that Richmal revealed herself fully to no one: genuinely sociable, she remained intensely private. A few 'friendly acquaintanceships' would endure beyond college days; but the guard on that 'innermost room' was evidently maintained throughout her three years at Holloway.

The college days of Bridget, introvert heroine of Richmal's first novel, were to be briefly irradiated by the occasional 'rapturous thrill of happiness' that had lightened her early, fearful perspective on life. But 'the enemy', too, would remain with her, always ready to spring out and catch her unawares:

> Sometimes, when she had read or heard of any cruelty, it haunted her day and night with the old horror . . . always cruelty and suffering . . . Cowardice . . . a woman robbed and killed horribly in a field only last week . . . it might have been herself . . . the thought of the suffering of children . . . people ill-treating or neglecting children somewhere every minute of every day . . . Sometimes the thoughts of evil and suffering did not come near her for weeks. Sometimes she fought against them – saying little verses of poetry, going over her work in her mind. Sometimes she couldn't keep them off and they came upon her, crowding over her like evil things, leaving her white and exhausted.[3]

Richmal was similarly incapable of an objective contemplation of suffering. In her sixties, she read with empathetic anguish, in Fitzgibbon's *Life of Dylan Thomas*, of the poet's 'heartrendingly pathetic inability to cope with the practical side of life'. And where most would consider Mr Bennet in *Pride and Prejudice* remarkably restrained in his conduct towards his wife, Richmal thought him cruel. But it was inevitable that, unable to diminish her capacity for vicarious suffering, she would nevertheless recognize absurdity in its manifestations. In 1955 she wrote to a friend: '. . . I've also been reading a diary of an archaeologist-cum-doctor who lived about 1840 . . . He was very thin-skinned and suffered terribly at real or imagined slights. I was so distressed that I could hardly sleep, the night (I read) that he was refused admittance to Covent Garden Theatre "with great insolence" . . . because he wore light-coloured trousers instead of black!'

Academically, the 'conscientious, hard-working' Miss Lamburn continued to shine. At the end of her first year she won a year's University scholarship, usually awarded to students of longer standing; and in her final year won the Driver Scholarship in Classics. J. W. Allen, Holloway's visiting Oxford professor of Greek, regarded Richmal as an excellent scholar, of 'very considerable ability'; and Margaret Ramsey and Margaret Taylor, Lecturer and Senior Lecturer in Classics, also recorded their belief in her 'marked ability'. She was to tell one of her own pupils, however, some ten years later, that she had found the teaching of Greek at Holloway very uninspiring; which suggests that she regretted not having taken up the Cambridge scholarship. Edward Lamburn is said to have considered London academically superior to Oxbridge; and Mrs Ashbee feels that her aunt had no 'lasting sense of regret' at having accepted the Holloway place before the Newnham offer arrived. But Richmal was not one to dwell on regrets; and certainly would not have invited sympathy. She once noted, however, 'how awe-inspiring are the moments of decision, which we never recognise for what they are: everything can go irretrievably the wrong way; and so often does.' Significant, too, may be the fact that she was to steer her own classics pupils toward the Cambridge course.

Whatever the shortcomings of the Holloway classics course, Richmal was to retain her deep love of Greek; and in her later years to reread Homer and the dramatists. Her classical knowledge was 'staggeringly comprehensive'; Paul Ashbee, an archaeologist and her nephew-by-marriage, believes she would have been a notable classicist, had she chosen that path instead of teaching. And since that retrospective assessment endorses Professor Allen's prediction of a distinguished career for Richmal, there can be little doubt that her classical ability was, indeed, considerable.

The senior classics lecturer, Margaret Taylor ('a grand fighter for causes she approved of, such as Women in the Church and Women's Suffrage'), evidently made a less favourable impression on Richmal than on Ivy Compton-Burnett, who had gone down five years before Richmal arrived at Holloway. Miss Compton-Burnett was soon to immortalize Miss Taylor in *Dolores*; Richmal was to portray her, as classics lecturer Miss Gill in *The Innermost Room*, much less flatteringly:

Miss Gill... was an intense feminist and she considered that one of her duties in life was to rend the veils of ignorance from the eyes of the young. She considered that half the evil in the world arose from ignorance and 'false modesty'. She had none herself. Her translations of certain portions of the classics would have made a Mormon blush... She deplored the social evils with Bridget, and Bridget agreed gravely, instinctively shielding her ignorance from those hard eyes and little rasping mouth.

'The state of things in some of our big towns,' said Miss Gill, 'is terrible. In spite of all laws women are still underpaid. And you know what that leads to?' Bridget didn't know, but she nodded wisely, and Miss Gill was satisfied. 'Why, I heard of a case only the other day... The woman said she'd been to her employer and told him she couldn't live on what he paid her, and he said to her – he *said* to her in so many words, "No one expects you to live on that. You have your nights." Isn't it scandalous?'

Bridget agreed. The words conveyed nothing to her. Very tentatively she broached the subject that night with Susan over a Greek dictionary. She repeated the anecdote.

'Susan, what does it mean?'

Susan turned her dark mournful eyes to her – as clear as a child's.

'I don't know. It sounds rubbish.' Then she added – irrelevantly: 'My mother's frightfully old-fashioned.'

Bridget sat on the hearthrug, her chin on her knees, her eyes on the fire.

'I believe it's something horrid. I don't think I want to know. You see, Susan, if once one knows horrible things, one always knows. They're *there*! They're always ready to come in and spoil things...'

So gross a state of ignorance in young women (it is perhaps worth noting that Richmal was almost 21 when she went up) invites incredulity; until one reflects that, in the earliest years of this century, few mothers and even fewer fathers would have dreamed of sullying the innocence of girlhood with an explanation of basic sexual facts. Nor could much be gleaned from school gossip, if the listener, panicking, closed ears and mind. In *The Innermost Room*, undergraduate Bridget, terrified and disgusted by an attempted seduction (the villain a friend's father, a man she has previously admired and respected), makes a desperate if belated attempt to solve for herself the problem of acquiring facts:

They worked in silence for about an hour, then Bridget said:

'Susan, I'm going to buy one of those books that tell you things. It's easier than asking people, I think, and I don't know whom to ask.' Wonderful things, friends! Susan didn't ask her what she was talking about. She said: 'Yes. Then you can just read it and chuck it away.'

Miss Taylor – known as Cato 'because her standards were Roman' – respected scholarship; had she been less alarmingly forthright in her approach, Richmal might have established an easier relationship with her. As it was, the older woman's uncompromising frankness evidently caused Richmal agonies of embarrassment – and no doubt provided 'the enemy' with yet more weapons for the assault on that 'innermost room'.

Members of the family old enough to recall those days are emphatically agreed that there was no love affair in Richmal's young womanhood. Bury had not yielded up a kindred soul; and Royal Holloway College took very seriously its role *in loco parentis*: 'Students must consult the Principal or her assistant before giving or receiving invitations, before going on the river unless with a lecturer, or undertaking expeditions. They are requested not to walk or bicycle alone beyond the grounds and to be within the grounds by sunset.' Life after university would be hardly less circumscribed, there being for a resident teacher in a girls' school few opportunities for social contact with men. There was, in any case, less pressure on educated women of her generation to find a husband. Richmal must have been aware of the contrast between her own prospects at 21 and those of her mother at the same age. Clara Crompton at 21 had another six years to wait before Mr Right arrived; and if he had failed to arrive, she would doubtless have remained at home, a dutiful daughter occupied with domestic affairs and charitable works.

Richmal clearly had come to the distressing realization that not every marriage was as happy as that of her parents. The idealistic view expounded by her young heroine Bridget, for the benefit of a young man anxious to deliver himself into the married state, may here be of significance:

'You can't marry just because you want to marry. You've got to wait till you meet the *person* you want to marry. And then you must marry because you feel you simply couldn't live without her. It doesn't matter how long you wait. Wait till you're thirty or forty or fifty. It doesn't matter how old you are. Age has nothing to do with it. And don't go out of your way for it. It will come. Just try to keep yourself fit for it, so that when it comes you won't have things to regret, things that spoil it...'[3]

One of Bridget's college friends, Diana, offers her own observations, palpably deficient in idealism:

'From what I've seen of the state of Holy Matrimony it's a wash-out all round!... My cousin married three years ago and the young man was most obligin'. It was to be an equal partnership, don't you know, and she was to have an equal say in everything. I *don't* think! Now he stands in front of the fire and says, "I don't wish you to, my dear, and that's sufficient and I don't intend to discuss the matter," and he says, "I am the master of this house and I insist on being obeyed," and, when she treads on his precious corns, he sulks for weeks or takes it out of the kid. She gives a sigh of relief every morning when the front door closes on him. That is Holy Matrimony.'

Clinging to her illusions, Bridget tentatively suggests that happy marriages do exist; but another friend's contribution, while less cynical than Diana's, is hardly less depressing:

'It doesn't seem to last, whatever it is,' said Susan with her gravely considering air. 'I mean – Mums is quite fond of dad, but she hates the days he's at home all day and she looks forward to the week he goes to Granny's in the summer. She doesn't say it, but we know.'

Gwen's remark that her sister, when young, 'couldn't bear men near her' is countered by the observation of a friend, that Richmal was 'always most unfeignedly friendly' towards any man with whom she came into contact in her adult life. The opinion expressed by a former pupil, however, is equally uncompromising: Miss Lamburn 'obviously hated men' and 'clearly thought women superior'. One suspects that Richmal did consider the female of the species more courageous and distinctly less selfish than the male (her novels certainly indicate that she had come to this then entirely reasonable conclusion). But the youthful physical shrinking detected by her sister doubtless owed less to a hatred of men than to fear of a single aspect of the male creature: the 'something more sinister than death', long shrouded in the 'thousand dark whispers to which she had shut her ears'.

The attempted seduction in *The Innermost Room* is chronicled with a bitter intensity and realism uncharacteristic not only of Richmal but also of most other writers of the period. Bridget's terror on realizing the would-be seducer's intention is starkly portrayed and remarkably convincing: 'It seemed almost as if the enemy who had haunted her all her life was revealed face to face in final horror at last . . . ' Justifiable disgust and anger are subsequently distorted into self-disgust and disillusion:

> The whole race of man stood condemned. He had been a prince of men and he had fallen. Then what of lesser men? . . . After that night she was always ready, always on her guard . . . she could recognize that subtle change of voice and look that heralded its coming and, beneath her smiling politeness, she was ready on the defensive, every nerve taut. That is one of the lessons Life teaches women and one that it teaches least gently. The memory of that night became one of the most potent weapons of the enemy. With that vivid imagination which is as great a curse as it is a blessing, she lived it over again in the fastnesses of her fiercely fastidious little soul with hot torturing waves of shame . . .

What more likely than such an experience to foster a growing conviction that her father alone stood above the baseness of men? It is interesting that those of her novels' male characters possessing the qualities – sensitivity, idealism, intellect – that might have attracted Richmal herself are, almost without exception, flawed by neurosis or effeminacy; while her upright, 'starkly honest', uncomplicated men could be guaranteed to bring any woman with a spark of intelligence to screaming point within minutes. Richmal herself, in a rare confidence years later, said she had never been in love: no other man, perhaps, could encompass all the virtues of Edward Lamburn.

The formidable Miss Taylor's advocacy of women's rights is said to have been forceful and unremitting; but there is little evidence that it bore much fruit at Holloway. The battle for female suffrage was nearing its height when Richmal went up in 1911, yet undergraduate feeling on the issue does not appear to have run very high. W. E. Delp, in her booklet on the college, observed: 'Coming as I did from Cambridge, it seemed to me that politics aroused less passion at Royal Holloway College than at Girton . . . '; and, from a contemporary of Richmal: 'All I now remember of women's suffrage was a mock election and candidates addressing all from every vantage point – and great fun! I can remember feeling running much higher on the vexed question of "whether to allow smoking or not"!'

Richmal's own sentiments were firmly pro-feminist. Feeling it beyond dispute that women should have the vote, however, she was less convinced of their right to stop at nothing to achieve their end. Nevertheless, references in her novels to the battle for suffrage are legion; and in *Abbots' End* (1929) she wrote of a woman's hiding behind 'the authority that still vaguely invests the father of the family, a legacy from that hey-day of the domestic bully, the Victorian age'. Fully committed to the cause, she made her own small sacrifice: conquering her ingrained horror of being in the public eye, she distributed suffragist literature to passersby. By these late pre-war years,

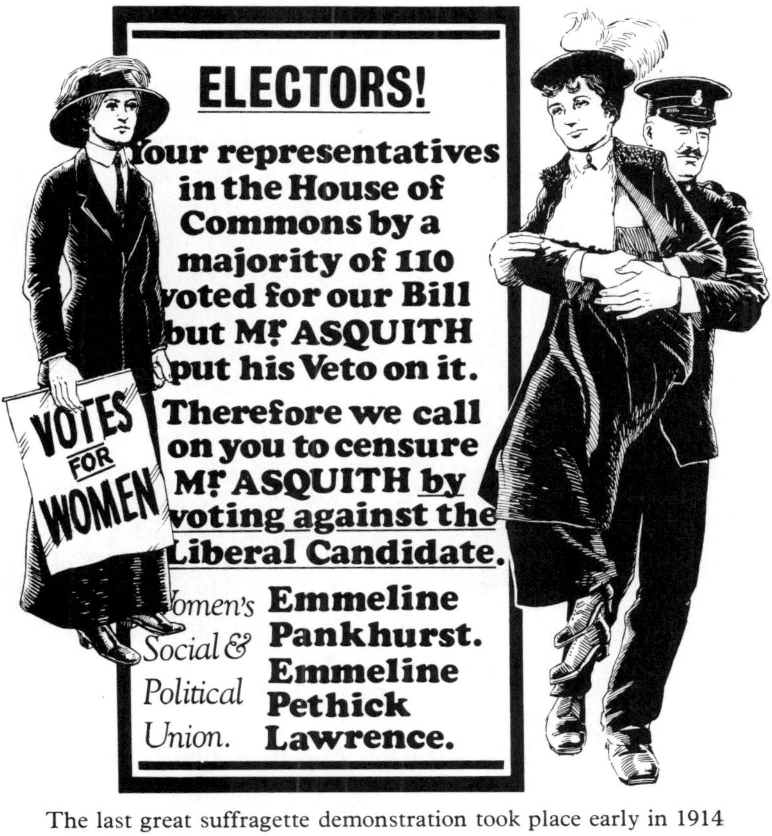

The last great suffragette demonstration took place early in 1914

however, there existed a considerable gulf between the suffragists, who still hoped for a peaceful constitutional victory, and the suffragettes, who recognized the inevitability of militant action. While remaining in the first camp, Richmal was nonetheless shocked by the brutality legally inflicted on her militant sisters; and felt a 'horrified admiration' for the former St. Elphins pupil who courageously invoked the anger of family, Crown and court by pleading at her presentation for an end to the forcible feeding of imprisoned suffragettes.

It is not unreasonable to suppose that the anguish of the eponymous heroine of *Anne Morrison* reflected Richmal's own inner conflict on the issue of militancy in the cause of women's rights. When a friend in the Movement calls to recruit Anne to the cause, she is swayed despite her doubts and dread:

> 'Look here, Anne, do you think men will ever bring in a Bill to help a class that hasn't got a vote?'
>
> 'I know that, Sylvia. I'd do anything, but is it the right way? That's what worries me.'
>
> Sylvia's lips closed together tightly.
>
> 'It's the *only* way. They'll never give it to us unless we make them... They won't *listen* to us...'
>
> Anne considered, very pale, her chin still in hands, eyes fixed on the empty grate, half convinced already, steeling herself, but still shrinking, shrinking with almost physical sickness from the thought of what it meant.
>
> 'I can't do anything – yet, you know, Sylvia.'
>
> 'I know – not till after Finals... It's for afterwards I want you.'
>
> 'What will you want me to do?'
>
> 'Interrupt in some big meeting, I think – go on interrupting whatever they do... What are sticks and stones? It's human lives we're trying to save. Look here, Anne, it's not pleasant... they don't use the London policemen for us now because they are too gentle – they deliberately get brutes and tell them to be brutal... Anne, don't stand out... don't sell your soul for a mess of pottage.'
>
> Anne was silent. The thought of Aineen and Timothy... Timothy sympathised with the militants. 'The men got the vote by rioting,' he said; 'why do they object to women doing the same?' But Aineen –

Edward, essentially just (he had been, for instance, strongly pro-Boer), may well have been as sympathetic as his counterpart in *Anne Morrison* to the women's cause; and one suspects that Clara's attitude to the 'unwomanly' suffragettes could indeed have been an effective brake on her daughter's following the forbidding path of conscience.

> Tentatively and indirectly she asked advice, but it was never satisfactory.
>
> 'A set of shrieking hoydens – their fathers and husbands ought to horsewhip 'em and keep 'em at home – that's a woman's place.'
>
> And that was useless. Or:
>
> 'They've got reason on their side, but they're losing their heads. They ought to wait.'
>
> 'But – they've tried waiting. They've waited for years,' Anne would say.
>
> 'Then let 'em wait again.'
>
> And that was useless. Or:
>
> 'I hope they'll get men under – *keep* 'em under.'
>
> And that was useless.
>
> Anne was still undecided when she finally went down, yet she knew that Sylvia's plea was drawing her . . . Over and over again (she) steeled herself in spirit to rise in a crowded meeting and shout. Over and over again cheeks flamed in agonized shame at the very imagination . . . The thought began to exercise a nightmare horror . . . She awoke perspiring from dreams of struggling with policemen . . . and again she hated herself for her weakness.

The dilemma facing Richmal at this period is manifest: like every other committed feminist who yet hesitated to take that giant step for womankind, she was impelled in two directions. Conscience dictated that violent action was never justified; yet denied her peace of mind while others were entering into battle on her behalf. For Anne Morrison, however, the outbreak of war was to resolve this particular dispute between conscience and duty:

> It was Aineen who looked up from the paper one morning after reading out the war news, and said:
>
> 'The militants have called a truce.'
>
> Timothy said casually: 'They'll have the vote before the war's over.'
>
> 'Why, Anne, darling,' said Aineen, smiling, 'what's the matter?'

'Nothing, said Anne, whose eyes were suddenly misty. 'Only – I'm so frightfully relieved.'

A pointer to the likelihood that Anne Morrison's heart-searchings over joining the suffragettes were indeed Richmal's own experience is the fact that she took a second-class honours degree, when, gifted and hard-working, she might well confidently have expected a first. Mrs Ashbee once ventured to ask her aunt why she had not taken a first. Richmal, 'rather indignant', pointed out that she had been top of her university (best candidate of her year) and that October 1914, when she sat her Finals, was 'a very unsettled time'; as of course it was, war having been declared only a few weeks earlier. But the war for women's rights, and perhaps Richmal's own agonizing over a personal commitment to militant action, had also reached its peak in those vital weeks before Finals.

More Richmal

V

Armed with her degree and glowing testimonials to her character and ability, Richmal returned to St. Elphins. Though the school could not match Holloway's standards of creature comfort, the new classical mistress was to find life at Darley Dale less austere than it had been during her own schooldays there. In these early days of the war, St. Elphins' rations were not much affected by shortages and, tucked away in the Derbyshire Peaks, the school was reasonably safe from air attack. There was only one real alarm: when, during Richmal's first term on the staff, Zeppelins heading for Sheffield dropped their loads well south of the target. The staff were roused from their beds, in case evacuation from dormitories to basement should prove necessary; it didn't, however, and everyone – relief tinged with a sense of anticlimax – went back to bed. But before long, the school was sharing in the nation's deprivations. Parents helped where they could, but the diet became increasingly insufficient and unpalatable; and the strain of war began to tell, even on those far removed from its devastations. Richmal's alter ego, Anne Morrison, felt

> . . . a continual heaviness of spirit . . . a dragging blackness of the soul. She did not wish to be free from this suffering of spirit . . . she felt that the world was suffering and that it was right that she should suffer too.

Gwen, now married and living in London, was expecting her first child in the summer of 1915, and Jack was in Rhodesia. Only Richmal, therefore, was able to return to Bury early in March, when her father developed pneumonia following an attack of pleurisy. Over the ensuing days, the Malvern Villas house saw a steady flow of callers, most of them strangers to Clara and Richmal; people of every age and circumstance who had reason to be grateful for Edward's past kindnesses and who now came anxiously to enquire after him. The 'something internal' the doctor diagnosed, when his patient had passed the pneumonia crisis yet still grew weaker, was empyema, a serious complication now preventable with antibiotics. In 1915, the only hope medical science could offer the 61-year-old Edward was surgical draining. He was taken by ambulance to a Manchester nursing home for immediate surgery; but the primitive anaesthetic methods of the day imposed additional strain on his already damaged lungs and he died without regaining consciousness after the operation.

Much of Bury shared the family's grief. Staff and pupils, past and present, attended the funeral to pay tribute to his 39 years as 'kind and fatherly friend' to two generations of Bury Grammar School boys; his parishioners and many others, genuinely saddened by the loss of this little man who had epitomized selflessness, came to stand with Edward Lamburn's family in their sorrow. After the funeral, Richmal helped her mother to settle her Bury affairs and saw her established with Gwen and her husband in London. Richmal then returned to Darley Dale; and for the next two years spent school holidays at Gwen's, making only the occasional visit to Bury to see the Crompton aunts.

Her teaching career had begun promisingly. In addition to demonstrating an ability to inspire interest and enthusiasm in both beginners and more advanced students of Latin, she proved herself 'an excellent organizer of dramatic entertainments, having considerable talent in this direction', a good disciplinarian and 'a most pleasant colleague'. It is not surprising that Miss Flood should have expressed deep regret at the prospect of losing her classical mistress at the end of the 1917 summer term. Visiting Clara in London, however, had involved travelling back and forth from Derbyshire several times a year, and a new position at a school down south must have seemed an attractive alternative. During the long summer holiday, Richmal moved with her mother into No. 9 Cherry Orchard Road in Bromley Common, Kent; and at the beginning of the autumn 1917 term took up her post as senior classical mistress, with some English teaching, at Bromley High School.

Her new job and environment quickly proved congenial. It was easier, at a day school, to see the girls not merely as pupils but also as members of local families. Among Richmal's pupils at Bromley High was a grand-daughter of the Hodder-Williams publishing family, whose home at Bromley Common, with its large family and 'wonderful Christmas and tennis parties', is believed by another former pupil to have contributed much to the settings of Richmal's novels. Living at home also ensured both greater privacy and increased opportunity for establishing social contacts. Richmal and Clara found themselves in especial demand whenever Jack returned briefly from abroad (in 1919 he was to leave Rhodesia to work in China). His looks and charm are said to have set local hearts aflutter: the social calls and invitations flooded in the moment it became known that he was due home on leave. The facilities for public worship, however, proved less than satisfactory, the local vicar failing dismally to attain the eloquence of Edward Lamburn's pulpit delivery. Presumably lacking Edward's inspiration, the local man read his weekly sermon; and Richmal was much amused one Sunday to hear him drone: 'In this dreadful nineteenth century of ours . . . '

While never sentimental in her dealings with children, Richmal had evidently inherited her father's gift for inspiring a lasting affection. The more outgoing of her pupils responded to her gift for rendering a potentially dull subject full of interest; the shy or sensitive gained confidence through her encouragement and understanding. The question of discipline, it seems, rarely arose in Richmal's classes: 'She had the gift of holding her pupils' attention, and it would never have occurred to anyone, even the most rebellious, to "play her up".' It did, however, occur to one pupil: an unhappy new girl, who at first refused to go in to prayers. But Richmal, with that delicate combination of concern, tact and reason it takes many a parent years to acquire in dealing with the 'difficult' child, deflected the challenge without loss of face to child or to adult. She 'pointed out the superb English of the Collects' and the rebel was won over.

The teaching of Greek had begun its decline, and she had few pupils for the subject at Bromley High. For those few, however, her classes were 'a truly thrilling experience, for Miss Lamburn adored Greek and it seemed like entering another world'. To her students of Latin, many of whom had previously regarded the subject as 'a drudgery of declension & conjugations, irregular verbs, the ablative absolute – a dead language to be learnt without any particular purpose', she gave the key to the 'fascinating classical world': under the guidance of an inspired teacher, 'there was a satisfaction in working out the writer's meaning, and in putting words together to make fine-sounding prose'. There was, it seems, no sting in her observation that one girl's Latin translation resembled 'the schoolboy's definition of a sponge: a lot of holes joined together'; and she often produced a funny story to drive home a point and 'impress it for ever on the memory'. (One former pupil attributes Richmal's 'facade of humour – a cynicism and wit above most of us' to a desire to hide 'her nervousness and real feelings'. But there was probably quite as much altruism as self-protection in the 'facade'.) In those days when the school outing was a rare treat, Richmal took her students of Ancient Greek to The Old Vic, to see Sybil Thorndike in *The Trojan Woman* and *Medea*, and her senior Latin pupils to classical plays performed at the Mary Datchelor School in Camberwell.

In February 1918, the law generously decreed that women who had passed their thirtieth year might henceforth vote. Miss Lamburn, then twenty-seven, 'obviously thought it wrong that women should have to wait till they were thirty'; as well she might, seeing that this privilege for which she must continue to wait had for thirty-four years been the right of every ignorant or illiterate adult male who happened to fit the legal definition of 'householder'.

Of Richmal's writing during the decade following her first acceptance, there is no record; the earliest published piece to have been traced to her authorship is a short story entitled 'Thomas', which appeared in January 1918 in *Girls Own Paper and Woman's Magazine*. Being a sentimental tale entirely typical of the period, 'Thomas' is of little interest beyond the fact that it contains a small boy called William – who suffers a thrashing at the hands of seven-year-old Thomas. Another of her stories, 'Mrs Tempest', was published in the April edition of the same magazine. Of much greater interest is the Richmal Crompton story that appeared in the September 1918 edition of *The Ladies Home Magazine* (more commonly known simply as *Home*): 'One Crowded Hour', whose protagonist, Robert Green, is manifestly William Brown in embryo. Misogynistic (but susceptible to pretty females in tears), boastful, totally lacking in refinements ('always rude, always rough, always dirty, and always greedy'), Robert at seven or eight years old is fully as lawless as William was to be at eleven: 'Mothers who wished for well-behaved children kept their offspring away from Robert Green as carefully as if he had measles or the whooping-cough.' There is even a Violet Elizabeth lookalike, complete with carefully tended curls and starched frilly skirts; though the Marie Elizabeth of 'One Crowded Hour' patently lacks her successor's termagant nature.

The earliest appearance of William himself has been variously ascribed in print to 1915, 1917, 1920, 1922 – even to 1924, by which time he had appeared in four hardback volumes. In fact, he was born in February 1919, in a story called 'Rice Mould'[5], in the monthly *Home* magazine. Literary midwife to William was *Home*'s assistant editor, now Mrs Constance Hall, one of whose duties was the selection of potentially suitable material; final decision on 'possibles' rested with the editor, Mary Cruikshank (a descendant of Victorian cartoonist George Cruikshank; but more proud of the fact that she was London's first female editor). *Home* and the other Newnes publication for which the pair were responsible, the weekly *Woman's Life*, were then largely committed to the publication of 'dramatic love stories and womanly articles'; but the young assistant editor 'giggled over William' and placed 'Rice Mould' at the top of the pile of manuscripts awaiting her chief's attention: 'I handed them over, saying I thought she would enjoy the top one, even if we couldn't use it.' Miss Cruikshank, however, 'loved it', and a cheque for three pounds winged the good news from London to Bromley.

Much encouraged, though still diffident, Richmal submitted a second story about the same boy. And in that second story, 'The Outlaws'[6], the *Home* editors saw fulfilled the promise they had glimpsed in 'Rice Mould': this time, the cheque was accompanied by a request for more stories about William. For a while, Richmal was happy to comply. But she 'preferred writing love stories', and soon began to demur at his encroachment on her time; and before long, William's further adventures were being preceded by 'regular small battles' between his creator and the *Home* editors. Each time Richmal rebelled, William was saved by an act of blackmail: *Home* would accept a romantic short story provided it came accompanied by a William story. (*Home*'s circulation figures, which had increased dramatically from his first appearance, no doubt contributed to Newnes' solicitude in the matter of William's continued existence.) By early 1920, the magazine seldom appeared without William; and by the time, a couple of years later, Constance Hall left Newnes

This illustration by L. Hocknell accompanied the first William story, 'Rice Mould', published in February 1919 in *Home* magazine. Thomas Henry's illustration of the same scene (shown in Chapter VII) first appeared in June 1922, in *More William.*

to marry, her office desk contained a drawerful of Richmal's unpublished, non-William stories. Fortunately for the *Home* editors, Richmal was not a 'typical' contributor: 'She never called in or telephoned to enquire when a particular story would appear, or what we thought of her latest contribution.' William's first battle for survival was over; it had been but a brief skirmish, his ultimate victory in little doubt.

It was perhaps inevitable that, over the years, several contenders for the role of 'the original William' would be suggested. The favourite, Richmal's brother, had indeed in boyhood shared some of William's interests and characteristics: Jack, too, was non-academic, demonstrated a passion for collecting the more revolting species of insect life; preferred rough companions to civilized company, hated being fussed over by women (and with greater reason, since he was much better-looking than William). But essentially there is not much of a likeness. For instance, the difficult relationship with his father caused Jack at least some degree of unhappiness, if only through frustration; whereas there are no hang-ups in William's relationship with his male parent. It was always William versus the entire, incomprehensible adult world; and it was usually the world, not William, that suffered. The second-favourite candidate, Richmal's nephew Thomas Disher, was some months short of his fourth birthday when William first appeared and therefore surely too young to have been the model. Richmal did, however, make use of some of Jack's and Tommy's interests and escapades: such as Tommy's provision of marmalade for the stag beetle residing in his underwear drawer, which appeared as one of William's lesser misdemeanours in 'William and Saint Valentine'[7].

One would hardly be inclined to look further, were it not for an assertion by Jack himself that William was 'not original'. Though Richmal's fierce family loyalty remained unshakeable to the end of her life, her relationship with her only brother was sadly strained during her final years; and it was during this period, in the late 1960s, that Jack told his son that William had been based on 'a turn-of-the-century boy character', whose name Jack could not remember.

The candidate who springs first to mind, if Jack's statement is to be given serious consideration, is Eden Philpotts' Human Boy, who appeared first in 1899 (*The Human Boy*) and in four subsequent volumes over the ensuing thirty years. Richmal's library contained a copy of the collected edition, *The Complete Human Boy*; and in the 1930s she introduced a young niece to Philpotts' agreeably tongue-in-cheek prose. The Human Boy, however, confines himself to recounting – in the first person – the lawlessness of his fellow pupils. He reveals no anarchic tendency on his own part and his general attitude to life, reflective and mildly ironical, is not at all reminiscent of William.

The American Peck's Bad Boy, resurrected in November 1967 to join William in a *Reader's Digest* magazine Book Supplement entitled 'Boys will be Boys!', proves an equally improbable source. Peck's Bad Boy ('Hennery') originated in George W. Peck's newspaper in 1874, appeared in book form in 1883 and was portrayed on stage by the young George Cohan; but his popularity did not spread beyond North America and in any case had faded by 1910. Beyond the inevitable fact that each is a severe trial to his father, there is little resemblance between Hennery and William; and Richmal Crompton's style is not even remotely suggestive of Peck's.

A third contender sprang from the Letters page of *Radio Times* in 1977, in the wake of a discussion on BBC Television of the first commercial-television William series[8]. In response to a letter asking whether any other 'middle-aged viewers' had been struck by the 'close similarities' between William and an earlier, American fictional character called Penrod, a Belfast reader claimed that details, incidents, even complete episodes had been 'lifted wholesale' by Richmal Crompton from the Penrod stories by Booth Tarkington.

The few references to Penrod to be found in standard works on children's literature are very brief; and while many of those who were reading six or seven decades ago remember Booth Tarkington's *Monsieur Beaucaire* and *The Magnificent Ambersons*, hardly any can recall his Penrod stories. Nevertheless, Penrod's adventures did appear in book form in Britain. Hodder & Stoughton published the first volume, *Penrod*, in 1914; five years before William's first appearance in the pages of *Home* magazine.

Richmal – the Pirate?

VI

Penrod, too, made his first appearance in a magazine: defunct within the decade and now anonymous, it presented him to an immediately appreciative American public in 1913. Receiving thereafter 'from affable readers, strangers to him, encouragement to discourse further upon the subject', Booth Tarkington expanded his theme of Boy versus Adult World to fill three volumes: *Penrod* (1914), *Penrod and Sam* (1916) and *Penrod Jashber* (1929). An abridged omnibus edition, PENROD *His Complete Story*, with illustrations by Gordon Grant, was published in 1931 and is still in print (Doubleday, N.Y.).

The style of the Penrod stories – narrative, episodic, prolix – is unfamiliar; their matter – 'a boy's doings in the days when the stable was empty but not yet rebuilt into a garage' – at times very familiar. Penrod Schofield, scourge of his middle-class family and neighbours, is eleven years old. He has a sister ('a pretty girl of nineteen') and a dog (Duke: a name 'undescriptive of his person, which was obviously the result of a singular series of mesalliances'). There is no gang, but Penrod does have a regular partner in crime:

> Mr. Samuel Williams, aged eleven, and congenial to Penrod in years, sex and disposition, appeared in the doorway, shaking into foam a black liquid within a pint bottle, stoppered by a thumb.
> 'Yay, Penrod!' the visitor gave greeting.
> 'Yay,' said Penrod with slight enthusiasm. 'What you got?'
> 'Lickrish water.'[9]

The pair meet in 'a one-storied wing of the stable, consisting of a single apartment, floored with cement and used as a storeroom'; and Sam's older brother, Robert, figures largely in Penrod's life.

The minor traits of character and behaviour shared by

Penrod and William are many and striking. It is evident from the beginning that book-learning holds as little charm for the former as for the latter:

> To Penrod school was merely a state of confinement, envenomed by mathematics. For interminable periods he was forced to listen to information concerning matters about which he had no curiosity whatever; and he had to read over and over the dullest passages in books that bored him into stupors, while always there overhung the preposterous task of improvising plausible evasions to conceal the fact that he did not know what he had no wish to know . . .[10]

Penrod Schofield

Parental exhortation to study is as ineffective with the one as with the other. William's reluctance to accept his mother's word that French verbs will one day be useful to him forcefully echoes Penrod's unwavering resistance to his elders' assurances that school is for his own good:

Pictures from a family album

John Lamburn (1791-1860),
Richmal's great-grandfather

Edward J. S. Lamburn (centre) in 1868,
with his parents and brothers

The Cromptons c. 1883. Front row: Hannah, Mr Crompton, Jack, Mrs Crompton.
Back: Harry, Re, Ada, Lizzie, Clara (Richmal's mother).

Clara's sister Re wilting beneath a tall curate during an outing of family and friends c. 1884

Clara (top left) displaying her new engagement ring in picturesque setting, with her sisters and a friend in the summer of 1886

Richmal
with older
sister Gwen
in 1891

Richmal at two and a half with her parents, sister Gwen
and new brother Jack

The Crompton family in early 1894. Standing: the Rev. E. J. S. Lamburn (Clara's husband), Hannah's husband and daughter, Ada's husband, Re, Jack, Harry. Seated: Clara, Hannah, Mrs Crompton with Ada's baby, Ada with her older son, Lizzie with John Wrigley (Hannah's son). Front: Jack, Richmal and Gwen Lamburn.

The Lamburn children in 1895: Gwen holding
Phyllis (died November 1895), Richmal, Jack

Richmal (centre, middle row) at her first school, with Gwen on her left

Gwen, Jack and Richmal (right) in 1896

The Lamburns (Richmal seated) in the garden of No. 4 Malvern Villas, c. 1897

Richmal (left) and Gwen at the Clergy Daughters School, Warrington

Richmal (right) and family c. 1904, on one of Edward's 'locum holidays'

Clara and Richmal, photographed by Jack on a Lincolnshire holiday c. 1905

Richmal (left), Gwen and parents c. 1906

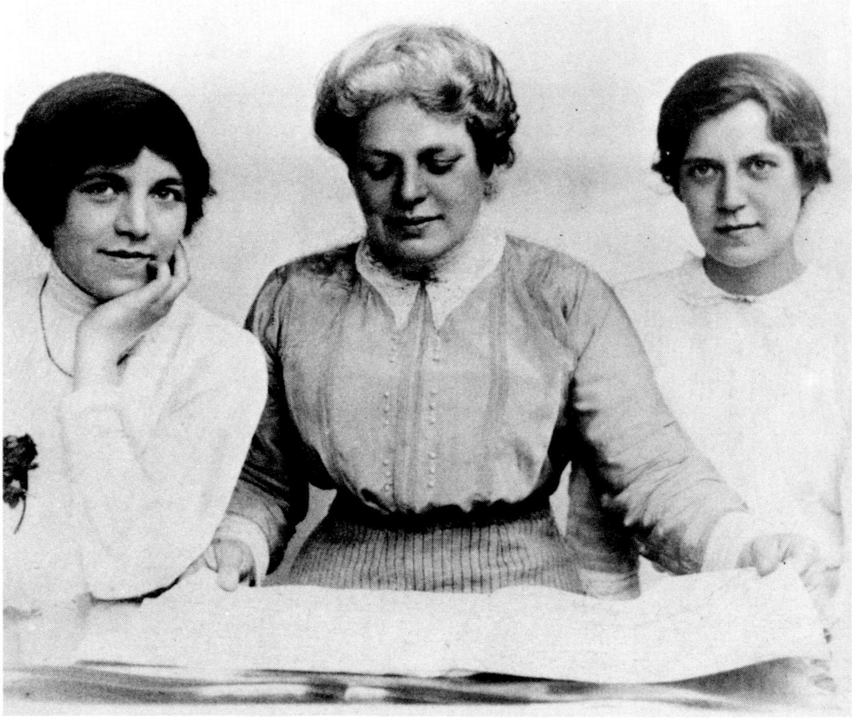

Gwen, Clara and Richmal (right) c. 1908

Penrod was wholly unable to imagine circumstances, present or future, under which any of the instruction and training he was now receiving could be of the slightest possible use or benefit to himself; and when he was informed that such circumstances would frequently arise in his later life, he but felt the slur upon his coming manhood and its powers to prevent any such unpleasantness . . .[10]

'Well, I never *will* wanter use 'em,' said William to his mother when she brought forward the time-honoured argument, 'I don' wanter talk to *any* French folks, an' if they wanter talk to me they can learn English. English's 's easy 's easy to talk. It's *silly* havin' other langwidges . . .'[11]

And Penrod's singing voice, 'shrill, loud, incredibly piercing and incredibly flat', has much the same effect on the hearer as William's:

Invalids murmured pitifully as Penrod came within hearing; and people trying to think cursed the day that they were born when he went shrilling by. His hands in his pockets, his shining face uplifted to the sky of June, he passed down the street, singing his way into the heart's deepest hatred of all who heard him . . .[9]

Inhabitants of the street along which William was passing hastily shut their front windows or fled from their front rooms or uttered loud objurgations of William according to their characters . . . William passed along, singing and unmoved . . .[12]

Unmusical, unacademic, Penrod is nevertheless subject to occasional attacks of creativity. At such times, he retreats to the solitude of the stable, there to struggle with his Muse:

Soon the two men were struggling together in the deathroes but soon Mr. Wilson got him bound and gaged his mouth and went away for while leavin our hero, it was dark and he writhd at his bonds writhing on the floor wile the rats came out o their holes and bit him and vernim got all over him from the floor of the helish spot but soon he manged to push the gag out of his mouth with the end of his tongue and got all his bonds off[9]

The superior punctuation of William's first recorded literary effort may safely be credited to an over-zealous proofreader.

The theme makes it plain that he shares Penrod's predilection for melodrama:

For a minit they stood trembling, then one, bolder than the rest, lept forward and tide Dick Savage's hands with rope behind his back. Another took from his pockets bottles of beer and tobacco in large quantities.

'Ho!' they cried exulting. 'Ho! Dick Savage the smuggler caught at last!'

Dick Savage gave one proud and defiant laugh, and, bringing his tide hands over his hed he bit the rope with one mighty bite.

'Ho! Ho!' he cried, throwing back his proud hed, 'Ho! Ho! You dirty dogs!'

Then, draining to the dregs a large bottle of poison he had concealed in his bosum he fell ded and lifless at there feet.[13]

Penrod's dog, Duke

The opening paragraphs of *Penrod*, the first volume, establish him as soulmate to William:

Penrod sat morosely upon the back fence and gazed with envy at Duke, his wistful dog.

A bitter soul dominated the various curved and angular surfaces known by a careless world as the face of Penrod Schofield. Except in solitude, that face was almost always cryptic and emotionless; for Penrod approached his twelfth year wearing an expression carefully trained to be inscrutable. Since the world was sure to misunderstand everything, mere defensive instinct prompted him to give it as little as possible to lay hold upon. Nothing is more impenetrable than the face of a boy who has learned this; and Penrod's was habitually as fathomless as the depth of his hatred this morning for the literary activities of Mrs Lora Rewbush – an almost universally respected fellow-citizen, a lady of charitable and poetic inclinations, and one of his own mother's most intimate friends.

Mrs. Lora Rewbush had written something which she called "The Children's Pageant of the Table Round"; and it was to be performed in public that very afternoon . . . And if any flavour of sweetness remained in the nature of Penrod Schofield after the dismal trials of the school-week just past, that problematic, infinitesimal remnant was made pungent acid by the imminence of his destiny to form a prominent feature of the spectacle, and to declaim the loathsome sentiments of a character named upon the program the Child Sir Lancelot . . .

In the story 'William and White Satin', an equally humiliating role is forced on William: he is to be a page at his cousin's wedding. His reaction to this news is precisely Penrod's reaction to the prospect of being dressed as the Child Sir Lancelot:

(Horrible were) the sentiments which animated Penrod's bosom when the instantaneous and unalterable conviction descended upon him that he was intended by his loved ones to make a public spectacle of himself in his sister's stockings and part of an old dress of his mother's . . . The frantic youth's final submission was obtained only after a painful telephonic conversation between himself and his father, the latter having been called up and upon, by the exhausted Mrs. Schofield, to subjugate his offspring by wire.[9]

'I've got a pair of lovely white silk stockings,' said (William's) mother. 'They'd do for tights, and Ethel has got a satin petticoat that's just beginning to go in one place. I should think we could make some sort of costume from that, don't you? We'll buy some more white satin and get some patterns.'

'No, I won't wear Ethel's ole clothes,' said William, smouldering. 'You all jus' want to make me look ridiclus. You don't care how ridiclus I look. I shall be ridiclus all the rest of my life goin' about in Ethel's ole clothes. I jus' won't do it. I jus' won't go to any ole weddin'. No, I *don't* want to see Cousin Sybil married, an' I jus' *won't* be made look ridiclus in Ethel's ole clothes.'

> They reasoned and coaxed and threatened, but in vain. Finally William yielded to parental authority and went about his world with an air of a martyr doomed to the stake.[14]

Not only do Penrod and William react similarly, the same possible means of escape occurs to each of them:

> Penrod had rather vaguely debated plans for self-mutilation such as would make his appearance as the Child Sir Lancelot inexpedient on public grounds; it was a heroic and attractive thought, but the results of some extremely sketchy preliminary experiments caused him to abandon it.[9]
>
> Life became very full. It was passed chiefly in the avenging of insults. William cherished a secret hope that the result of this would be to leave him disfigured for life and so unable to attend the wedding. However, except for a large lump on his forehead, he was none the worse. He eyed the lump thoughtfully in his looking-glass and decided that with a little encouragement it might render his public appearance in an affair of romance an impossibility. But the pain which resulted from one heroic effort at banging it against the wall caused him to abandon the plan.[14]

Fate spares William the threatened humiliation. Penrod is less fortunate; but the subsequent disaster recalls many a chaotic finale engendered by William's participation in such an affair:

> They made a brief, manful effort (to go on with the Pageant). But the irrepressible outbursts from the audience confused them; every time Sir Lancelot du Lake the Child opened his mouth, the great, shadowy house fell into an uproar and the children into confusion. Strong women and brave girls in the audience went out into the lobby, shrieking and clinging to one another. Others remained, rocking in their seats, helpless and spent. The neighbourhood of Mrs. Schofield and Margaret became, tactfully, a desert. Friends of the author went behind the scenes and encountered a hitherto unknown phase of Mrs. Lora Rewbush; they said, afterwards, that she hardly seemed to know what she was doing. She begged to be left alone with Penrod Schofield for just a little while . . .[9]

Penrod's sister, Margaret, is more kindly than William's sister; and Mrs Schofield, like Mrs Brown, is simply A Mother. Penrod's father, however, has a great deal in common with Mr

Brown. Not the least of each father's afflictions is the sound of his son's voice raised in song:

> Mr. Brown opened the library door.
>
> 'Will – you – stop – that – confounded – noise!' he demanded emphatically.
>
> 'I'm sorry,' said William amicably. 'I forgot you din't like musick.'[12]

> 'Pen-*rod*!'
>
> Mr. Schofield appeared at an open window upstairs, a book in his hand.
>
> 'Stop it!' he commanded. 'Can't I stay home with a headache *one* morning from the office without having to listen to – I never *did* hear such squawking!'[9]

Penrod is as much inclined as William to make the most of any rare genuine infirmity; and Mr. Schofield as little inclined as Mr. Brown to extend a tender paternal sympathy:

> Penrod entered the schoolroom, Monday morning, picturesquely leaning upon a man's cane shortened to support a cripple approaching the age of twelve. He arrived about twenty minutes late, limping deeply, his brave young mouth drawn with pain, and the sensation he created must have been a solace to him, the only possible criticism of this entrance being that it was just a shade too heroic. Perhaps for that reason it failed to stagger Miss Spence, a woman so saturated with suspicion that she penalised Penrod for tardiness as promptly and as coldly as if he had been a mere, ordinary, unmutilated boy...
>
> However, the distinction of cane and limp remained to him, consolations which he protracted far into the week – until Thursday evening, in fact, when Mr. Schofield, observing from a window his son's pursuit of Duke round and round the backyard, confiscated the cane, with the promise that it should not remain idle if he saw Penrod limping again.[9]

Frequently confounded by his son's skill in prevarication, Mr. Schofield, like Mr. Brown, is nevertheless occasionally allowed his revenge:

> 'Where did I get what, papa?' asked Penrod meekly, depositing the accordion in the hall, just outside the dining-room door.

'That da- that third-hand concertina.'

'It's a 'cordion,' said Penrod, taking his place at the table...

'Who *was* he?'

'Who do you mean, papa?'

'The man who gave you that ghastly Thing.'

'Yessir. A man gave it to me.'

'I say, who *was* he?' shouted Mr. Schofield.

'Well, I was just walking along, and the man came up to me – it was right down in front of Colgates', where most of the paint's rubbed off the fence –'

'Penrod!' The father used his most dangerous tone.

'Sir?'

'Who was the man who gave you the concertina?'

'I don't know. I was walking along and –'

'You never saw him before?'

'No, sir. I was just walk-'

'That will do,' said Mr. Schofield, rising. 'I suppose every family has its hidden enemies, and this was one of ours. I must ask to be excused!'

With that he went out crossly, stopping in the hall a moment before passing beyond hearing. And, after lunch, Penrod sought in vain for his accordion; he even searched the library where his father sat reading, though, upon inquiry, Penrod explained that he was looking for a misplaced school-book. He thought he ought to study a little every day, he said, even during vacation-time. Much pleased, Mr. Schofield rose and joined in the search, finding the missing work on mathematics with singular ease...[9]

And under extreme provocation, Mr. Schofield and Mr. Brown reach an identical conclusion:

Mr. Schofield's version of things was that Penrod was insane. 'He's a stark, raving lunatic!' declared the father, descending to the library from a before-dinner interview with the outlaw that evening. 'I'd send him to a military school, but I don't believe they'd take him...'[9]

Inside the house, (William's) father, reclining at length in an armchair, discoursed to his wife on the subject of his son. One hand was pressed to his aching brow, and the other gesticulating freely. 'He's insane,' he said, 'stark, raving insane... They're the acts of a lunatic – you ought to have his brain examined.'[15]

One does not have to read very far into *Penrod* to be struck by the number of incidents and situations common to the early William stories. Penrod, for example, visits a sweetshop and buys a five-cent sack of candy . . . :

> . . . so generously capable of resisting solution that the purchaser must needs be avaricious beyond reason who did not realise his money's worth.
>
> Equipped with this collation, Penrod contributed his remaining nickel to a picture show . . . in cosy darkness, he placidly insulted his liver with jaw-breaker upon jaw-breaker from the paper sack, and in a surfeit of content watched the silent actors on the screen.
>
> One film made a lasting impression upon him. It depicted with relentless pathos the drunkard's progress, beginning with his conversion to beer in the company of loose travelling men; pursuing him through an inexplicable lapse into evening clothes and the society of some remarkably painful ladies; next, exhibiting the effects of alcohol in the victim's domestic disposition, the unfortunate man was seen in the act of striking his wife and, subsequently, his pleading baby daughter, with an abnormally heavy walking stick. Their flight – through the snow – to seek the protection of a relative was shown, and, finally, the drunkard's picturesque behaviour at the portals of a madhouse.[9]

In the third William story published, he, too, has visited a sweet-shop ('In the matter of sweets, William frankly upheld the superiority of quantity over quality') on his way to the Picture Palace:

> Sitting quite motionless, he watched, with wide, fascinated eyes, though his jaws never ceased their rotary movement and every now and then his hand would go mechanically to the paper bag on his knees and convey a Gooseberry Eye to his mouth...
>
> Lastly came the pathetic story of a drunkard's downward path. He began as a wild young man in evening clothes drinking intoxicants and playing cards, he ended as a wild old man in rags still drinking intoxicants and playing cards. He had a small child with a pious and superior expression, who spent her time weeping over him and exhorting him to a better life, till, in a moment of justifiable exasperation, he threw a beer bottle at her head. He then bedewed her bed in Hospital with penitent tears, tore out his hair, flung up his arms towards Heaven, beat his waistcoast, and clasped her to his breast, so that it was not to be wondered at that, after all that excitement, the child had a relapse and with the words 'Good-bye, Father. Do not think of what you have done. I forgive you.' passed peacefully away.[15]

Penrod, though dazzled by the young sophisticate who parades her familiarity with Paris and the French language and offers to teach him the latest dance step, does his best to appear unimpressed. William, equally dazzled and equally determined not to show it, also resorts to taciturnity in the face of the female phenomenon:

> 'Do you like Paris?' she asked William.
>
> 'Never been there,' said William stolidly, glancing surreptitiously round to see that Jumble was following.
>
> She shook her dark curly head from side to side – a little trick she had.
>
> 'You funny boy. *Mais vous parlez Français, n'est-ce pas?*'
>
> William disdained to answer. He whistled to Jumble, who was chasing an imaginary rabbit in a ditch.
>
> 'Can you jazz?' she asked.
>
> 'I don't know,' he said guardedly. 'I've not tried. I expect I could.'
>
> She took a few flying graceful steps with slim black silk-encased legs.

'That's it. I'll teach you at home. We'll dance it to a gramophone.'[16]

The sixth story published, 'William Joins the Band of Hope', recalls the passage in which Penrod meets the Rev. Mr. Kinosling. Penrod has recently been the subject of persecution: contemporaries have been taunting him with the vile epithet of 'little gentleman'. Though partially avenged, he is still smouldering and the rest of the family is therefore apprehensive as they all sit down to dinner with their reverend guest:

"It has been a delicious day," said Mr. Kinosling presently; "warm but balmy." With a benevolent smile he addressed Penrod, who sat opposite him. "I suppose, little gentleman, you have been indulging in the usual outdoor sports of vacation?"

Penrod laid down his fork and glared, open-mouthed, at Mr. Kinosling.

"You'll have another slice of breast of the chicken?" Mr. Schofield inquired, loudly and quickly.

"A lovely day!' exclaimed Margaret, with equal promptitude and emphasis. "Lovely, oh, lovely! Lovely!"

"Beautiful, beautiful, beautiful!" said Mrs. Schofield, and after a glance at Penrod which confirmed her impression that he intended to say something she continued, "Yes, beautiful, beautiful beautiful . . . !"

It is not known in what light Mr. Kinosling viewed the expression of Penrod's face . . . it is oftener than is suspected the case that extremely peculiar expressions upon the countenances of boys are entirely overlooked, and suggest nothing to the minds of the people staring straight at them. Certainly Penrod's expression – which, to the perception of his family, was perfectly horrible – caused not the faintest perturbation in the breast of Mr. Kinosling . . .[9]

In 'William Joins the Band of Hope', Mrs Brown, having insisted on William's transformation to a model of cleanliness and tidiness, suffers an equally well founded anxiety as her guest departs:

(Mrs. de Vere Carter) stretched out her arm with an encircling movement, but William stepped back and stood looking at her with a sinister frown.

"I *have* so enjoyed seeing you. I hope you'll come again," untruthfully stammered Mrs. Brown, moving so as to block out the sight of William's face, but Mrs. de Vere Carter was not to be checked. There are people to whom the expression on a child's face conveys absolutely nothing . . .[6]

In 'The Best-Laid Plans', the eleventh story published in *Home* (Jan. 1920), William is bribed by an admirer of his sister. Penrod also is bribed by an admirer of his sister, who here relates to her boyfriend the disastrous results of his bribe, spent by Penrod at the fair:

" . . . water-melon, and chocolate creams, and licorice sticks, and lemon-drops, and peanuts, and jaw-breakers, and sardines, and raspberry lemonade, and pickles, and popcorn . . . and papa said, 'Who gave you that dollar?' Only he didn't say '*who*' – he said something horrible, Bob! And Penrod thought he was going to die, and he said *you* gave it to him; and, oh! it was just pitiful to hear the poor child, Bob, because he thought he was dying, you see, and he blamed you for the whole thing. He said if you'd only let him alone and not given it to him, he'd have grown up to be a good man – and now he couldn't! I never heard anything so heartrending – he was so weak he could hardly whisper, but he kept trying to talk, telling us over and over it was all your fault."

In the darkness Mr. Williams' facial expression could not be seen, but his voice sounded hopeful.

"Is he – is he still in a great deal of pain?"[9]

William's half-crown goes the way of Penrod's dollar; and Ethel's admirer has quite as much cause as Margaret's to regret his bribe:

. . . Having now completely recovered from the sensations caused by the merry-go-round, (William) purchased a large bag of pop-corn and stood leaning against a tent-pole until he had consumed it. Then he purchased two sticks of nougat and with it drank two bottles of ginger-beer. The remaining 4d. was spent upon a large packet of a red sticky mixture called Canadian Delight.

Dusk was falling by this time and slowly, very slowly, William returned home. He firmly refused all food at supper. Mrs. Brown grew anxious . . .

When pressed, he admitted having gone to the fair.

'Someone gave me half-a-crown,' he excused himself plaintively. 'I jus' had to go somewhere.'

'It's perfectly absurd of people,' said Mrs. Brown indignantly, 'to give large sums of money to a boy of William's age. It always ends this way. People ought to know better.'

As they passed out from the supper-table, William whispered hoarsely to Mr. French:

'It was that half-crown what you give me.'

'Don't tell them,' whispered Mr. French desperately.

'What'll you give me not to?'

Furtively Mr. French pressed a two-shilling piece into his hand.[6]

Between Penrod and Georgie Bassett ('the Best Boy in Town'), as between the Outlaws and Georgie Murdoch ('the Perfect Boy'), unfavourable comparisons are inevitable:

'Everywhere I hear wonderful reports of him,' said Mr. Kinosling. 'I may say that I understand boys, and I feel that he is a rare, a fine, a pure, a lofty spirit. I say spirit, for spirit is the word I hear spoken of him.'

A chorus of enthusiastic approbation affirmed the accuracy of this proclamation, and Mrs. Bassett flushed with pleasure. Georgie's spiritual perfection was demonstrated by instances of it, related by the visitors; his piety was cited, and wonderful things he had said were quoted.

'Not all boys are pure, of fine spirit, of high mind,' said Mr. Kinosling, and continued with real feelings: 'You have a neighbour, dear Mrs. Bassett, whose household I indeed really feel it quite impossible to visit until such time when better, firmer, stronger handed, more determined discipline shall prevail. I find Mr. and Mrs. Schofield and their daughter charming, but-'

Three or four ladies said 'Oh!' and spoke a name simultaneously. It was as if they had said, 'Oh, the bubonic plague!'

'Oh! Penrod Schofield!'[9]

And then George Murdoch came to live at the Laurels and Georgie Murdoch was the Perfect Boy.

The effect upon the Outlaws' parents was dynamic.

No longer did they view their offspring with resigned disgust and tell themselves and each other that boys would be boys, for was not Georgie Murdoch a walking refutation of the theory. Georgie Murdoch's whole existence proved conclusively that boys needn't be boys...

> As Ginger had predicted, they all had to have him to tea, and on each occasion Georgie remained clean and tidy and immaculate in his white suit and said at the end to his host's mother, 'Yes, I told him not to. I *said* you wouldn't like it.' And when the guest had departed the host's mother said to the host:
>
> 'How I *wish* that you were a little more like Georgie Murdoch.'[17]

The ultimate downfall of the paragon is in each case satisfyingly total. Georgie Bassett, having misguidedly revealed his ambition to become a minister, is persuaded (by Penrod) that his only hope of ordination lies in acquiring the uninhibited style of a pole-climbing, hollering, revivalist preacher-man. Taunted beyond endurance, Georgie frenziedly insists on proving his suitability for the ministry by climbing the maple tree under the critical eye of Penrod. The tree stands only a few feet from the drawing-room wherein Georgie's mother is entertaining guests to tea:

> 'Going to heaven!' shrieked George, squirming up another inch. 'Going to heaven, heaven, heaven!'
>
> His mother's frenzied attempts to attract his attention failed utterly. George was using the full power of his lungs, deafening his own ears to all other sounds. Mrs. Bassett called in vain; while the tea-party stood petrified in a cluster about the window...
>
> He tried to climb higher, but began to slip downward, his exertions causing damage to his apparel. A button flew into the air, and his knickerbockers and his waist-band severed relations.
>
> 'Devil's got my coat-tails, sinners! Old devil's got my coat-tails!' he announced appropriately. Then he began to slide. He relaxed his clasp of the tree and slid to the ground.
>
> 'Going to hell!' shrieked Georgie, reaching a high pitch of enthusiasm in this great climax. 'Going to hell! Going to hell! I'm going to hell, hell, hell!'
>
> With a loud scream, Mrs. Bassett threw herself out of the window, alighting by some miracle upon her feet, with ankles unsprained...[9]

The mother of Georgie Murdoch, William's *bête noire*, is similarly engaged when the blow falls. She is giving a garden party, at which a children's prize has been offered for the best-acted scene from English History. Georgie has attached himself to William's group; and William, 'sphinx-like', suggests they enact King John's 'losing his things in the Wash': a scene that involves the protagonist's covering himself in mud and then calling for his servants, Dam and Blarst. Georgie, determined to acquire the prize of chocolate creams, demands to be King John . . . :

> Just then William and Ginger appeared. They had replaced their stockings and shoes and looked for William and Ginger unusually neat and tidy.
>
> 'Well, dears,' said Mrs. Murdoch, smiling, 'have you chosen your little scene yet?'
>
> 'No,' said William, 'we can't get on with it with Georgie messin' about the pond all the time.'
>
> At that moment Georgie, imagining that William and Ginger had heralded his approach with all ceremony, came proudly into view from behind the bushes, followed by Douglas and Henry. The mud from the pond was a peculiarly concentrated kind of mud and Georgie had wallowed in it from head to foot. One could only guess at his white suit and glinting curls. But through it shone Georgie's eyes in rapturous anticipation of a two pound box of chocolate creams.
>
> William and Ginger gazed at him in well simulated horror.
>
> 'Oh, Georgie, you *naughty* boy!' said William.
>
> 'What *will* your mother say?' said Ginger.
>
> Douglas and Henry stepped forward.
>
> 'We *told* him not to,' said Douglas.
>
> 'We *knew* you wouldn't like it,' said Henry to the speechless Mrs. Murdoch.
>
> Georgie felt that something had gone wrong somewhere but he was determined to do his part at any rate to win those chocolate creams.
>
> He looked at Henry and Douglas. 'Oh, Dam and Blarst-' he began, but the uproar drowned the rest.
>
> With a scream of horror audible a mile away Mrs. Murdoch seized the perfect little gentleman by the arm and hurried him indoors.[17]

Penrod's public humiliation of another saintly thorn in his flesh, Roddy Magsworth-Bitts (a 'fat, torpid acquaintance' reminiscent of Hubert Lane) produces a parental reaction wholly unexpected:

Singularly enough, Mrs. Williams did not look troubled; she looked as if she were trying to look troubled. Mrs. Schofield wore a similar expression. So did Mr. Schofield. So did Mr. Williams...

'I never did hear anyone in such a state before,' continued Mrs. Williams. 'So furious-'

'Quite justly, of course,' said Mrs. Schofield...

'She said one thing I think rather tactless,' interrupted Mrs. Williams. 'Of course, we must allow for her being dreadfully excited and wrought up, but I do think it wasn't quite delicate in her, and she's usually the very soul of delicacy. She said that Roderick had *never* been allowed to associate with – with common boys –'

'Meaning Sam and Penrod,' said Mrs. Schofield. 'Yes, she said that to me, too.'

'She said that the most awful thing about it,' Mrs. Williams went on, 'was that, though she's going to prosecute the newspapers, many people would always believe the story... I'm afraid it will be a great come-down for them.'

'I'm afraid so,' said Mrs. Schofield gently. 'A very great one – yes, a very, very great one.'[9]

The annihilation of Georgie Murdoch affords a comparable satisfaction to the parents of the Outlaws:

... Georgie's reputation was gone. It had so to speak vanished in a night. Georgie might have paraded his clean white-clad figure and smug smile and golden curls before the eyes of the village for a hundred years and yet never wiped out the memory of that mud-caked little horror uttering horrible oaths before the assembled aristocrats of the village... The Outlaws, clean and neat and sphinx-like and silent, accompanied their parents home.

'*Well*,' said the parents, 'I'd never have believed *that* of Georgie Murdoch!'

'*Caked* with mud!'

'And such *language*!'

'It shows that you never can *tell*.'

A close observer might have gathered that at heart the Outlaws' parents were almost as jubilant over Georgie's downfall as were the Outlaws themselves...[17]

For Penrod, as for William, 'punishment and clemency are alike inexplicable'. After the Magsworth-Bitts fiasco, Penrod and Sam expect the parental conclave to be followed swiftly by retribution:

> 'Well,' observed Mrs. Williams, after a thoughtful pause, 'there's only one thing to be done, and I suppose it had better be done right away.'
>
> She glanced toward the two gentlemen...
>
> Thus, in the early twilight, the now historic stable was approached by two fathers charged to do the only thing to be done... With hanging heads and despondent countenances, each still ornamented with a moustache and an imperial, Penrod and Sam awaited sentence...
>
> Mr. Williams took his son by the ear.
>
> 'You march home!' he commanded.
>
> Sam marched, not looking back, and his father followed the small figure implacably.
>
> 'You goin' to whip me?' quavered Penrod, alone with Justice.
>
> 'Wash your face at that hydrant,' said his father sternly.
>
> About fifteen minutes later, Penrod hurriedly entering the corner drug store, two blocks distant, was astonished to perceive a familiar form at the soda counter.
>
> 'Yay, Penrod,' said Sam Williams. 'Want some sody? Come on. He didn't lick me. He didn't do anything to me at all. He gave me a quarter.'
>
> 'So'd mine,' said Penrod.[9]

In 'The Show', the fifth story published (*Home*, June 1919; *Just – William*), William has been caught in the act of admitting a paying public to the bedroom in which his aunt lay snoring, false teeth and hairpiece on display beside her. He, too, apprehensively awaits the parental wrath:

> Aunt Emily fixed her eye upon (Mr. Brown).
>
> 'Will you be good enough to procure a conveyance?' she said. 'After the indignities to which I have been subjected in this house I refuse to remain in it a moment longer.'
>
> Quivering with indignation she gave details of the indignities to which she had been subjected. William's mother pleaded, apologised, coaxed. William's father went quietly out to procure a conveyance. When he returned she was still talking in the hall.
>
> 'A crowd of vulgar little boys,' she was saying, 'and horrible

indecent placards all over the room.'

He carried her bag down to the cab.

'And me in my state of health,' she said as she followed him. From the cab she gave her parting shot.

'And if this thing hadn't happened, I might have stayed with you all the winter and perhaps part of the spring.'

William's father wiped his brow with his handkerchief as the cab drove off.

'How dreadful!' said his wife, but she avoided meeting his eye. 'It's – it's *disgraceful* of William,' she went on with sudden spirit. 'You must speak to him.'

'I will,' said his father determinedly. 'William!' he shouted sternly from the hall...

William slowly removed the barricade and descended the stairs. He had remembered to take off the crown and dressing-gown, but his one-sided moustache still hung limply over his mouth.

His father was standing in the hall.

'What's that horrible thing on your face?' he began.

'Whiskers,' answered William laconically.

His father accepted the explanation.

'Is it true,' he went on, 'that you actually took your friends into your aunt's room without permission and hung vulgar placards around it?'

William glanced up into his father's face and suddenly took hope. Mr. Brown was no actor.

'Yes,' he admitted.

'It's disgraceful,' said Mr. Brown, '*disgraceful*! That's all.'

But it was not quite all. Something hard and round slipped into William's hand...[18]

Many an adult male has confessed to the astonishment (occasionally tinged, one suspects, with outrage) he experienced when first informed that the creator of William was female. Indeed, it is hardly surprising that Richmal Crompton – unmarried, childless, her education and early professional life confined to all-female establishments – should seem to some an improbable source of so profound a knowledge, so great an understanding of the eleven-year-old male. Few familiar with her other work would claim originality to be a significant feature of the forty adult novels, or of the many short stories and sketches; and the conclusion that Richmal Crompton possessed a gift rather interpretative than original must, for many, serve to underline the enigma: whence William?

The evidence for Penrod as progenitor of William, however, arresting though the similarities are, remains entirely circumstantial. Grant the virtual inevitability in each case of the rebel's sex (determined by the period), class (respectability and convention being a necessary foil to his eccentricities) and age (a point on the short bridge between childhood and adolescence); and the coincidences seem at once less startling. The world of the middle-class pre-adolescent child being then in most respects very much circumscribed, it would surely be more surprising if the two writers had failed to employ a number of near-identical situations and incidents.

On the issue of whether or not Richmal had Penrod in mind when she first wrote of William, the facts of her general aversion to American writers and her poor opinion of contemporary children's literature may weigh as little with the sceptic as her niece's assertion that Richmal was incapable of 'lifting'. Her library did contain *Little Orvie*, another of Booth Tarkington's books about a boy; but that – inscribed 'For Richmal Crompton, who will understand Little Orvie' – was given to her in 1960. That she had once read a Penrod book and forgotten it is, of course, possible: unconscious memory was certainly the culprit in one affair that caused her much embarrassment. (Having bestowed an improbable-sounding name on an unsympathetic character in an early William story, she was horrified to be reminded, via a letter of complaint, that she had been at school with the original owner of the name. There was no response to her immediate letter of apology; and the thought that she might be believed to have caused distress deliberately, continued to haunt her.) That she had once read a Penrod book and not forgotten it, is also possible. But it seems much more probable that William simply evolved as the Mark II version of Robert Green, who (as discussed in the previous chapter) had appeared four months before him in *Home*, in the story 'One Crowded Hour'.

Robert Green was, indisputably, William Brown in prototype. In devising any further adventures for Robert, however, Richmal would undoubtedly have been inhibited by his extreme youth; and if she represented him as having aged four years in as many months, she would certainly have to rename him. William – at that time performing an annual seesaw with John as the most popular male given name (Robert, too, consistently made the top ten) – may well have been the first name that came to mind; and the transition from Green to Brown was no doubt equally uncomplicated. However random its derivation, the name had a singularly apt pedigree: history records many a villainous namesake transported or hanged. (William's own choice of ancestor would surely have been William Brown, *Bounty* mutineer.)

Worthy of note are several instances in which Booth Tarkington might be thought to have been influenced by Richmal Crompton. For example, it was not until 1929, in *Penrod Jashber*, that Penrod turned his hand to detection; whereas William had set out in pursuit of a 'criminal' as early as 1922 (in 'The Great Detective',[19] April *Home*) and again six years later ('The Mystery of Oaklands'[20], *Happy Mag*, September 1928). Richmal was first also with the incident in which the boy listens in to one of his sister's romantic interludes: William eavesdropped in February 1925, in 'William and Saint Valentine'[21], Penrod not until four years later in *Penrod Jashber*. There is, in short, a wealth of circumstantial evidence on both sides.

Penrod has his twelfth birthday; William, despite the passage of several birthdays and Christmases, remains eleven. But it is not only his attaining the age of twelve that suggests that Penrod will, eventually, grow to reasonably civilized adulthood. Discernible beyond the eye-catching similarities is an unbridgeable gulf: between the idealism of Richmal Crompton and the realism of Booth Tarkington. Penrod, surely, is rather descendant of Tom Sawyer than ancestor of William. The latter's unfailing courage and scrupulous honesty in money matters argue an improbably well developed moral sense in one of eleven years. Penrod, more realistically, is allowed to appear at times cowardly, and even dishonest:

> When the teacher of his class in Sunday School requested the weekly contribution, Penrod managed to look so embarrassed that the gentle lady told him not to mind, and said she was often forgetful herself. She was so sweet about it that, looking into the future, Penrod began to feel confident of a small but regular income.[9]

Cruelty, too, was for Richmal an unacceptable face of boyhood.

GEORGE B JASHBER
DETECTIVE OFICE
WALK IN

While William may inadvertently cause a beetle, a spider, a rat to suffer, his concern for its general well-being is indisputable, his distress when it fails to survive the new diet and 'training', genuine. Penrod's more truly scientific researches into insect and animal life make less pleasant reading:

> Penrod's efforts – with the aid of a pin – to effect a transference of living organism were unsuccessful; but he convinced himself for ever that a spider cannot walk with beetle's legs. Della then enhanced zoological interest by depositing upon the back porch a large rat-trap from the cellar, the prison of four live rats awaiting execution.
>
> Penrod at once took possession, retiring to the empty stable, where he installed the rats in a small wooden box with a sheet of broken window glass – held down by a brickbat – over the top. Thus the symptoms of their agitation, when the box was shaken or hammered upon, could be studied at leisure. This Saturday was starting splendidly.[9]

It is the element of fantasy in William that enables us to share his objective enjoyment of other people's afflictions. His fascination with the symptoms manifested by a 'nervous breakdowner' is undeniably callous, yet its presentation does not offend. The unfortunate victim is kept at a remove: the harsh realities of mental illness, physical handicap, social disadvantage, poverty, death, are never permitted to intrude on the fantasy. The Penrod books, in contrast, contain episodes calculated, one might think, to raise rather a shudder than a laugh. Penrod's envious admiration of the lifestyle of two new black acquaintances – Herman and his (literally) tongue-tied brother, Verman – rings unpleasantly true. The savagery of boyhood is deftly and shockingly laid bare when Herman points northward in the course of conversation, and in so doing reveals that his right hand lacks a forefinger:

> 'Look there!' exclaimed Penrod. 'You haven't got any finger!'
>
> '*I* mum map,' said Verman, with egregious pride.
>
> '*He* done 'at,' interpreted Herman, chuckling. 'Yessuh; don chop 'er spang off, long 'go. He's a playin' wif a ax an' I lay my finguh on de do'-sill an' I say, "Verman, chop 'er off!" So Verman he chop 'er right spang off up to de roots! Yessuh.'
>
> 'What *for*?'
>
> 'Jes' fo' nothin'.'[9]

To Penrod, it rapidly becomes apparent that the entire family is bathed in glamour:

> 'Ow sistuh Queenie, she a growed-up woman; she got a goituh.'
>
> 'Got a what?'
>
> 'Goituh. Swellin' on her neck – grea' big swellin'. She heppin' mammy move in now. You look in de front-room winduh where she sweepin': you kin see it on her.'
>
> Penrod looked in the window and was rewarded by a fine view of Queenie's goitre. He had never before seen one, and only the lure of further conversation on the part of Verman brought him from the window.
>
> 'Verman say tell you 'bout pappy,' explained Herman. 'Mammy and Queenie move in town an' go git de house all fix up befo' pappy git out.'
>
> 'Out of where?'
>
> 'Jail. Pappy cut a man, an' de police done kep' him in jail evuh sense Chris'mus time; but dey goin' tuhn him loose ag'in nex' week.'
>
> 'What'd he cut the other man with?'
>
> 'Wif a pitchfawk.'[9]

The crowning touch is added by Penrod's suggestion that his new friends name their newly acquired pet raccoon Sherman – after their dead brother.

Grisly detail notwithstanding, *Penrod* is very funny; much funnier, indeed, than the two subsequent books. And the fact that the best of Penrod is confined to the first book is significant, for Richmal did not consistently produce the best of William until she had been writing about him for several years; and it is unlikely that any writer could sustain for so long another's relatively short-lived inspiration.

A charge of plagiarism always fascinates, not least because such a charge can rarely be satisfactorily disproved. It is reassuring, therefore, to find that Constance Hall, on whose desk the first William manuscript arrived more than sixty-five years ago, has no doubt at all of William's originality. 'This is not a thing I have to rake my memory for,' she added with finality. 'Miss Cruikshank [the *Home* editor] was very down on anything that even remotely sounded like plagiarism.'

Richmal herself said more than once that the earliest William stories were inspired by incidents she recalled from her brother Jack's childhood. But she acknowledged that William very quickly became a character in his own right, and the extent of his independence is perhaps reflected in her subsequent non-explanation of the phenomenon: 'Once you've thought of a boy, the rest is easy . . . ' Few would dispute that the Savoy operas – which abound in echoes of earlier composers – stand as sole witness to the original genius of Sir Arthur Sullivan. Is it not equally reasonable to accept that the genius of Richmal Crompton survives in William?

Thomas Henry's illustration of William's first encounter with the mongrel that was to become his pet: from the story 'Jumble', published in *Home* magazine (May 1919) and in *Just – William* (1922).

Richmal's Crowded Hours

VII

From the very beginning, William had a fine supporting cast: the Brown family, united in its opposition to the anarchy in its midst. In 'Rice Mould', the first story, the mere existence of Robert, Ethel and the Brown parents was established; their personalities would become more distinct as each new story appeared. William's milieu, too, was established in that first story: with library, cook and housemaid, he was well placed to plague the inhabitants of the middle middle class. Mrs Brown, in 'Rice Mould' as in other of the early stories, was made a mouthpiece for a few unpleasing small snobberies of the period (as when she remonstrates with the hysterical housemaid: 'You're always imagining things. If you'd read the [books] I recommend, instead of the foolish ones you will get hold of–'[5]); but then, most contemporary magazine stories for women featured at least one half-witted domestic whose solecisms could be counted on to provoke a condescending chuckle. Before long, however, Mrs Brown had settled comfortably into a bland imperturbability which only domestic crisis could penetrate; and that but briefly. Cornerstone of the family unit, she darns socks, makes new garters and entertains to tea with inexhaustible placidity.

Mr Brown bears up throughout his younger son's half-century-long eleventh year with occasional outbursts of baffled anger and more frequent sardonic thrusts, the beauty of which invariably escapes William. Robert was early established as a susceptible, rather humourless youth of limited intellectual capacity: born fall-guy for William. Ethel, pretty, shrewd and mercenary, is perhaps more nearly equal than any other member of the long-suffering Brown family to the challenge of her younger brother.

William himself may at first appear revolutionary. Preferring dirt to cleanliness, noise to peace, ruffians to little gentlemen, he

patently spurns the ethos of middle-class existence; and he displays no musical, artistic or literary talent to compensate for his lack of academic ability. But he is also arrogant, and determined to have for himself the best of anything going; it is with envy of their ragged clothes and coarse accents and comparative freedom, not with pity for their deprivations, that he regards 'the poor'. Richmal is reported to have told an interviewer in later years that she had released all her criminal tendencies in William; which may have been the simple expression of a complex truth. William shared her own contempt for those wrapped up in material possessions; but in all other respects he is everything that Richmal at eleven was not: unimaginative, lacking in sensitivity, totally unacademic, boastful, scornful of all things cultural, unable to see any point of view but his own. Perhaps William was fired by a coruscant anti-authority spark, flickering deep beneath the binding influences of her upbringing; certainly, the stories reveal a profound delight in adult discomfiture. One thing is indisputable: though her attitude to him was constantly to veer between affection and irritation, William was real to Richmal.

The second William story, 'The Outlaws', published in

March 1919 in *Home*, introduced Ginger, Douglas and Henry and established the site ('about a quarter of a mile from William's house') of the old barn, scene of many an Outlaw plot. This was the story that prompted the astute Miss Cruikshank to ask for more: funny and inventively plotted, 'The Outlaws' survived a very old-fashioned ending to set William and his gang irrevocably on their long warpath. The third story, which identified the previously unnamed little girl next door as Joan Clive, was a gem: 'William Goes To The Pictures', first published in April 1919. (The *Home* editors were sufficiently impressed to give it pride of place three years later in the first hardback volume.)

The fourth story introduced, in May 1919, the final permanent addition to the Brown household: Jumble, of the 'fox-terrier ears, retriever nose, collie tail and slightly dachshund body' – surely a challenge to any illustrator. L. Hocknell, who had illustrated Richmal's pre-William stories in *Home* (there had been at least two, in late 1918: the Robert Green story, 'One Crowded Hour', and a typically dreadful seasonal offering entitled 'On Christmas Eve'), had been commissioned to provide the illustration for 'Rice Mould'; but his interpretation of William had failed to appeal to Richmal. Newnes had then approached Thomas Henry, a 40-year-old designer and cartoonist whose work regularly appeared in leading periodicals of the day. (His full name was Thomas Henry Fisher: the son of an engineer, he was born in Eastwood, Nottinghamshire, in the house opposite that in which D. H. Lawrence was born six years later. One of Henry's first jobs, when apprenticed to Formans, the Nottingham newspaper proprietors and printers, was on the lithographic work for the original colour production of the 'Sailor' trademark of Player's Cigarettes.) Henry was sent galley proofs of one of the earliest William stories, and asked to submit his ideas. Richmal said Henry's illustrations were 'just as she imagined William to be'; and Thomas Henry continued to portray William until the artist's death in 1962. Despite their celebrated partnership, author and artist did not meet until 1954 (when Richmal presented him with an engraved silver pencil to mark the occasion), by which time Thomas Henry had been illustrating William's adventures for 35 years.

Throughout the early months of his existence, William continued to delight – in 'The Show', 'William Joins the Band of Hope', 'William – the Intruder' and 'William and White Satin' (*Just – William*), and in 'William's Burglar' (*More William*) – the growing number of *Home* readers. While his disregard for convention must have been a novel attraction, the most important factor in his instant popularity was undoubtedly the stories' refreshing lack of the sentimentality that still pervaded most stories and articles written for women's magazines. With the tenth story, however, Richmal took, perhaps again in deference to seasonal tradition, what can only be regarded as a retrograde step. 'William's Christmas Eve' (*More William*, unabridged edition), in which he brings succour to the poor and is rewarded with their feudally expressed gratitude ('"It's real kind of yer, sir!"), is not only excessively sentimental; it also lacks the timeless quality of the better William stories.

The *Home* editor accepted this tenth story for publication in the December 1919 issue, but with some reluctance; and her request that Richmal should avoid pathos in future was instrumental in keeping William firmly to humorous lines thereafter. For this, we should be eternally grateful to Miss Cruikshank: after so glorious a beginning, how ignominious an end would William's permanent descent into sentimentality have been! (The publishers of the most recent Czech translation of William stories were insistent that 'William's Christmas Eve' be included; their translator, who was working from the abridged edition of *More – William*, wrote anxiously after the story's whereabouts. One can only think that they intended to use it as anti-capitalist propaganda.)

William made his last appearance in *Home* in October 1922, in 'Not Much'[19], and reappeared two months later, in 'Just William's Luck'[19], in another Newnes monthly: *The Happy Mag*, whose motto was 'every story has a happy ending'. Earlier that year, in May, Newnes had brought out the first volume of collected stories, *Just-William*; and now, in December, as William transferred from *Home* to *Happy*, they published a second volume, *More William*. Within a month, they were printing a second impression of *More William*, a third impression of *Just-William* – and Richmal had unwittingly sold all the copyrights with each story.

It is not known whether she turned for advice to the Society of Authors (which she had joined two years earlier); whether she was prompted by Clara, now her daughter's business manager;

Thomas Henry's version of the scene from 'Rice Mould' earlier illustrated by L. Hocknell (see Chapter V)

or whether her own indignation was sufficient to spur Richmal to action. In any event, she acquired an agent early in that year. (Though her own agent/writer relationship – with A. P. Watt & Son – remained entirely amicable throughout 46 years, Richmal was later to urge a friend to 'consider the pros and cons' before asking an agent to handle a short story. The cons, she warned, far outweighed the pros: '... it disappears into a sort of void for months and months – maybe a year or more. They don't let you know how it's faring. They just submit it to – say – 10 periodicals and each may keep it a month or more before coming to a decision and you've no idea how it's getting on in its journeying... I began by writing short stories and I submitted them and placed such as I did place by myself and had personal contact with the editors, who were most helpful to me.')

In the four years since William's first appearance, his creator's identity had remained almost unknown outside her family. Throughout her life, Richmal maintained a strong aversion to discussing her work, particularly the novels; and in any case, a teacher employed by the Girls' Public Day School Trust was not at that period permitted an outside occupation. Since at Bromley High she was 'Miss Lamburn' to pupils and 'Ray', her family name, to friends on the staff, she had run only a slight risk of being identified as Richmal Crompton, author of the frivolous literary efforts printed in publications high in circulation but low in brow, such as *Home*, *Happy* and *The Humorist*. Her articles and stories that graced the pages of *Punch* and other of the more highly regarded magazines, however, were credited, usually in an index, to 'Miss R. C. Lamburn'; and discovery came when Miss Hodge, headmistress of Bromley High, happened to scan a *Punch* index. Fortunately for Richmal, the two were on very good terms, and Miss Hodge confined herself to a reproachful: 'Why didn't you *tell* us?' Richmal's inner reaction to this unmasking by her employer, however, was probably at least as uneasy as that of Bridget, heroine of her first novel:

> 'Er – I – we saw a little sketch in the *Helicon* last month... with your signature. It is not a common name. May I – er – ask whether you –'
>
> 'Yes, I wrote it.'
>
> She wished he hadn't found out. It made her somebody definite, it gave her a personality. She'd liked having no

personality there. It had been so restful... she ought not to have used her own name, then it would not have happened.

'Excellent – er – excellent,' he said, leaning back in his chair and joining the tips of his fingers together. 'My – er – wife and I enjoyed it immensely.'

'I'm so glad.'

Her voice was gentle and remote, her face was still pale and serene, just a tint of anxiety in her eyes. She hoped he wasn't going to talk to her about it...[3]

Richmal's protective cloak of anonymity, already slipping, was soon to be wrenched from her for ever by another Bromley High detective. Her pupils had long endeavoured to discover what the 'R. C.' stood for in Miss Lamburn's name. Then Richmal lent a book, an old school prize inscribed with her full name on the flyleaf, to a pupil who had only the previous day enjoyed the latest William story in *Happy Mag* and wondered at the unusual name of the author. It is hardly too strong to say that Richmal was betrayed by William; and that this betrayal confirmed the ambivalence of the relationship between author and character. She bore her unmasking with a good grace, however, and even signed first editions of *Just-William* (soon to go, just a year after first publication, into its fifth impression) for the girls.

In April 1923, *The Innermost Room* was published by Andrew Melrose. It was not the first novel she had written; she was to tell a friend she had written three before she had one published. Her third published novel (*Anne Morrison*) was to be more obviously autobiographical; many Bury people recognized themselves and others within its pages, and it mirrored more accurately Richmal's own family circumstances and childhood experiences. Nevertheless, the heroine of *The Innermost Room*, Bridget – imaginative, painfully sensitive, affectionate yet reserved – is clearly identifiable as Anne/Richmal in a different setting.

This first novel is – as, indeed, is more than one of the later novels – an odd blend of perception and naivety. From a distance of sixty years, it is impossible to take seriously the nobility, not to mention the patience, of the shadowy male figure who wins Bridget on the last page; and the passage describing the reunion of Bridget's brother (newly returned from proving himself worthy in South Africa) and his intended bride is, today, hilarious. Gladys, during her fiancé's six-year absence, has kept herself busy: she has gone through art school, found fame and fortune as a sculptor and acquired an exalted circle of arty friends; and by the time solid old Derek returns, she has decided that Life holds more than housekeeping and children. With suitably dramatic mien, she tells him she still loves him – but then comes up with a most unladylike proposal:

> 'I'll agree to any other arrangement you like to propose, but I won't marry you.'
>
> 'I don't know what you mean by that,' he said, and his lips hardly moved as he said it.
>
> Gladys laughed.
>
> 'Oh yes, you do,' she said.
>
> 'Good God!' he said, laughing in his turn... 'To think I've kept myself clean all these years – for this.'
>
> His face was ashen white. He looked round the room as if he noticed it for the first time – with its beautiful furniture and masses of flowers. His eyes went from those to the framed photographs of men on the mantelpiece...
>
> 'Presents from friends of yours, I suppose,' he said with a twist of his lips.

No hint there of the gentle derision of sentimentality and cliché that was simultaneously delighting readers of *Just-William*:

> Next came another love-story – this time of a noble-hearted couple, consumed with mutual passion and kept apart not only by a series of misunderstandings possible only in a picture play, but also by maidenly pride and reserve on the part of the heroine and manly pride and reserve on the part of the hero that forced them to hide their ardour beneath a cold and haughty exterior. The heroine's brother moved through the story like a good fairy, tender and protective towards his orphan sister and ultimately explained to each the burning passion of the other.
>
> It was moving and touching and William was moved and touched.[15]

Yet through Bridget and her undergraduate friends in *The Innermost Room*, Richmal roundly derided the sentimentality and cliché of another romantic author:

> (Diana) looked out of the window. 'If this foul weather goes on much longer, I shall go mad. Where's that priceless Charles

Garvice I brought down? Read it out loud to us, Elf. It's an absolute scream. It beats even Stephen Leacock hollow.'

The plots of Charles Garvice, who dominated Hodder and Stoughton's Sevenpennies in 1914 with such titles as *In Cupid's Chains*, *Staunch As A Woman* and *Once In A Life*, were undeniably mirth-provoking. The heroine of *Once In A Life*, for example, is tricked into a false marriage with a bounder who has promised to pay her father's debts in return for her hand. Despite the effort he's put into planning the consummation of his evil designs, however, the villain goes missing immediately after the ceremony; which of course ensures that the heroine remains virginal and therefore still a fitting bride for the titled hero. Through Bridget and her friends, Richmal laughed at such nonsense; yet many of her own novels, at least superficially, were not to be so very different from Charles Garvice's: her heroines would be quite as beautiful and pure, her heroes as handsome and noble, her occasional villains as deviously lustful and as invariably thwarted.

On a deeper level, however, Richmal's first novel sheds light on a fear that was evidently ever present to her, as well as to each new heroine she created. The book returns again and again to the title theme: the innermost room, to which one admits at peril even the most affectionately regarded friends; the innermost room, one's last defence against the instincts of passion:

> The mere sense of his nearness brought it to her – something she had never known before ... that mad, surging, thrilling sting of happiness ... his tall well-proportioned figure, strong profile, kindly curving lips, his gloved hands – strong capable doctor's hands. This was what people felt ... then they married and they found that it had tricked them ... It didn't last ... They gave up everything for it – their privacy, their most precious secret thoughts, they gave somebody else the right to criticise and question every interest, every ideal, to hurt them every minute of every day ... 'till death do us part' – and did even Death part? – all because of that beating of the pulses, that sense of ecstasy ... that didn't last ... She fought against it hard, setting her lips ... He held the key to the innermost room of all. She seemed to throw herself against it to stop him – stop him coming in.

But even as she stands guard over that innnermost room, Bridget is fully aware of all it denies her; even as she seeks refuge, she despises herself for cowardice:

> Oh, it must be lovely to have children . . . to be loved like that . . . If one had the courage to take the risk and pay the price, how lovely that would be! *Courage* . . . that was it . . .

Clearly, she believes that for woman there exist only two alternatives: remain childless and therefore incomplete, or become a mother and be torn to pieces:

> Mrs. Tracey had told Bridget about their little boy who had died of fever. Mrs. Tracey had said she had nearly gone mad with grief. 'I was as thin as a pole, my dear.' She sat there, fat and placid, and told of how she'd nearly died of grief and how she'd been as thin as a pole. That was it . . . 'giving hostages to fortune' . . . always anxious or suffering for those you loved . . . never secure again . . . Everything that hurt them hurt you a thousand times more and they would be right in the innermost room . . . with power to hurt you always . . .

Woman's obsession with woman's destiny: an extraordinary foretaste of the feminist literature of half a century later. It is unlikely that Fay Weldon's novel, *Female Friends*, would have appealed to Richmal; yet she would surely have recognized its passionate echoing of her own theme:

> Oh my friends, my female friends, how wise you are to have no children or to throw them off. Better abort them, sterilise yourselves, or have your womb cut out. Give birth, and you give others the power to destroy you, to multiply your hurts a thousand times, to make you suffer with them.[22]

The Innermost Room, sufficiently popular in the early 1920s to warrant a cheap edition four years after first publication, has long been out of fashion and out of print. It is nevertheless worth pursuit through the usual secondhand-book sources, if only for its autobiographical element.

By June 1923, when the third hardback collection, *William Again*, appeared, Richmal was producing at least one new William story a month for *Happy Mag*. Her existing account book, which also dates from June 1923, reveals that each story now earned her twenty pounds. (Clara, a most efficient manager, kept the account book up to date with admirably clear and detailed entries.) Life that summer must have seemed to Richmal very agreeable. Her teaching career was increasingly satisfying, and she was rapidly becoming established as a writer. Advance royalties were paid in respect of *William Again*; one novel had been published and another was under way; and she had a steady market for all her articles and short stories. Her income from writing, from early June to the end of July alone, was nearly £150 – thirty pounds more than a full term's salary.

But success is said to bring its own problems; and for Richmal it certainly did. The plea from Miss Hodge, her headmistress, that Richmal should now give up writing lest it interfere with her teaching career, was no less urgent than the simultaneous exhortation of the Newnes editors: 'Give up teaching – it will interfere with your writing.' Richmal, however, though malleable enough normally in the cause of peaceful relations, was not to be swayed on this issue: she loved teaching and she loved writing, and no amount of pressure from any direction was going to persuade her to give up either pursuit. Nevertheless, she was not one who thrived on discord or opposition, and it must have been with some relief that she boarded the train with Clara, towards the end of August 1923, for a well-earned holiday in Norfolk.

Richmal – the Conqueror

VIII

The resort they had chosen was peaceful Cromer, renowned for the restorative effect of its sea breezes and quiet charm. After a few days, however, it became apparent that, far from being invigorated by the bracing Norfolk air, Richmal was feeling increasingly unwell; indeed, was developing feverish symptoms at an alarming rate. Clara's request for the attendance of a doctor was not graciously met; and when the doctor confided his suspected diagnosis – infantile paralysis (poliomyelitis) – the hotel proprietor abandoned all pretence of solicitude and made it callously clear that his sole concern was to rid the hotel at once of the possibility of infection.

Richmal was by now very ill indeed, and Clara, aided by porters and improvised stretchers, struggled desperately through the nightmare train journey back to Bromley. A few days later, Gwen and her two children, just returned from an overseas voyage, called at the house in Cherry Orchard Road to exchange news with her mother and sister. Expecting to find Clara and Richmal fit and rested after their holiday, Gwen was shocked to find herself denied admittance: the disease was still in its primary, infectious stage and Richmal's life was in the balance. Clara's devoted nursing is said to have saved her; but when the pain and fever of the acute phase had subsided, the ravages of the disease became appallingly clear: Richmal was paralysed in all her limbs.

She was at first unable even to turn over in bed without assistance, but electrical treatment, massage and exercise over the ensuing weeks restored the use of one side; and by great application she further managed to bring her writing hand back to life. A return to full-time teaching, though, was out of the question; the school was four miles away and, clearly, Richmal could no longer cycle eight miles a day. Yet her immediate enforced retirement would be a severe blow to those pupils she had been preparing for university scholarships. Richmal's relationship with her scholarship students was strongly founded on her rare ability to build confidence and inspire enthusiasm (at a Board of Education inspection later that year, the school's standard in Latin – 'by far the best of any of the Trust Schools' – was attributed to Richmal's teaching) and a temporary classics mistress from the beginning of the autumn term proved an inadequate replacement. A solution was found by Miss Hodge, who arranged for Richmal's few senior classics students to visit her home for coaching; and thus she recommenced teaching Greek and Latin language and history, from an armchair in the sitting-room.

One of those who benefitted from the coaching sessions at Cherry Orchard Road is convinced that her being subsequently offered a place at Girton, after only five terms' work on the language and history of Ancient Greece, was entirely owing to the quality of Richmal's teaching. She had recommended the Cambridge course to another of her classics students; but the temporary mistress at Bromley High had thought otherwise, and by the time the coaching sessions at Richmal's home began, the student was already working for the Oxford scholarship. On the first visit to Cherry Orchard Road, she brought with her the Somerville reading list. Richmal 'hardly glanced' at it. Together they read 'a bit of Catullus and the Greek Anthology, Aeneid IV, the best bits of Homer'; in short, the girl 'simply had a lovely time'. When she went up, well read but undeniably ill-prepared for the Oxford course, she was taken aback by the Somerville tutor's 'scathing' comment: 'You have certainly picked the plums.'

As soon as Richmal was able to get about a little on crutches, she went to Bromley High by taxi two or three mornings a week for the benefit of her Latin-only senior classics pupils, one of whom recalls: 'It was plainly an effort for her to manoeuvre herself and her crutches in and out of the taxi, up the steps to the front door, and into the classroom set aside for her (where her lunch was brought to her by one of the staff), and to grapple intensively with high-level work, filling every moment with the riches of her knowledge and enthusiasm; but her spirit was undiminished, her knowledge and skill at imparting it unimpaired. Her courage and unshakeable cheerfulness taught us far more than Latin.'

Richmal's own reaction – after the instinctive fight for

survival – to her illness and subsequent incapacity may at first appear surprising: 'It was wonderful,' she said, in response to a direct question some years later. 'It was like going into a new world.' She added that the attack of polio had, by obliging her to give up teaching, resolved the professional dilemma she had attempted to ignore. But it may be that she was released also from deeper anxieties. Her capacity for courage, so rigorously tested, was now beyond dispute; and personal relationships, including the physical intimacy so much dreaded by her novels' heroines, perhaps now seemed less threatening a prospect. The guard on that 'innermost room' might at last be relaxed a little.

Three William stories written in advance of the disastrous Norfolk holiday ensured that *Happy Mag* did not have to disappoint its readers while she was ill; and within three months of her contracting polio, Richmal's output was again rising. Articles, short stories and a multitude of sketches poured forth from the Cherry Orchard Road house to the pages of *The Humorist*, *Passing Show* and *London Opinion* (then her three most enthusiastic patrons, at three guineas a sketch); to *Pearson's*, *Cassell's Weekly*, *British Weekly*, *The Sphere*, *Time and Tide*, *John o'London*, *Windsor*, *Sovereign*, *Premier*, *London* magazine, *Strand*, *Nash*, *Ladies' Home World* and *The Novel*. The market in the 1920s was a writer's dream. Readers, too, were spoiled for choice: each month's William story excepted, there was generally at least as much entertainment in *Happy Mag*'s advertisements as in its stories. 'Are You Unable to Walk?' cheerily enquired Jas. P. Witham in the July 1924 issue. If so, you were urged to acquire one of his hand tricycles, 'world-famed for hill-climbing'; and if the copy didn't inspire you, the illustration surely would, with its team of Jas's satisfied hand-tricycled customers apparently about to tackle, with every sign of confidence and anticipatory enjoyment, a hill of Everest proportions.

In March 1924, Richmal's second novel, *The Hidden Light*, was published by Hodder and Stoughton. Its theme – the light within that can never be extinguished – strongly echoed that of her first novel. *The Hidden Light*, however, is the most cloyingly sentimental of all Richmal's novels and inspires little in today's reader beyond an overpowering desire to throttle the heroine as she bravely endures each new humiliation thrust upon her by her well-born cad of a husband, and languishes (purely) after the hero who has come Too Late into her life. This one apart, Richmal's heroines – for all their irritating predisposition to self-sacrifice and stiff upper lip – are generally quite credible. But her hero (there *is* only one) is never believable, having no substance at all beyond his 'long, mobile mouth', his 'indefinable air of breeding' and his capacity for infinitely deep, nonerotic passion. (The 'baddies' among her male characters, though often stereotyped, were much better drawn.) Yet even as the hero was expressing, in the most conventional of terms, his creator's intensely romantic idealism, William was simultaneously laying bare her gentle scepticism, her irrepressible sense of the ridiculous, her matter-of-fact Lancastrian view of life's absurdities.

In the April, Newnes brought out *William – the Fourth*. Staggered by the success of *Just-William*, for which they had selected the plums from a three-year *Home* crop, the publishers had hastily gathered the remainder – regardless of quality – for the second and third volumes, *More William* and *William Again*. Sales at this period seem to have been unaffected by the standard of individual stories: these early books were riding the wave created by the popularity of *Just-William*. *William – the Fourth*, while not particularly distinguished, was yet an improvement on the two preceding volumes. Perhaps its best story is 'William Makes A Night Of It', in which he takes revenge on one of Ethel's admirers, a child-care expert, who has committed the unforgiveable offences of calling William 'Willie' and pressing on him 'A Child's Encyclopaedia of Knowledge'. By the time William has finished with him, Mr. Bennison has rescinded his belief that 'little hearts should be won by kindness', and that 'innocent curiosity should always be promptly satisfied'; he is, in fact, a satisfactorily broken man.

That summer, having graduated from dependence on crutches to walking with the aid of a stick, Richmal embarked with a former Bromley High colleague, Decima Leake, on a trip to the Continent. They sailed to France for a month-long tour of France, Belgium, Italy and Switzerland. At Versailles, Richmal relived Marie Antoinette's 'four moments of agony':

1) Her rooms at Versailles invaded by mobs;
2) The arrest and dragging back of her family to danger after attempted flight;
3) The sight of the head of P. de Lomballe and
4) The taking away of the daughter.

'For a strong nature,' Richmal concluded in her travel notebook, 'one would mind less.' The spectacle of boys and young men at prayer, 'rapt and silent' in a Paris church, inspired a more fervid passage. Having noted the 'utter abandon and want of self-consciousness' of the worshippers, she added:

> 'There must be a fount of devotion and piety in boys and young men in England, untapped and wasted. All the natural chivalry and devotion, repressed by training, blazed forth at the call of the war. To many, it was a religious war, needing a religious fervour. As the rich and idle young flocked to the Crusades in the old days and sacrificed ease and luxury and comfort and life, so would the young do now – if modern life made any call for it, if that wonderful fount of devotion and self-sacrifice and idealism of youth were not allowed to die unused. Religion is too much repressed – our clergy are too fond of trying to pose as men of the world.'

Italy brought a less spiritual experience. Having decided not to accompany Decima to Capri, Richmal went alone to San Martino, where she was conducted round the church by a 'beastly and amorous guide who insisted on placing me in best position for each picture with a lot of mauling and pawing'. At Fontainebleau, on their way home, she noted appreciatively (and used in her novel *The Four Graces*, published four and a half years later) an American tourist's obvious relief when he remarked: 'This is our last day of hard work. Tomorrow, we're going to begin to enjoy ourselves.' There is little reference in the travel diary to the physical difficulties of the long journey. Gwen, however, recalled that her sister returned exhausted from the tour.

In January 1925, *Anne Morrison* was published by Jarrolds. Many Bury acquaintances of Richmal's childhood spotted themselves and each other in this third novel; and if Aunt Lizzie, Clara's older unmarried sister, failed to see herself in the carping, frustrated Aunt Susannah, the rest of Bury certainly recognized her. The Bury aunts, it seems, were never much impressed by their niece's literary success. They allowed William a degree of credit; but the romantic nature of the novels savoured too much, perhaps, of an unworthy frivolity of purpose. (Bury's motto, Vincit Omnia Industria, might have been designed expressly to discourage any tendency to the anguished self-examination so frequently indulged in by

Richmal's heroines.) There seems to have been, too, that slightly offended suspicion of family members who, fortunate enough to have been born Northerners, have voluntarily relinquished their birthright by effecting a permanent removal southward; and who, to add insult to injury, do not appear to regret having made the move. On their occasional visits to Bromley, Clara's unmarried sisters, Lizzie and Re, are recalled as having consistently demonstrated the traditional Northern 'carefulness'; the thrift that was to occupy several of Richmal's fictional spinster aunts to the point of obsession. To be sure of getting their full pennyworth, they would stay on buses past their destination and walk back; and Lizzie once brought with her from Bury an 'incredibly holey' umbrella that reduced Gwen's children to a state of barely containable hysteria.

With its sound basis of fact and its excellent picture of life in a girls' boarding school at the turn of the century, *Anne Morrison* is one of the more readable of Richmal's early novels. It was written with greater assurance, and in a mercifully lighter tone than that of her first two novels. But from the point, some threequarters of the way through the book, where fiction completely takes over from fact, it is much less convincing. Within the last few pages of the book, Anne's brother and younger sister (Richmal's frequent use of sibling quartets in her novels suggests she had not forgotten Phyllis, the sister who had died so young) both find True Love; Anne herself receives a marriage proposal (Stanley Rowland, Edward Lamburn's young colleague at Bury Grammar School, recognizing himself as the suitor, ungallantly let it be known that he had not proposed to Richmal); and on the last page, her future is secured by news of an unexpected £10,000 legacy.

Three months after *Anne Morrison* came *Still-William*, thirteen of whose stories had appeared in *Happy Mag* between mid-1923 and the end of 1924. The remaining story, 'An Afternoon With William', was the only early William story not to have appeared first in *Home* or *Happy Mag*; it appeared instead in another Newnes publication, *Tit-Bits Annual*. This fifth volume recalled the standard of *Just-William*: 'The Bishop's Hankerchief', 'Henri Learns The Language', 'William Turns Over A New Leaf', 'William the Matchmaker' (originally entitled 'William Dabbles in Matrimony') and 'William Spoils The Party' are the best of an excellent vintage. Violet Elizabeth, lisping six-year-old daughter of the *nouveaux riches* Botts, makes her début in 'Sweet Little Girl In White' (originally 'Enter Violet Elizabeth'); and the last story in the book, 'William and Saint Valentine', had been the first to command the increased fee of twenty-five pounds. The Colonel R. E. Crompton, CB, RE, to whom *Still-William* was dedicated, had written after the publication of *Just-William* to ask if Richmal were 'really a Crompton'. Though they never managed to trace a relationship they assumed that one existed, since he also was from Lancashire and Crompton was a Bury name; and they continued to correspond until his death in 1940.

In July, Hodder and Stoughton published *The Wildings*, the first volume of a mildly ambitious trilogy. Separately and together, the volumes of the Wildings saga stand as proof of Richmal's natural craft in story-telling. A significant factor in the trilogy's durability is the solid, hardworking Northern family's 'trade' background, which carries immeasurably greater conviction than the upper-middle-class setting of so many of her novels. By the time *The Wildings* was published, however, Richmal was wishing she had devised a different pseudoynm for the novels. To her, William was much less important than the novels; and to see displayed on the frontispiece of each new novel 'by the author of *Just-William*' must have been a constant vexation.

Of her three books published in March of the following year, 1926, *William – the Conqueror* is the most worthy of mention; another collector's piece, it introduced (in 'The Wrong Party') the boy we all loved to hate: Hubert Lane. The gems of this sixth volume are 'A Birthday Treat', 'The Leopard Hunter', 'William Leads A Better Life' and 'William and the Lost Tourist'. Judging by the generally high standard of stories in this and the preceding volume, one assumes that Richmal had recently been going through a fonder stage in her turbulent relationship with William. Indeed, it was at about this period that she said, 'with a twinkle in her eye', to a former pupil: 'A very naughty little boy, but oh! I love him!' The remark was uncharacteristically expansive: generally, the most Richmal would say – and that reluctantly – about William was: 'When you've thought of a boy, the rest is easy.'

WILLIAM HAD A VISION OF HUBERT'S FAT PALE FACE STARING OPEN-MOUTHED THROUGH THE WINDOW.

The March issue of *Happy Mag* advertised *Just-William* in its 15th edition in less than four years, the 12th edition of *More William*, the ninth of *William Again* and the sixth of *William – the Fourth*; and the third edition of *Still-William* had appeared in the previous month, just ten months after its first appearance. Richmal's own contribution, 'William and the Fairy Daffodil', to that March 1926 *Happy Mag* provided welcome contrast to such offerings as 'Bravo, Belinda!', the 'magnificent new serial' by Keble Howard (who, as a 'Master of Humorous Fiction', rated a larger type size than Richmal in the index). Notwithstanding the fact that servant-girl Belinda, stranded on a desert island with her master, has demonstrated (through a multitude of dropped aitches and double negatives) her undoubted superiority in intelligence and ingenuity, the reader is left comfortably assured that Breeding Tells and a good servant Knows Her Place. William shone like a beacon from the

bog of ponderous humour; today, the William story apart, only the advertisements would tempt one to linger within *Happy Mag*'s pages. For 3s 10d, the 'latest and most illuminating' of Mr Walter M. Gallichan's 'Racial Health Books', *Pitfalls of Marriage*, could be yours; Sphere Oval-Octo Suspenders, it was unblushingly claimed, POSITIVELY CANNOT CAUSE LADDERS; and Mrs Whittington of Bolton beamed healthfully in endorsement of the claim that URACE, and URACE alone, could cure Rheumatism. *Happy Mag*'s advertising pages offer a rich harvest to those who feel that life has become less colourful since the introduction of consumer-protective legislation.

Also in March 1926, Hodder and Stoughton published *Kathleen & I and of course Veronica*, a collection of whimsical sketches, most of which had previously appeared in *Punch*, *The Humorist* or *London Opinion*; and Richmal's fifth novel, *The House* (published later that year in America, under the title *Dread Dwelling*). Though the intended sense of evil fails to permeate *The House*, a certain interest lies in the resemblance of the 'dread dwelling' to Borley Rectory, which was later to share the fate of Richmal's fictional haunted house: destruction by fire.

In August, *David Wilding*, second volume of the trilogy, appeared; and from the end of 1926, Newnes began to publish, in *Happy Mag* and *Tit Bits* Christmas Extras and Summer-holiday annuals, two or three 'William articles' a year. Written as if by William himself, the articles expounded his views on a

The Happy Mag.

variety of subjects, including education, Christmas, pets, the seaside, careers and holidays. Richmal earned between six pounds and eight guineas for each. The articles appeared intermittently for at least five years; but they lacked the appeal of the stories. Deprived of the fringe characters – Miss Milton, General Moult, the Botts, etc. – of his village environment, William remained one-dimensional.

February 1927 saw the publication of *Leadon Hill*, Richmal's seventh novel; Hodder & Stoughton published it and Newnes brought out a cheap edition five or six years later. The story is told from the viewpoint of Marcia, a pleasant, intelligent woman who, temporarily rid of her insensitive clod of a husband, is at leisure to observe the effect on the village of the arrival of Helen West, a young woman who embodies all the nobler virtues. Though Helen herself, the focal point of the novel, never really comes to life, the village prejudices and bitcheries could hardly have been better drawn; and Marcia's children, particularly the arrogant Hugo, are sketched with the very sure touch that characterizes Richmal's every portrayal of childhood.

In March, *William – In Trouble* and the novel *Millicent Dorrington* were published. The former, to be reprinted three times within the year, achieved a standard higher even than that of *Conqueror* and *Still*: 'William and the Chinese God', 'William Among The Poets', 'William At The Garden Party' – but one would have to list every one of the ten stories. *William – In Trouble* is William at his inimitable best. For the setting of *Millicent Dorrington*, Richmal had returned to Lancashire. Again, the heroine is overwhelmingly beautiful:

> The golden pallor of her oval face showed up the vivid blue of her eyes; her lips were exquisite – dreamy, unawakened, wistful; her hair – of a gleaming gold – curled softly about her face and hung in a plait over her shoulder; the line of her chin was lovely and immature; her body was slight and nervous; her feet and hands were shapely;

passionate:

> The memories that Millicent had been struggling against all the morning returned in a sudden flood – memories of his eyes, his lips, the indescribable thrill that his look and touch had given her. Her heart beat unevenly;

'innocent':

> She was terrified of this new thing that had come to her. Her thoughts, trained both by her own instinct and by the trend of the time not to dwell on eroticism in any form, suddenly refused to obey her. Strange instincts unknown before sprang suddenly to life. She fought unavailingly against the ecstasy that swept over her;

and reserved:

> '... There's something in all of us that nobody else on earth could ever understand, and we all have a right to keep that to ourselves, we all ought to keep that to ourselves. A friend who wants it, who asks for it – isn't a friend.'

Millicent shares, too, the deep religious faith of Anne Morrison, and of *The Innermost Room*'s heroine, Bridget:

> And there was also, hidden away in the most secret place of her heart, her religion – a curiously childlike religion, a thing apart from creeds and doctrines... and somehow, despite her grief, she had preserved her spirit from bitterness and self-pity.

The story begins with the young Millicent's dream of leaving her mill-town (though not materially deprived) environment, and details reasonably entertainingly over the ensuing 450 pages the aetiology of the dream's frustration.

In July, Newnes brought out *Enter – Patricia*, a collection of sketches (written as if by a young husband), illustrated by Moorsom and mostly previously published in *The Humorist*. Dedicated to 'THE READER, with a respectful recommendation not to read all the following sketches at one sitting', the book is worthy of note if only in its prescience of Stephen Potter's Lifemanship:

> MEETING THE SITUATION
>
> I rushed down the platform as usual, attaché case in one hand, evening paper in the other. I'd seen Jones at the barrier and greeted him in the hasty way one does greet people at barriers, then I fled down the platform closely pursued by him. Jones and I live near each other in the country and work near each other in the city, so it sometimes happens that without any previous arrangement we travel together. I hurled myself into a carriage just as the train was starting, and Jones hurled himself in at my

heels. We picked ourselves up, sorted out our attaché cases and evening papers, and sat down. The train seemed to be going faster than usual. A station flashed by. I couldn't see what it was, but I saw a look of dismay overshadow Jones' frank and manly countenance.

'Pardon me,' he said to a young lady opposite, who, in the manner of young ladies nowadays, might have been anything from fifteen to fifty. 'Pardon me, but could you tell me the name of the station we have just passed?'

Frontispiece for *Enter – Patricia*, illustrated by Geoffrey Moorsom

At the young lady's answer Jones' jaw dropped open and a horrible suspicion began to form at my heart.

'W-where is the next stop?' stammered Jones.

'Margate,' said the undated young lady. 'It's the Margate express. Didn't you know?'

Jones' eyes bulged. He gazed round helplessly at every one in the carriage in turn.

'N-no,' he said. 'I must have got into the wrong train.' Everyone laughed. Of course, there's nothing quite so excruciatingly funny as someone else's having got into the wrong train. Lastly, Jones turned and gaped at me.

'It g-goes to Margate,' he said.

Now I'd had a nasty shock, but I'd had time to get over it while Jones was gaping around at the others, and I believe that the whole art of life lies in meeting situations with an air. So I met this with an air.

'Yes, of course it does,' I said. 'Didn't you know?'

'N-no,' said Jones, 'I thought it went home. I just followed you. I thought you were going home.'

I laughed.

'I'm so sorry,' I said. 'No, I was just having a run down to Margate. I often think that there's simply no tonic like a run down to Margate at the end of a day's work.'

Jones blinked and didn't say another word till we reached Margate.

I got out jauntily and asked the porter the time of the next train to London. He said that there was one in an hour's time.

'Just nice time,' I said to Jones. 'Time to buy some fish and get a breath of sea air.'

I dragged him, still speechless, down to a fish shop.

'There's nothing like the fish you get here,' I said. 'London fish doesn't compare with it. As a matter of fact I don't think I'd ever bother to come down here like this, if it weren't for the inducement of real Margate fish for breakfast the next morning.'

Jones blinked, lost his head, bought a lobster and staggered back to the prom.

'There's generally time,' I told him, 'to walk to the end of the prom. and back before the train goes.'

I didn't tell him that it was the first time I'd ever been to Margate in my life.

Since then Jones' manner to me has changed. He looks on me with awe. He treats me with respect. Only yesterday I heard him

murmur impressively to one of his friends as I passed:
'He goes to Margate for his fish . . . '

Forty years on, Richmal wrote to a friend: 'When I re-read [*Enter – Patricia*] it seemed, as you say, to be out of a completely different world. I can't believe that we ever lived in it.'

In October, *William – the Outlaw* appeared. (This book and its predecessor, *William – in Trouble*, are always transposed in the sequential list on the book-jackets.) Of this latest collection, 'Georgie and the Outlaws', 'William Plays Santa Claus' and 'William Finds A Job' are outstanding; but all are vintage William, and the sixth story, 'Finding A School For William', certainly justified the increased rate, established in the August, of thirty pounds for each William story. A week after *Outlaw* was published, Hutchinson brought out Richmal's first book of short stories, *A Monstrous Regiment*. In addition to her six hardback publications, she also produced during 1927 magazine stories, articles and sketches at an average rate of ten a month. Her total earned income for 1927 was £2,336.11.5d, of which William contributed more than £1,300.

Plans had been made during that year for a larger house to be built, in Oakley Road, still in the Bromley Common area. On completion of the house – The Glebe, set in an acre of garden – the removal was made in 1928, an equally prolific year for Richmal. It began with the publication in January of *Mist & other stories*, a foray into the macabre. Though the book is irritatingly peppered with members and residences of the aristocracy (one would have welcomed the occasional plebeian hauntee), one or two of the stories do fleetingly provoke that physical chill that marks the writer's success. April saw the completion of the Wildings trilogy with *The Thorn Bush*; and in May, *William – the Good* further delighted readers of all ages with 'William – the Great Actor', 'William – the Money Maker', 'Parrots for Ethel', 'One Good Turn' and the title story.

In July, another volume of short stories, *The Middle Things*, appeared; and in August, Newnes brought out *Felicity Stands By*, a collection of short stories (previously seen in *London* magazine, which had paid eighteen guineas for each) about a sixteen-year-old female impersonation of William. The tomboyish Felicity does wreak a fair amount of havoc; but never could she even briefly have threatened to rival William's popular appeal. Her grandfather, Sir Digby Harborough, engages in the lowly capacity of valet a young man with an 'unmistakable air of breeding'. One is unsurprised later to find the new valet revealed as an impoverished aristocrat, whose father was at Harrow with Sir Digby; and the book ends with Felicity's submitting to presentation at court. In the following month, September, Richmal's tenth novel in five years appeared: *Roofs Off!*, written in the style of the earlier *Leadon Hill* – an account of the interaction of neighbouring families rather than the story of one family.

It was during this year that the only real female challenge to William first appeared on the literary scene, in *Just – Jane*. Jane Turpin's creator, Evadne Price, claimed never to have heard of William, and to have based the Jane stories on her own experiences. Whether or not one can accept the first of these claims, it is a fact that Jane did emerge forcefully, with a personality and a will of her own. Jane, too, as the undisputed leader of a small gang of boys, wrought constant chaos and embarrassment among her middle-class family and neighbours. Where William was in permanent revolt against civilization itself, however, Jane was required to devote too much of her energy to belying her very feminine appearance; and thus, while boys and girls read William with equal enjoyment, the Jane books – ten in all – could really appeal only to girls.

From early in 1928, the three-guinea fee appeared but rarely in Clara's black account-book; seven guineas was now the average paid for shorter pieces, and each non-William short story now earned Richmal twenty-four pounds. Her prodigious output was at its peak; though her preference for writing novels, combined with the security of increasing royalty payments in respect of the William books, would encourage her to eschew the shorter, more whimsical pieces in future. In February 1929 the novel *The Four Graces* was published. The 'four Graces' are the beautiful Warden sisters, who by the end of the story are virtually reduced to two, one having killed herself for love of a married man and another having hied herself to a nunnery for love of a woman. This was not one of Richmal's better efforts; most of the characters are overdrawn, several are recognisable from her earlier novels, and none of them is more than fleetingly convincing.

The next William hardback saw Newnes temporarily bereft of their original touch. Entitled simply *William*, this tenth volume appeared in March 1929. It was now exactly ten years and one month since William had made his début in *Home*, and

The Glebe, Bromley Common

his popularity showed no sign of waning. Nor did the Brown family's prosperity yet show signs of diminution: Mrs Brown still darned and read in the morning-room, dined in the dining-room and spent her afternoons in the drawing-room; the kitchen was still occupied by a cook; visitors for afternoon tea were still announced by a maid; and Robert and Ethel still lived in a whirl of parties and fancy-dress dances. Maiden aunts, vicars' wives, retired army officers and curates continued to throw themselves in William's path; speakers still spoke to the Temperance Society, the Literary Society, societies for the encouragement of Higher Thought or Advanced Thinking; bazaars, fêtes and sales of work continued to support the Choir Fund, the Women's Guild, the Church Repair Fund (not a cause dear to William's heart, since broken church walls made for easier illicit access) and the Conservative Party. Life went on, undisturbed except by William, in his unnamed, vaguely Home Counties village.

William in trouble again

In May, *Sugar and Spice*, another volume of short stories, was published by Ward, Lock & Co. Though one or two of the stories are enjoyable, Richmal had again planted most of her characters in a sludge of snobbery and sentiment. The romantic improbabilities of 'Maeve', a story in which man and maiden are kept apart by manly pride and reserve and maidenly pride and reserve respectively, immediately recall – and invite unfavourable comparison with – the *Just-William* story earlier quoted, 'William Goes To The Pictures'. But the indulgent smile with which we rightly put sentimental excess into historical perspective becomes a little strained when we confront that other basic ingredient of 1920s romantic fiction, snobbery. While most of the snobbery detectable in Richmal's novels and short stories is defensible as intrinsic to individual characters, one is occasionally struck by a blatant servility toward the presumed prejudices of the reader. Richmal's next novel, *Abbots' End*, published in July by Hodder and Stoughton, was marred by just such a gesture:

> You could still see what it was that had made Maurice Lattimer marry his landlady's daughter. It was blousy now and run to seed, but it was still there. Her hair retained its sheen of gold, her eyes their vivid blue, but she had grown enormously stout, was too tightly corseted, and her once exquisite complexion was mottled and coarsened. She greeted Beatrice affectionately with the easy familiarity of the class to which she belonged.

Inevitable that the attractive, comfortably off Mrs. Lattimer should become 'blousy', her figure stout, her complexion coarse; that she should remain insensitive to the finer points of social intercourse: those old working-class genes again . . .

Such lapses irritate; the more so because Richmal herself, despite an ineradicable if unobtrusive respect for rank (surely detectable in her confiding that she would prefer the antiques she'd bought to have been inherited from forebears), was in everyday life utterly unsnobbish. Far from judging by externals, she responded instinctively to kindliness, to quiet humour, to a love of books, to a sense of the ridiculous; and would as readily privately dismiss, as 'not on the same wavelength', Lady Smythe as Joe Smith. *Abbots' End* survives, however, on its excellent portrait of possessive motherhood, and on an enjoyable crisis of clerical conscience that unmistakably recalls Trollope's *Framley Parsonage*; and though the last-page evaporation of maternal possessiveness fails to convince, the book nonetheless remains a good read.

Richmal's final hardback publication in 1929 was *Ladies First*, short stories published by Hutchinson in October. Since the beginning of this year, her monthly output of non-William magazine stories, articles and sketches had slackened considerably. This may be attributable to her desire to concentrate on the novels; though her mother's failing health was probably also a factor. Clara, now 67 and suffering from arteriosclerosis, was relaxing her grasp on household and business affairs. In the December, Richmal took over the account-book records (evidently without enthusiasm – the entries became increasingly spasmodic and ceased altogether within eighteen months); and during 1930, her fortieth year, she seems to have written very little for magazine publication apart from the William stories, most of which were still first appearing in *Happy Mag*.

The novels, however, continued to appear regularly. In *Blue Flames*, published in April 1930 by Hodder & Stoughton and later reissued by Newnes, Richmal returned to a favourite theme: one family's vicissitudes throughout two generations. The 'blue flames' motif is maudlin and obtrusive; the power of this book lies in the Oedipal struggles between mother and sons. Richmal outwardly expressed little sympathy with Freud's work (though much with Jung's), yet she frequently employed Freudian theory in the writing of her novels. Among her surviving notes (scrawled, in best writing tradition, near-illegibly on odd scraps of paper) on themes, characters and settings for her novels is a set of jottings, clearly taken from a Freudian textbook, on the psychology of family life. 'I think her religion and love of the arts precluded too sexual a view of human behaviour,' comments a friend with whom she often discussed psychology. 'However, she was never mealy-mouthed and her opinions were delivered in frank terms unusual for one of her religion and class.'

The previous month had brought forth *William – the Bad*, which saw Richmal again in top form, guying as she alone could the over-enthusiastic exponent of the latest 'crank' movement. The mind-over-matter brigade constituted the first target:

> '. . . It's closely allied to Christian Science, of course, but it's wider. It embraces more spheres, so to speak. It begins with that of pain, of course, teaching that there's no such thing. No such thing at all. I never feel pain. Never. Why? Because my thoughts know that there's no such thing as pain so naturally they don't feel it. Never.'
>
> At this moment the prize cat who had made its way under the Chesterfield and discovered one of Miss Messiter's ankles on the

other side put out an exploratory paw and touched it with extended claws. Miss Messiter uttered a scream.

'Whatever's the matter?' said Mrs Brown.

The visitor was clutching her ankle.

'A sudden excruciating pain,' she said.

'Neuritis perhaps, or arthritis,' suggested Mrs Brown soothingly. 'They do come on suddenly.'

'Where had I got to?' said the visitor, still rubbing her ankle.

'About your never feeling pain,' said Mrs Brown.

'Oh yes... well the *reason* I don't feel pain is simply that I've trained my thoughts to ignore it. My thoughts mechanically reject the notion of pain. It's all so simple.' She withdrew her hand from her ankle to wave it in the air. 'All so simple and so beautiful. The lecturer will put it to you in all its beautiful simplicity. You will never feel pain again. When people say to me that they are in pain I say to them: "Pain? What is pain?"'

At this minute the prize cat put out his paw again in order to experience a second time the delicious sensation of sinking his claws through Miss Messiter's woollen stockings into her skin beneath.

'*Whatever's* the matter?' said Mrs Brown when Miss Messiter's scream had died away.

'Another of those excruciating pains,' said Miss Messiter. 'I can't explain it. I've never known anything of the sort before. Excruciating.'

'Neuritis probably,' said Mrs Brown, showing more interest that she had shown in the Thought Mastery Movement.[23]

And return-to-the-soil adherents were sitting ducks:

> 'It is the ugliness of modern life,' she said, 'that shocks Adolphus and me so terribly . . . In the evenings, when Adolphus and I are alone at home, we go back to the morning of the world, and wear the clothes that nature intended us to wear,' seeing a question in Mrs Brown's eye, Mrs Pennyman explained hastily, 'flowing robes completely covering the human body and combining beauty with grace and harmony . . . We tried the experiment of going out in them, but the result was not encouraging. We met with what I can only describe as a hostile reception . . . '[24]

Richmal enjoyed, too, in *William – the Bad* a dig at political expediency:

> 'Do shut up int'ruptin',' said Henry. 'I'm tryin' to tell you 'bout this gen'ral election. There's four sorts of people tryin' to get to be rulers. They all want to make things better, but they want to make 'em better in different ways. There's Conservatives an' they want to make things better by keepin' 'em jus' like what they are now. An' there's Lib'rals an' they want to make things better by alterin' them jus' a bit, but not so's anyone'd notice, an' there's Socialists, an' they want to make things better by taking everyone's money off 'em an' there's Communists an' they want to make things better by killin' everyone but themselves.'[25]

Ginger having promptly bagged Communism on the strength of its gory appeal, William is in a quandary over which of the remaining three avenues to political glory he should choose. He conceives a violent antipathy to Liberalism over tea when Robert, a declared Liberal, appropriates most of the doughnuts; and of the two remaining ideologies, Socialism definitely sounds the more attractive. Then he recalls a recent house guest, who had shot big game in Africa and altogether revealed himself as William's ideal of manhood; and decides that what is good enough, politically speaking, for his hero will be good enough for him:

> 'Mother, you remember that Mr Martin what stayed here last month?'
>
> 'Yes, dear.'
>
> 'Well, what was he?'
>
> 'He was a friend of your father's, dear.'

'I mean, was he a Communist?'

If Mr Martin were a Communist, William had decided to fight Ginger for the post of head of the Communist party.

'Of *course* not, dear,' said Mrs Brown, deeply shocked, 'he was a Conservative.'

'Then I'm one, too,' said William importantly.[25]

A considerable contrast to the gentle cynicism of *William – the Bad* was provided by Richmal's next novel, *Naomi Godstone*, published in the September by Hodder & Stoughton and later reprinted by Newnes. Richmal dedicated the book to the memory of her father; and he appears in the story as he appeared in *Anne Morrison*: as a learned, almost saintly priest with the symbolical name of Timothy (from the Greek *Timotheos*: 'honour' + 'God'). The plot of this later novel, however, is

a truly breathtaking tangle of tear-jerking cliché. Naomi compensates for maternal rejection by lavishing on her brother a love of startling intensity; indeed, so impassioned is her regard for Roddy that one begins uneasily to anticipate revelations of incestuous love. But suddenly, as the plot thickens, the truth is uncovered: Imogen is not Naomi's real mother – and Roddy, Imogen's son, is therefore not Naomi's brother. This naturally does not mean that the path of true love can henceforth run smooth; what, after all, could any self-respecting proud beautiful passionate girl do in the circumstances but rush out and offer herself in marriage to the nearest self-made uncultured wealthy man? Of course, Naomi soon regrets this act of proud revenge: in best Victorian tradition, she faints on her wedding night; and after their return from honeymoon to The Towers, the tasteless edifice (shades, perhaps, of Royal Holloway College) erected in vulgar celebration of Humphrey's acquisition of wealth, countless small revelations of his essential coarseness and ill-breeding grate daily on her rarefied sensibilities. She continues to languish after Roddy, who has by now cast his affections elsewhere; and spends an inordinate amount of time pondering the romance of her true parentage (aristocratic poet 'had his way' with proud and beautiful gipsy girl under a hawthorn bush – hardly a memorable romantic experience for either, one would think) as the story proceeds through further dramatic revelations to a predictably anodyne end. The absurdities of plot and stereotyping of character do not, however, render *Naomi Godstone* unreadable. The appeal, skilfully conveyed, is not to reason but to emotion; and as pure melodrama, the book may fairly be said to succeed.

Also in September, *William's Happy Days* came out. This was a good average collection, 'William and the School Report', 'William's Birthday' and 'William the Superman' being the stories most worthy of note. In writing the penultimate story, 'William Puts Things Right', Richmal appears to have suffered a temporary mental aberration: with no reference whatever to the Botts (who, with an army of servants, had been in permanent residence for six years) she placed in the Hall a Mrs Porker, 'large and stout and wealthy' and irredeemably common; in fact, a facsimile edition of Mrs Bott. Mrs Porker never appeared again and the Botts were reinstated at the Hall without explanation in the next-but-one volume. Eagle-eyed William fans wrote to point out less obvious discrepancies: Robert's and Ethel's ages (which ranged between 17 and 19, and 19 and 21, respectively while William remained 11); the colouring and surname of William's golden-curled/dark-haired favourite, Joan (sometimes Clive, sometimes Parfitt, once Crewe); Ginger's surname (Merridew/Merrydew/Flowerdew). But the discrepancy that seemed most to grieve was the variety in location of the Outlaws' meeting place, the old barn, which was situated sometimes behind William's house, sometimes as

far away as the other side of the village. (One exasperated reader went to the length of sending Richmal a detailed map of the imaginary village to ensure future accuracy.) There were noticeably fewer inconsistencies in the novels, probably because Clara subjected their final manuscripts to a rigorous search; only once was a 'howler' picked up by a proof-reader, who pointed out that daffodils did not usually decorate the church at Harvest Festival.

Richmal's novels, being too well written for the vast slush market yet too romantic for the more critical reader, had to date attracted a following devoted but insufficient to ensure more than fairly respectable sales figures. At around this period, the chairman of Hodder and Stoughton, Ernest Hodder-Williams, offered his professional advice: if Richmal would make certain changes in style, notably with regard to the endings, her novels 'could be best-sellers'. This well-meaning suggestion roused Richmal to indignation. The 'spineless amiability' to which her mother had more than once referred reflected not a masochistic acquiescence to being pushed around but simply an innate aversion to discord. Invasion of privacy, however, in this case via the novels that meant so much to her, was a threat that demanded a rare fighting response. She accepted with resignation the fact that William subsidised the novels; she would continue, albeit reluctantly, to produce William stories on demand; but of all her writing, only the novels really mattered to her now. The financial aspect of becoming a best-selling novelist held no appeal; William 'provided very nicely' for her needs. Now that she was established as a novelist, she could and would continue to write her books exactly as she wanted to write them. The Hodder and Stoughton chairman may well have regretted having raised the issue. In any event, he had no further opportunity to offer advice, for Richmal's next novel was to go to Macmillans.

IX

It had long been a sorrow to Clara that her daughter, despite her fortune, could not be induced to spend freely on herself, and particularly not on her clothes. Though one would hardly think it from reading her novels, whose heroines' attire is often almost obsessively recounted, Richmal had never been much interested in clothes; as long as old, familiar garments would wear (or as long as Clara would consent to mend them) Richmal would continue to wear them. Her only real personal indulgence was in buying books; and even in that she was far from extravagant.

The material rewards clearly were, to Richmal, much the least important aspect of her success. While her generosity to family, friends, acquaintances and many charitable institutions was unbounded and unsung, she herself had much of her father's unconcern with worldly goods. The lines she marked in a shabby black book of translations from Ancient Hebrew literature are no doubt significant:

> There is contempt for misfortune in the thought of him that is at ease:
> It awaiteth them who are slipping with their foot.
>
> Lose thy money for thy brother and thy friend, And let it not rust under a stone to be lost.
>
> He that loveth gold shall not be justified.
>
> The rich man shall lie down, but he shall not be gathered:
> He openeth his eyes, and he is not.

Nor was fame very welcome, with the Bible no less uncompromising on the sin of pride than on the possession of wealth. One line, from Proverbs 29.23, is heavily underscored in the black book:

> A man's pride shall bring him low: but honour shall uphold the humble in spirit.

Not that pride or vanity can have been besetting sins: Richmal had a lifelong antipathy to being the centre of public attention. Quite early in her fame, finding herself ill with a bilious attack on the morning of a day she was to attend a dinner, she had thought 'what a pity', made her excuses and stayed at home. On the day of the next similar function, however, she suffered an identical attack; and this time recognized that the illness might be a manifestation of her dread of the occasion. Thereafter, she sensibly accepted the disinclination and agreed to as few public appearances as possible; though she always made a special effort if there were a family connection, or if she felt the cause to be particularly worthwhile.

In January 1931, Hutchinsons published another volume of Richmal's short stories, under the title of *The Silver Birch*. The tinge of contempt apparent in her portrayal of middle-class womanhood (so prone to faint or throw hysterics at the least provocation) in the William stories is discernible also in *The Silver Birch*. In one of the stories, the picture is quite bluntly presented:

> Deep down in her heart Janet knew that Mother was rather stupid. And she knew, too, that Father liked her to be rather stupid, that he liked all women to be rather stupid. He liked them to listen to his views and ask his advice about things. He hated their having views of their own and not asking his advice.
>
> It flattered him to feel himself definitely their superior, and on that understanding to load them with pretty things for which they had to be very, very grateful . . .[26]

William's Crowded Hours, published in the July, proved a middling good volume; and September brought *Portrait of a Family*, a novel described by Ralph Straus in the *Sunday Times* as 'a delightful little study of "ordinary" people who, of course, are not ordinary at all'. The story centres on a widower's agonized search for the meaning of his wife's last words: 'Did you – never guess – about Charlie and me?' One is disappointed, though not surprised, to discover that in the end he settles for remaining ignorant about Charlie and her. As usual, the children's characters and relationships are much more convincingly drawn than those of the adult family members. One knows from the beginning that Olivia's burgeoning love affair with the 'distinguished looking' Stephen will never be consummated, that she'll decide ultimately to remain faithful to her disagreeable husband. The sympathy and perception at times apparent in the writing are small compensation for the predictability of this novel.

The Odyssey of Euphemia Tracey (Macmillan), published in April 1932, is no more probable but considerably more enjoyable than its predecessor. This story of a woman who, freed from servitude by the death of her tyrant father, sets out at the age of forty to seek Life was described by the *Punch* reviewer as 'genial, likeable and amusing'. The following month brought publication of *William – the Pirate*, whose penultimate story, 'Aunt Arabella in Charge', clearly was inspired by the contemporary A. A. Milne cult. William and the Outlaws have already met and recoiled from Anthony Martin, an obnoxiously self-possessed six-year-old who gives public recitals of poems his mother has written about him. Aunt Arabella, however, adores the poems (the latest of which has every verse ending in 'Anthony Martin is milking a cow'), and her reaction to the prodigy's arrival in the village is ecstatic:

> 'My dears!' she said, 'you'll never *guess* who's come to stay in the village. Anthony Martin!'
>
> 'We've seen him,' said William dejectedly.
>
> 'But, my dears, aren't you *thrilled*?'
>
> 'No,' said William.
>
> 'You know his *sweet* things, don't you?'
>
> 'No,' said William.
>
> 'Oh, I must read some to you. I've got them nearly all here. I never go anywhere without them.'
>
> The dejection of the Outlaws deepened still more.

When a friend asked whether Anthony Martin was based on Christopher Robin, Richmal 'smiled the bright, hunted smile' with which she invariably parried direct questions about her writing, and expressed sympathy with Christopher Robin's being forced to attend 'terrible children's parties'.

There is a wealth of quiet enjoyment, too, in the description of William's visit to one of his many formidable aunts:

> The house was depressingly clean and tidy. Everything in it had its own place and was not to be moved or touched . . . She met all his suggestions for the employment of his time with an unfailing: 'No, William, *certainly* not.' . . . She found a friend for him, a nice quiet boy whose interests centred entirely in the study of

geography and the making of maps. After one meeting William announced to his aunt that he would not go out with that boy again, not if he was to be put to death by torture for it...

She had plenty of suggestions in answer to William's demands as to what there was for him to do.

'Well, dear, there's a lot for you to do. You can sit quietly in the morning-room and read. I've got a complete set of the *Encyclopaedia Britannica*, and I'm sure you'd find it interesting. One sees quite young children reading it in the advertisements. And, when you're tired of reading, you could go for a nice walk. There's a very interesting church in the village. Part of it Early Perpendicular. I'm sure you'd find that *most* interesting. You could spend a few hours looking round it, and then you could come home and read the article on Architecture in the *Encylopaedia Britannica*. Then in the afternoon you could go out with a notebook and make notes of all the wild flowers you see – keeping to the roads, of course, because the grass is always apt to be damp – and then you could spend the evening reading the article on Botany in the *Encyclopaedia Britannica*. And you could make a little collection of wild flowers. I think that you would find the time pass very quickly in that way.'[27]

William bests Aunt Jane and her deadly programme, of course, just as he ensures Anthony Martin's come-uppance; and *William – the Pirate* provides, if not the best of William, at least very good entertainment.

Richmal's seventeenth novel in eleven years, *Marriage of Hermione*, came out in the September. Again, her predilection for the late-Victorian era is apparent: the story begins in 1882, when Hermione is seventeen; again, the husband is insensitive, dogmatic, near-stupid; again, the heroine discovers the maternal instinct to be infinitely stronger than (and by implication superior to) the sexual instinct. Sensuality is transmuted into an acceptable sensuousness in Hermione's contact with her children:

She... loved the feeling of warm little arms clasped around her neck, and the familiar tea-time smell of the nursery – a mingled smell of toast and dripping, of damp gaiters drying on the fire-guard, of healthy, perspiring little bodies, of well-washed and powdered babyhood...

...Then followed the elder ones' hour when she would read to them – Vere, and sometimes Alan as well, on her knee, John and

Monica sitting on the floor, their heads leaning against her. Before they went to bed she let them take down her hair, each drawing out a hairpin in turn till the whole mass of it fell in silky golden curls down her back and over her shoulders. Then they would hold up the golden mesh and let it fall slowly in shining single curls, pressing their hot little cheeks against its silky coolness. She felt their love – the fervent, whole-hearted, uncritical adoration of childhood – as if it were some radiant mist enclosing her, shutting out the rest of the world.

Again, the more sensitive, highly strung of the children – Alan and Vere – are the best portrayed of all the characters. Vere, in particular, almost breathes from the page:

When she had been naughty and was sorry for it she would try to show her penitence by small unobtrusive services, but nothing would ever induce her to utter the conventional nursery apology, "I'm sorry I've been a naughty girl". Punishment only made her more stubborn and obstinate, and she possessed a strength of enduring, unyielding obstinacy that was amazing in so young a child. To join issue with her was to court sure defeat.

In the confrontation between Vere and her father over a plate of uneaten rice pudding, it is apparent that the views expressed by Hermione were Richmal's own:

"They must be made to do as they're told," he said shortly.

Her eyes laughed at him.

"But, Charles, they're *people*, real people, not little puppets with strings that you make do just what you want. You see" – frowning, she searched for words – "the idea of *making* them do things is so futile. Only stupid people try to do it. Don't you see if you've made a child do something it doesn't want to, you're just where you were before? It still doesn't *want* to do it. You're worse off really than you were before, because you've hurt and angered it as well... If a child does something just because it knows that you'll hurt it physically if it doesn't – well, it's not even a sporting fight. Any grown-up fool can hurt a child. It's futile and despicable... a confession of weakness... I wouldn't eat rice pudding if I didn't want it, and neither would you. Why should you expect Vere to do something you wouldn't do yourself?"

For all their inherent weaknesses, Richmal's novels could not justly be dismissed as the fantasy fodder of a bygone era: the quality of her child characterization alone – that minute yet always compassionate observation of childhood idiosyncrasy, surely a major factor in her personal success as a teacher – would redeem them. The tenuous thread of feminism is equally intriguing: a maverick spirit that frequently belies the heroine's apparent acceptance of her predetermined role of passive femininity. She is never permitted, however, to translate her rebellious feelings into unfeminine action. Hermione, in common with most of Richmal's married heroines, resents much; but she is careful to contain her resentment:

> . . . As she listened to him her irritation had risen to fever pitch. Charles was, she knew, a good husband. The sowing of his wild oats – a mild enough proceeding on the whole – belonged completely to the past. He had never taken too much to drink since that fateful Christmas Eve. He had never been unfaithful to her since his affair with Mrs. Payne . . . She knew that, though often thoughtlessly inconsiderate, he would readily have given his life for her or for any of their children. But he was a man of set ideas and preconceived notions . . . With him a 'discussion' took the form of dogmatic pronouncements to which he obstinately adhered in the face of all argument. Moreover, his unspoken standpoint that because she was a woman her opinion on anything beyond the nursery and kitchen was unworthy of consideration, had infuriated her, and she had gone to bed feeling out of patience not only with Charles but with her whole life.

It is interesting to compare Hermione with Letty, a central character of fellow-Lancastrian Dorothy Whipple's novel *Greenbanks*,[28] also published in September 1932. After thirty years of submission to her husband, Ambrose (in pomposity, insensitivity and humourlessness the double of Hermione's husband), Letty rebels openly. Instead of gratefully accepting Ambrose's offer to invest for her the money she has inherited from an aunt, she asserts her right to manage it for herself. He is even more outraged when she proposes to spend it not as he recommends but on a trip to visit relations in Africa:

> 'Good heavens, you can't go to Africa alone!'
> 'Oh, yes, I can.'
> There was a pause.
> 'You're not like a woman,' said Ambrose bitterly.

'Now what exactly do you mean by that? What is it to be like *a* woman? Take the women you know: me, mother, Kate Barlow, Rachel – all different. Which is like a woman? You've got some pattern of a woman in your mind, and if women don't fit it, it is they who are wrong, I suppose, not you . . .'

Whether or not a real-life downtrodden wife could have found the courage to speak thus to a real-life Ambrose is beside the point, which is that Letty's rebellion gives a satisfaction that is denied the reader of *Marriage of Hermione* – a satisfaction that may account for the much greater popularity of *Greenbanks*, reprinted three times within the month.

Early in the following year, 1933, perhaps because, as her mother's health deteriorated (Clara was now suffering from heart trouble, and also underwent a mastectomy at around this period), she was finding less time for writing, Richmal made another attempt to eliminate William. This time, she took an unusually firm stance: he had been around fourteen years longer than she had intended he should be, and she was tired of having to devise new plots for him. But William, born in 'Rice Mould', baptized in 'The Outlaws', gloriously confirmed in 'William Goes to the Pictures' and in a hundred stories since, again put his faith in the agency of others. What pressure was brought to bear by publisher and agent, or even whether her resolution reached their ears, is not known; the pressure exerted by the family was sufficient to make her yield. Indeed, to anyone less indifferent than Richmal to wealth, the idea of her voluntarily relinquishing a character who had thus far ensured the sale of more than 700,000 volumes (not including *Just – William* and *More William*, from which, having sold all the copyright, she received no royalties – just an *ex gratia* payment, negotiated by her agents) must have seemed insane. Her brother Jack, who, now married and permanently settled in England, had drawn on his travel experiences to produce 'P.C. Wren-type' adventure novels, magazine articles and a 'fantasy' novel (*The Kingdom That Was*: described by one reviewer as 'a blend of Haggard, Wells and Kipling'), offered to 'take the pressure off pro tem.'. He did, in fact, ultimately supply about twenty detailed plots; Richmal wrote up the stories and passed on an appropriate proportion of the royalties.

It was William's final triumph; never again did his creator seriously attempt to rid herself of him. She regarded him thenceforth with an exasperated affection that remained constant in the face of her spirited denials to sentimentally inclined interviewers that William was the son she wished she'd had. (And who could honestly doubt the denials? William between the covers of a book is irresistible; William in the flesh, as son, brother or next-door neighbour, would be a very large thorn indeed.) In his next book, appropriately entitled *William – the Rebel*, William consolidated his triumph with such winners as 'The Outlaws and the Penknife', 'William and the Watch and Chain' and 'It All Began With the Typewriter'.

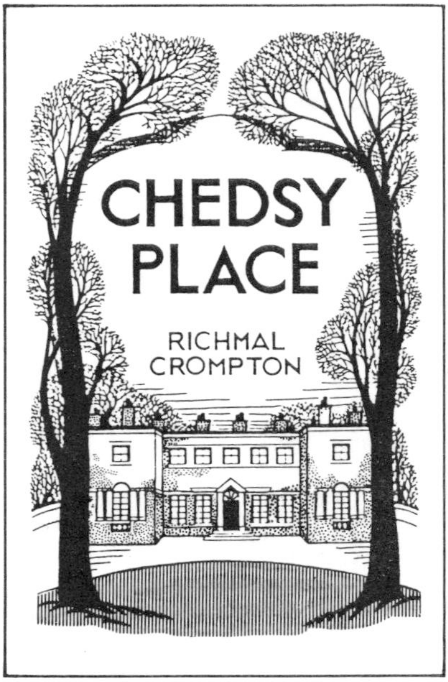

In the June of 1933, Macmillan published *The Holiday*, of which The Times review said: 'The interplay of character and the momentary revelation of other people's lives, accompanied by the young fluting of the children and their natural and amusing adventures, makes this novel the pleasantest possible light volume for holiday reading.' *Chedsy Place*, published in February 1934, also won kind reviews: 'The book is written with ease and brightness, and Miss Crompton's many admirers will read it with enjoyment' (Gerald Gould, The Observer). It is probable, however, that all but the most fervent of Miss Crompton's admirers were roused to exasperation by the predictability of Robert Beaton's appearance:

His brown suit was shapeless, his brown shoes worn and shabby, but there was an unmistakable air of breeding about him. He appeared at home and in his natural element in this rather stately setting of country mansion, broad terrace, and smooth sweeping lawns.

Chedsy Place relates, competently enough, the events ensuing on Celia Beaton's attempt to convert her husband's newly inherited stately pile into a superior guest house for the Christmas season. Among the guests who bring their personal problems to Chedsy Place for Christmas is Judith, a mannish female accompanied by an innocent young girl confusingly named Sidney. When it becomes apparent that the latter is falling heavily for Judith's new chauffeur, however, one is immediately assailed by scepticism. Could it be that this chauffeur was not, so to speak, born to chauffeurdom? Indeed it could: he is, in fact, a very well-connected former public-schoolboy temporarily on hard times. At the end of the story, he clasps Sidney to his manly, well-bred bosom, and the wicked Judith's jealous fury avails her nothing.

Richmal had made oblique reference in earlier novels to intense female relationships; indeed, in *Marriage of Hermione* (1932), she had at first left little room for doubt concerning the sexual proclivities of Hermione's sister-in-law:

> Maud did not return to Abbotford after the war. She took a flat in London with a girl of twenty-two whom she had met when engaged in land work. Maud had cut her hair as short as a man's, and kept it cropped, wearing always a dark coat and skirt with stiff collar and cuffs. Her striding gait and deep voice increased the impression of masculinity. The girl was of the ultra-feminine type with fluffy hair and saucer-like eyes. They went everywhere together, and were on cloyingly affectionate terms.

But in the very next sentence, perhaps apprehensive of presenting so unambiguous a portrait, she had taken care to blur her canvas:

> There was nothing wrong with the *ménage*, but its atmosphere was vaguely unhealthy, and Charles, who now disapproved of his sister as strongly as he had once admired her, did not like Hermione or the girls to visit her much.

The topically entitled *William – the Gangster* came out in May 1934 and delighted devotees with 'William and the Russian

Prince', 'A Night of Mysteries' and 'William the Sleepmaker'. In this last story, William's passion for experimenting (in this case with his aunt's medically prescribed opiate) leads to his killing, albeit accidentally, three rats and a cat and very nearly killing the teetotal Mr Forrester. Forty years on, when Collins were planning a new hardback edition, a well-meaning editor decreed that the more dangerous of William's exploits be eliminated lest they incite emulation. But in William's daring lay the fantasy: he fought *for us* against adult authority, against the irksome bans – which we knew, if did not acknowledge, to be reasonable – on playing with sharp knives, climbing tall trees, fooling around near ponds, setting off our own fireworks, and all the other potentially lethal pleasures of childhood.

William's unique appeal had by now spread far beyond Scandinavia, where the Danes and Norwegians had early taken him up with an enthusiasm almost equal to that of the Swedes, who regularly acquired new translation rights from 1925. Spain and Italy had fallen under his spell; he flourished in climes as diverse as Iceland and Portugal; and Holland and Germany were now producing many of his adventures in English-language textbooks for schools, which both gratified and entertained Richmal. A footnote in one such German edition, in a valiant attempt to decolloquialize 'Three Cheers for Sweetikins', translated Ginger's mild 'Gosh!' rather more forcefully as 'By God!' Foreign editions of William were the only aspect of her work Richmal would discuss without prompting; she seemed to revel in the sight of William in knickerbockers or lederhosen and would show the pictures to friends, a suppressed delight in her 'Look, isn't this amusing?'

In the September, *The Old Man's Birthday* was published. This was the best received, by critics, of all her novels and the second to enjoy subsequent publication in the States. The occasional short story made its way to America; but William had to be content with captivating the rest of the world. Richmal attributed his lack of popularity in the US to the American child's leaping 'straight from the cradle to adolescence' – or, in the unbowdlerized version, 'to the petting party'. The continued reign of Penrod, however, is likely to have been a more significant factor.

The following year, 1935, is probably the year in which Richmal herself had a mastectomy. (One wonders if this experience marked the genesis of her clairvoyant conviction that she would die as her mother had died: at the age of seventy-eight, from a heart attack.) She spoke so little of her health, depreciating every illness and accident, that it is difficult to identify the periods at which ill-health affected her output; but only one novel and one William book came out during this year.

The novel, *Quartet* (Macmillan), competently reiterated a well-loved theme: the development, from early childhood to early middle age, of four siblings. Jenifer, the central character of *Quartet*, has much in common with the heroine of *Anne Morrison* (1925) and with Bridget of *The Innermost Room* (1923). She displays the same unchildlike fastidiousness, guards quite as closely that inner preserve; and is equally haunted by memories of a disapproving spinster aunt, whose 'frightened shrinking' from the 'foul, veiled' subject of sex early left its mark. Jenifer, at 25, is ill at ease with men:

> She was vaguely worried by this and tried hard to overcome the secret shrinking that prevented her making men friends. It worried her because it made her feel that she was growing like Aunt Lena . . . She fought against it, but her whole being seemed to go tense and rigid when any man showed a special interest in her, while an attempt at love-making, however mild, would throw her into a blind unreasoning panic.

It is worthy of remark that though Bridget, heroine of Richmal's first novel, had worried herself frequently to the point of desperation over the same incapacity, it had never occurred to her to seek a solution; or, indeed, to wonder whether a solution might exist. Certainly, neither she nor Anne Morrison would have contemplated as therapy an illicit weekend, which a formerly platonic friend unexpectedly suggests to Jenifer. But a decade has passed since publication of *The Innermost Room* and *Anne Morrison*; and the heroine of *Quartet* is allowed at least to consider the proposition:

> She was silent for some moments. After all, why not? she thought. It would break down the exaggerated fear of sex that had become an obsession with her, making her shrink even from casual friendship with men, that was like a black river surrounding her. She'd swim through it and start fresh on the other side. It would mean nothing to Bobby, so it need mean nothing to her.

Richmal's awareness of changing mores, however, took her heroine no further than verbal acquiescence: the weekend evaporates, as does later a proposed marriage, and Jenifer continues to struggle unaided against the 'strange revulsion' she acknowledges bitterly as a 'heritage of prudery'.

There are other aspects, equally important if less striking, to Jenifer's view of the relationship between man and woman. To dismiss as merely symbolic the horror with which she contemplates loss of individuality through penetration of her inner being, would be facile: Jenifer, like Bridget and Anne and Richmal herself, sees Love as ineffable and indestructible, a force no ego could survive; and clearly she agrees with John Stuart Mill, that 'whatever crushes individuality is despotism, by whatever name it may be called'. Fleeting glimpses of the real thing evoke in her a poignant longing:

> Peter had a pleasant voice, and Jenifer listened idly, without hearing the words, watching Sylvia's brown head bent placidly over her work. The atmosphere of enclosed peace, of deep calm happiness, was so potent that it filled her with a sudden envy. It was what at the bottom of her heart she had always wanted, probably what every woman wanted...

Deep and lasting love between husband and wife is made the more precious in Jenifer's eyes by its evident rarity. But reality always intrudes upon the vicarious idyll. Ten years on, her friend's marriage is no less happy, yet its charm for Jenifer is flawed:

> Jenifer found (Peter) irritatingly slow and limited in outlook, and his Victorian attitude to his wife irked her feminist soul. Sylvia had surrendered her individuality and independence to him completely. She deferred to him and subjected all her plans to his wishes, yet she lived care-free and happy within the magic circle of his tenderness and devotion.

The longing to inhabit a 'magic circle' of her own, to experience 'what every woman wanted', would continue to plague Jenifer; but resistance to the idea of losing her own identity was to remain the stronger instinct.

The stories in *William – the Detective*, published in the July, were well up to standard; 'William and the Campers' (a title Richmal had used before), 'William the Rat Lover' and 'Waste Paper Wanted' are musts for the connoisseur. The same month's edition of *Happy Mag* (July 1935) carried the only William story to escape subsequent publication in a hardback collection: 'William on the Trail'. Three other stories bearing that title duly appeared between the familiar red covers; but this one was not republished until 1980, when it took pride of place in the very well researched private publication *William – a Bibliography*, by William Lofts and Derek Adley.

There has lately been much criticism of one of the stories in *William – the Detective*: 'William and the Nasties', in which William, having learned that in Germany Jewish shopkeepers are being hounded from their shops, reflects on the advantages of being a 'Nasty':

> 'Crumbs!' said William with a deep sigh of ecstasy, as there came to him glorious visions of chasing Jew after Jew out of sweetshop after sweetshop and appropriating the precious spoils. 'Crumbs! I jolly well wish I was one.'
>
> 'So do I,' said Ginger, 'an' if I'd got enough money I'd go to Germany an' be one to-morrow. I never remember in all my life,' he added pathetically, 'having as many sweets as I wanted.'

The story is indisputably tasteless. 'Miss Crompton must have been deplorably insensitive or completely innocent to have written it,' was the published comment of one longstanding William fan. 'It was meant to be funny, but even at the age of eleven we were politically conscious enough not to laugh.' Insensitive Richmal clearly was not. She may well, however, have been 'innocent': the story was written early in 1934, and at that time many Britons were either still unaware of or simply unwilling to believe the stories of Nazi persecution of the German Jews. It is also worth remembering that racial prejudices were freely voiced in the Britain of fifty years ago. (A friend writing to Richmal in 1938 mused on the virtues of a mutual acquaintance: perception, wit, charm, discernment, '*lovely* house and garden'. She concluded: 'What a pity he isn't English.')

Certainly no modern writer would permit his/her child character to plot the removal of a mean Jewish shopkeeper; indeed, the fictional shopkeeper would today be unlikely to be both mean and Jewish. But there is no evidence to suggest that Richmal was consciously anti-Semitic. Her equation of Jewishness with avarice in this story undoubtedly represents an inheritance from her family background. The class into which she was born has ever been a stronghold of conservatism; and the Cromptons, among whom she spent her childhood, were no exception, having for centuries belonged to the middle rank of a provincial middle class, keenly conscious of their superiority over that much larger rank of mill-workers below them. The rigid social observances of the day; the teaching of the Established Church; Clara's unremitting struggle to maintain 'standards' on a limited income; all had combined to ensure the acutely aware child's commitment to orthodoxy, in politics as in religion. And while Edward Lamburn was perhaps more sensitive than his wife to social injustice, his intense spirituality, in which the afterlife loomed so large, probably reinforced the message that humanity should concern itself not with its lot in this life but with its fitness for the next. It is therefore hardly surprising that Richmal was a 'staunch Conservative' all her life; and, moreover, very little inclined to question Conservative policy.

She had, however, no taste for political theory. Politics bored her: addressing (and licking) envelopes for the Party, which she had joined around 1920, fulfilled her sense of duty and left her free to remain otherwise uninvolved. Politicians bored her; she rarely missed an opportunity to deflate, as in the William story 'The May King'[5]:

> (William) disliked facts, and he disliked being tied down to

detail, and he disliked answering questions. As a politician, a great future would have lain before him.

An essential fair-mindedness enabled her to derive a mild enjoyment from observing minor absurdities in the established social order, even if she never seriously doubted that it was ordained by God. And by the time war came, she fully acknowledged the rightness of Britain's cause. Her novel *Weatherley Parade*, published in 1944, contains many references to atrocities committed by the Nazis in prewar years. One character in the novel says, in 1940: 'We're fighting something so monstrously evil that no one who hasn't lived with it can know how evil it is . . . This is beyond imagination, beyond hatred. We can only fight blindly . . .' The William books are currently being reissued, by Macmillan. Let us hope that this and any future edition of *William – the Detective* will not include the story 'William and the Nasties'.

The following year, 1936, began with the first production, at the Aldwych Theatre on 12th January, of 'Charity Begins . . .', a three-act comedy based on one of Richmal's short stories. Rex Harrison played the caddish Rodney in pursuit of Judy Deveral's virtue, Nigel Patrick the clean-cut Bobby in pursuit of her hand. The play was written by Ireland Wood, who seems also to have adapted for the stage at least three more of Richmal's works. 'Miss Tracey' (presumably based on the 1932 novel *The Odyssey of Euphemia Tracey*) and 'In Mrs 'awkins' Kitchen' (possibly based on the sketch 'Mrs Hawkins on the Drama', sold to *The Humorist* in 1924) have long since sunk into obscurity, but 'William's Half Holiday' (1960) is still occasionally performed by repertory companies. (Mr Wood declined to comment on his professional association with Richmal Crompton. She would, however, greatly have relished his brief assessment of her character: 'Sweet, but too *terribly* suburban.')

The rest of 1936 brought *The First Morning*, another volume of short stories; the novel *Caroline*, a competently reworked portrait of the havoc wrought by an abnormally developed maternal instinct; and in August, *Sweet William*, which, apart from its first story ('William and the Wonderful Present'), is average William. In the story 'Pensions for Boys', one senses a defensive undertone to the remarks of the sympathetic old lady who encounters the Outlaws on their march to a confrontation with Parliament:

> (William) explained the situation, and she listened with interest and sympathy.
>
> 'I'm very much afraid it's no use,' she said, gently, when he had finished. 'You see, I was one of them, too. A suffragette, I mean. I marched to London and made speeches at street corners and shouted "Votes for Women" all over the place, and – well we'd never have got it if it hadn't been for the war. It was the war that made them give it us, not anything we did.'

A reassurance to Richmal herself, perhaps, that the militancy she had not been able wholeheartedly to endorse would never have achieved its object.

The next year, 1937, brought publication of yet another novel whose heroine essentially remains in the late-Victorian era in which she was born: *There Are Four Seasons*, which The Times Literary Supplement described, with noticeable wistfulness, as 'a good picture of more stable times than these'. (Perhaps the reviewer approved of the servant Andrew's reliability: certainly, he knows his place quite as well in old age as he knew it when he first touched his forelock to the young mistress on page nine.) *William – the Showman* was published in the September, with 'William and the Little Strangers' and 'William Starts the New Year' the stars of a good collection. The latter story, in particular, highlights the weaknesses in critical analyses of William's appeal:

> '. . . it may be doubted whether children are ever well served by truly adult humour – that is, by humour deliberately keyed to adults.'
>
> . . . *Intent Upon Reading*
> (Brockhampton Press) by
> Margery Fisher
>
> 'More sophisticated authors like . . . Richmal Crompton made sure that their stories could be read on more than one level . . .'
>
> Books & Bookmen review of
> *The Schoolgirl Ethic* by
> Gillian Freeman

There was no such calculation in Richmal's writing of William. That he could be read with delight by children was purely fortuitous: '. . . the original stories were written for adults with no thought of child readers. It is possible that when the books were eventually accepted as "books for children" & gravitated from the "general library" to the "children's library", it affected my style without my realising it. But I tried never to "write down" to children, even when I realised that the children had accepted William as their own.'

Richmal's inadvertent discovery that children are in fact very well served by humour 'deliberately keyed to adults', and her subsequent decision not to alter the style of the stories, may well account for her prodigious success. Vindication of this theory may be found amid the glorious complications of 'William Starts the New Year', in which it is not the absurdity of childhood enthusiasms but the shibboleths of the adult world that are gently mocked. Having overheard Miss Milton advocating the full-scale adoption by well-to-do families of poor families, and much disappointed by his mother's uncharacteristically vehement rejection of the idea, William finds his own member of 'the poor'. For want of any more convenient place to keep Albert (becomingly clad in 'a baggy suit much too large for him and a man's cap pulled down low over his eyes'), William parks him in Miss Milton's bed – never doubting that she, who originated the idea, could be anything but delighted. But Albert soon grows bored with awaiting his adoptive parent and wanders into the vicarage garden, where he apprises the vicar's wife of his new status. The bewildered Mrs Monks rallies sufficiently to provide him with a meagre tea in the summerhouse, where he can do the least damage:

> She lifted him on to the seat and escaped indoors, pleased by her little manoeuvre. She disliked children at the best of times and found Albert a peculiarly unattractive specimen, which made it all the more wonderful of Miss Milton to have adopted him, of course. The child of some relative, perhaps. He looked terribly common, but even Miss Milton might have common relatives. The very best people had...[29]

That tickles the funny-bone of William fans of all ages, from ten to 100. As in Stephen Leacock's humorous writing, the appeal is to an ageless, universal sense of the ridiculous.

Richmal had much else in common with the English-born Canadian humorist. Both had been classical scholars; both taught and wrote with equal enjoyment. (Despite his huge success as a humorous writer and lecturer, Leacock retained his professorship at McGill University until compulsorily retired, to his bitter resentment, at 65.) He shared, too, Richmal's basic conservatism. The best of Leacock reveals, as does the best of William, the satirical humour of a 'very shrewd but essentially good-natured' human being, 'anything but an angry reformer'. J. B. Priestley wrote of Leacock:

> ... his serious writing seems to me quite commonplace, lacking originality and the insight that might have been expected of such a lively mind, just run-of-the-mill stuff, sufficiently responsible and conscientious but without distinction.[30]

Leacock's 'serious' writing was academic. If one extracts the reference to insight, however, this criticism could equally appropriately be applied to the novels of Richmal Crompton.

William – the Dictator, published in June 1938, underlined the topical allusion of its title with the story 'What's In A Name?', in which Richmal again appeared to flirt with fascism. This story, though, is much less offensive than the story published three years earlier, and can surely be taken as proof of her inherent lack of interest in politics: at a time when all but the most determinedly blind had become aware of the threat implicit in fascism, to Richmal the Blackshirts and Brownshirts were merely pegs on which to hang a story. The plot of the third story in this book, 'Agnes Matilda Comes to Stay', is the only one of the plots provided by Richmal's brother to have survived in its original, handwritten form. (It offers, incidentally, an entertaining sidelight on the relative strength of the male and the female sense of propriety. In Jack's plot outline, Agnes Matilda attaches herself to a tramp and passes the night in his hut; Richmal retained tramp and hut, but ensured that Agnes Matilda was safely out of the latter before nightfall.) The indisputable jewel of *William – the Dictator*, however, is 'William and the Old Man In the Fog', another perfect example of humour 'keyed to adults' yet equally irresistible to children.

Richmal's only novel published in that year, *Journeying Wave*, relates the story of Viola, whose husband leaves her briefly for another woman. In fact, very few of Richmal's married heroines were spared the odd adulterous escapade on the part of their husbands; and all who suffered it, accepted it – with varying degrees of anguish, but nonetheless without exception – as a moral lapse almost to be expected from the male creature. The occasional heroine who finds herself similarly tempted invariably summons all her moral strength to overcome the temptation and thus avoid inflicting on her husband, however unworthy, a like humiliation. One is not therefore surprised to learn that Richmal's 'answer to the problem of an unfaithful husband' (dragged from her, surely: impossible to imagine her volunteering advice to the lovelorn) was: 'He gets over it.' The basic orthodoxy of her view did not, however, preclude a belief that there was a limit to what a wife should be expected to endure. Her heroines would continue nobly to eschew divorce, which clearly Richmal saw as not only the sordid ending of a partnership destined to be indissoluble but also a cruel mockery of the essential infinitude of Love; yet she accompanied her sister to the harsh 1930s divorce court, and proved unwaveringly supportive throughout the ordeal. That fierce loyalty to family found its way into more than one of the novels. The little girl who lavished poetry and cuddles on her family of dolls in the seclusion of the Malvern Villas attic can often be glimpsed in the heroine whose tender, protective sympathy constantly overflows at the spectacle of brother or sister ill-used by unworthy spouse; though the strong maternal element in Richmal's own family affections is unlikely to have been a significant factor in her antipathy to her brother-in-law, or in her milder dislike of her sister-in-law. Simply, by an unfortunate coincidence, she had nothing in common with either.

Journeying Wave is, like most of her novels, very readable. It is not, however, the sort of book Richmal herself enjoyed reading. Of contemporary novelists, she seems most to have admired at this period Elizabeth Bowen, Rosamund Lehmann and Ivy Compton-Burnett; for the latter's work, in particular, she early conceived a respect that was to deepen almost to reverence. She was generally averse to humorous writers, confessing herself quite unable to read P. G. Wodehouse; though her bookcase did harbour the supreme humorist, Stephen Leacock, to whom she had made fleeting reference in her first novel. The only form of escapist literature she does seem to have enjoyed is the whodunit. She clearly did not squander her valuable reading time on light fiction; and yet her own novels, classic if superior examples of the genre, were not written as 'pot-boilers'. They were what she was driven to write; she was always 'much more pleased if someone had read the novels than if they had read William', and certainly they were much less profitable than the William books. Of the heroines identifiable at least in part as Richmal herself, two –

Bridget of *The Innermost Room* and Jenifer of *Quartet* – also become writers. Significantly, each is content with a modest success; neither strikes a lucrative vein of popular literature. Bridget, after university, supports herself by part-time secretarial work and writes in her spare time. Jenifer, having received a legacy, is able at 35 to devote all her working hours to writing:

> She was absorbed in her work (she had had several novels published) but not particularly ambitious, satisfied if each book maintained the reputation for readability that the first had won for her.[31]

The relative importance to Richmal of the novels and William bears analogy with Sir Arthur Sullivan's attitude to his musical compositions. Sullivan, too, derived much greater satisfaction from his 'serious' work. His musicianship – as undeniable as Richmal's craftmanship – earned him this uncharacteristically lyrical tribute from the feminist-composer Dame Ethel Smyth: 'A greater master of melody and of rhythm has never existed; and what is more, appraised by the organs we bring to bear on technical masterpieces like the canon in "Fidelio", for instance, his work survives the test.'[32] Yet Sullivan was, Dame Ethel admitted, 'only at his immortal best when tied to Gilbert'; his gift of originality, abundantly apparent in his music for Gilbert's comic-opera libretti, does not reveal itself in the oratorios and incidental music he believed more worthy of his art. And just as Sullivan's Savoy-opera music lives on when his nobler efforts are largely forgotten, so has William survived the novels that mean so much to Richmal. Sullivan, however, believed that his serious work would outlive his lighter creations. Richmal seems to have retained no such illusion. In 1957, in response to an admiring letter, she wrote: 'I feel deeply touched by what you say about my work. I know that it is in the "lower ranks" of literature but I think it was Chekhov who said that the "lower ranks" are as necessary in literature as in the army!'

Sullivan's partner, of course, shared many of William's attributes. Unlike Sir Arthur, who responded ecstatically to royal patronage, Gilbert was disinclined to reverence; he held a low opinion of most eminent figures of his day and a very high opinion of himself. (His aversion to Elizabethan drama would surely have endeared him to William. 'If you promise me

photo: *Bury Times*

The Rev. Edward Lamburn (front, right) minus his droopy moustache: in 1912, with other Bury Grammar School staff

Thomas Disher, Richmal's nephew, born 1915

Staff of Bromley High School c. 1920: Richmal second from right, back row

Early editions of the William books in their original dust-jackets are now almost impossible to find.

Richmal c. 1925

An early reprint of Richmal's first novel (first published 1923)

Advertisement in *Strand* for the first issue (June 1922) of *Happy Mag*

William on the cover of the November 1925 *Happy Mag*

Richmal c. 1930

Richmal entertaining the
niece named after her

Richmal (right) with
mother, niece and
a family friend, c. 1935

Richmal in a Surbiton
garden in August 1938

Richmal in the mid-1940s in severely tailored suit...
...and in softer Forties style

Richmal and her Peke, Ming, at the Glebe, c. 1951

photo: *Home Notes*

Richmal and her brother (left) before the microphone, with Alick Hayes (producer) and John Clark (star) of the first two BBC radio series, 1945-1947

Richmal with Thomas Henry in the mid-1950s

This card game appeared in 1952. William was not heavily marketed until 1977, when a number of spin-offs (paperback reissue, William annual, game and sweets) accompanied the first commercial-television series (LWT).

William in Merlin paperback, published in 1967 by Hamlyns. The first paperback edition was published two years earlier, by Armada (William Collins).

Richmal's fortieth and final novel, published in 1960 by Hutchinson

Richmal outside her bungalow in Petts Wood, c. 1963

Richmal among her roses, c. 1965

faithfully not to mention this to a single person,' he is said to have confided to a friend, 'I don't think Shakespeare rollicking.') While he deflated with relish the pompous or vain, he remained much inclined to avenge his own injuries, and caused many an enemy to retire in that state of impotent fury so familiar to victims of William's revenge. But it is Gilbert's iconoclasm that savours most strongly of William; and the source, albeit unconscious, of William's iconoclasm can only have been Richmal. Her preference for writing the novels may well have represented a triumph for the conventional influences of her upbringing; but the existence of William rendered it a hollow victory.

On the question of upbringing, Richmal herself remarked upon its importance in the matter of religious faith: 'If I'd been raised a sceptic – well, I don't know!' Her own faith ('such a real and deep part of me, the one thing that gives life meaning to me'), though much stronger than her political instinct, was yet channelled into the same unswerving orthodoxy. With the cheerful unconcern of the moderately High Anglican, she once admitted: 'I never have the faintest desire to convert anyone else.' She quoted Tennyson in condemning smugness and complacency in believer and unbeliever alike ('There is more faith in honest doubt, Believe me, than in half the creeds'), then promptly took issue with him: 'I'm not sure that I agree with him. "Faith" and "doubt" seem somehow incompatible!' Her interest in the theory of reincarnation seems at odds with her religious conformity; until one learns that the family has 'always more or less accepted its possibility; almost as if it *were* orthodox'. Richmal happily took part in the discussion of tenets and doctrine, absorbing it all with eager interest; but she was never more than momentarily diverted from the mainstream of traditional Christian belief. When, in later years, a psychically inclined friend informed her that the Rev. Edward Lamburn had come through at a seance with a message for her, Richmal was markedly sceptical. The 'message' – that she should cultivate more colour in her garden – 'in no way sounded like him or the sort of advice he would give'; and when pressed to seek a deeper meaning, along the lines of striving for a more colourful existence, she said flatly that her father would never have expressed himself so ambiguously.

Among the many benefits of her classical education was its power to remove from faith the stain of fear. Through scholarship, the fires of Hell could be rationalized, and others besides herself might be reassured:

> 'The idea of eternal punishment is quite incompatible with Christianity and I didn't know that anyone believed in it these days! Actually, the Greek word that is wrongly translated as "everlasting" in the Authorized Version, means "for a certain period" ... It's occasionally used to mean a long and indefinite period, but its actual meaning is just a period of time. In the Revised Version it's translated as "eternal" – not in the sense of "everlasting" but in the sense of the eternal world that impinges on this world but of course outlasts it. And the language of the East is full of symbolism so that "fire" doesn't mean the literal flames that burn in our sitting-room grate! The explanation, as I see it, is that a person who has lived a completely material life here, indulging his or her every lust and appetite, will, on leaving the material plane after death, suffer agonies of desire (comparable to consuming fire) when unable to indulge them ... but as Christ says (I forget where and can't quote it) that all mankind will eventually come to the knowledge of God, the refining process will gradually destroy the bodily cravings ... There's nothing cruel or vindictive about it.'

On 20 May 1939, having survived her husband by twenty-four years, Clara Lamburn died. In attempting, some years later, to give comfort to a friend whose mother was near death, Richmal could write from her own experience: 'Try to *accept* it as something natural and inevitable and part of the scheme of life, something even beautiful ... she goes to something much fuller and more perfect than this existence and you will meet her again when you've "awakened from the dream of life" – which sounds a bit sententious but is the only sane way of looking at it.'

Clara had come into her own at The Glebe, as her granddaughter Margaret recalls: 'Marvellous, very stern, she dominated that very female household. She inspected our hands at the table and sent us back if they were less than spotless. She was obsessive about punctuality, insisting that everybody must arrive half-an-hour early for trains, theatre, etc.' For twenty years Clara had been happily occupied with running a household again, keeping a watchful eye on Richmal's health and a competent hand on her financial affairs. Now, there was no one to apply a critical eye to the novels' manuscripts before they went to the publisher. (Gwen's third child, named Richmal after her aunt, later assumed this responsibility; though she was to entertain a permanent suspicion that her aunt was secretly untroubled by the prospect of a 'howler' in print.) Clara had been an able business manager; Richmal, though capable of a penetrating shrewdness in other directions, was not sufficiently interested in money to enjoy applying her energies to its management. She was reasonably methodical, and astute enough to recognize the professional as well as the social shark (the building firm that submitted a bill almost 300% higher than the estimate was destined to be disappointed); but Clara's practical presence was nevertheless sorely missed.

As time passed, however, it became apparent that Richmal now felt free to develop her own style, if only in the matter of clothes. Clara had been addicted to floral prints: 'You always saw Granny in large floral prints and Auntie in small floral prints.' It had probably been the least line of resistance on an issue to which Richmal was in any case largely indifferent. Now, though, she seemed to realize that, 'if she liked, she could perfectly well choose something that *hadn't* got flowers'. Otherwise, her life remained much as it had been before Clara's death. She continued to fulfil the role of Ideal Aunt, taking as much interest in her younger niece (Richmal) and nephew (David, Jack's firstborn) and in her several godchildren as she still took in the older children of the family. As Gwen's older daughter recalls, Richmal 'virtually took my father's place in my upbringing.' She visited them all at school, provided 'slap-up' teas out, arranged visits to zoo and circus and pantomime, to ballet, theatre and cinema; and demonstrated a generous willingness to provide autographs, which, in the economics of school life, were becoming increasingly valuable.

The William book published during May 1939, *William and A.R.P.*, was to have its title changed in 1956 – lest the new generation of William fans be mystified by 'A.R.P.' – to *William's Bad Resolution.* Dedicated to Dick Lupino, Roddy McDowall, Peter Miles and Norman Robinson, 'the William, Ginger, Henry and Douglas of the Screen' (the first William film was shortly to have its premiere), *William and A.R.P.* is given distinction by 'William's Day Off', 'William and the Vanishing Luck' and, best of all, 'William and the Begging Letter', whose genius London Weekend Television's carefully researched 1977 'Just – William' series did not fully convey. The novel *Merlin Bay,* also published in 1939, offers yet another minute examination of monstrous maternity in its portrait of Pen, uptight mother of six; and in the August, *Just William – The Book of The Film* appeared. This contained, in full but minus the Thomas Henry illustrations, 'The Outlaws and Cousin Percy'[33], 'William to the Rescue'[29], 'The Outlaws and the Triplets'[34], 'William and the Wonderful Present'[35], 'The Outlaws and the Fifth'[36] and 'William Enters Politics'[37]; and the film script, which was written by Doreen Montgomery, Graham Cutts and Ireland Wood. Produced by Associated British, this first of the William films was shown again at the National Film Theatre in November 1975. Though advertised on the Junior NFT programme, the showing attracted a considerable number of men and women between the ages of thirty and sixty-five; indeed, nearly every Junior present was accompanied by a Senior bearing an expression of excited anticipation.

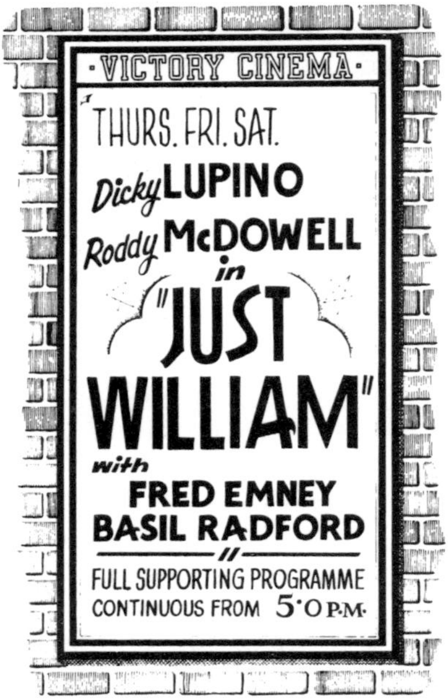

Alas, their hopes were unrealized. Fred Emney performed valiantly: he did manage, occasionally, at least to sound like Mr Brown. But William (Dicky Lupino) looked more like Hubert Lane; Mrs Brown, angular and singularly perturbable, was hopelessly miscast; Robert was much too self-assured. In the absence of Ginger's spasmodic challenge to William's hegemony, of Henry's (relative) erudition, of Douglas's apprehensive pessimism, the Outlaws lacked individuality; the Brown residence was far too imposing; and from the moment, early in the film, when 'William' self-consciously slid down the banisters and into a soppy embrace with his mother – well, one knew that all was lost. The children present seemed to enjoy the film; but it wasn't William.

During that last summer before the war, Richmal took a holiday: a cruise, on *S.S. Orion*, of Iceland and the Scandinavian countries. As always on her trips abroad, she made copious notes on landscapes, customs and inhabitants (who were generally recorded as being healthy and content, however extreme their poverty). More entertaining are her observations on the people she encountered abroad. In Oslo, an 'elderly hypochondriac' resident at the same hotel offered her a lift to the shops in the taxi he'd commandeered. Once she was inside, he ordered the taxi to be driven around for fifteen minutes and proceeded to expound at length on his many dreadful symptoms. As he drew breath to continue, Richmal told the driver to stop and escaped as rapidly as she could. Finding herself in unfamiliar surroundings, she asked for directions at a garage:

> He asked which ship I wanted to join & when I said 'Orion' he said, 'Oh... a foreign ship!' Felt most indignant. Nearly said that on the contrary his ships were the foreign ships.

At Åarhus, a party of sea scouts came aboard the *Orion*. Their Danish leader immediately held forth on 'international peace and goodwill in broken English' and later 'stood in front of our chairs and sang a song of his own composition and loaded us with literature dealing with his movement'. Everything was observed with enjoyment, and much with sympathy, particularly an unexpected meeting with a fellow-Lancastrian, a very homesick mother of ten Danish children.

Although the political situation had caused a change in the cruise's itinerary (she was to have seen Danzig and the Baltic), only one entry in this summer 1939 travel diary gives any indication of the rumblings of war. Of Iceland, she wrote:

> No army or navy. One cruiser to protect fishing. One sea plane to give notice to fishermen of movements of herring, etc. Day

> before, they'd taken a German cruiser for being within the 3 mile limit. Had to fire 12 shots... before she'd stop.

Yet war was coming; and with it would come – to William's village as to the rest of Europe – a gradual erosion of comfortable middle-class standards. The Brown's gardener was already less in evidence; though little else had changed over the twenty years of the family's existence. Robert's higher education remained subordinate to his kaleidoscopic love-life; as yet, no vulgar suggestion of gainful employment shadowed Ethel's decorative existence on her allowance; and cook and housemaid continued to ensure the supervisory nature of Mrs Brown's domestic duties. But these halcyon days were numbered. Before long Mrs Brown would be polishing her own furniture and baking her own cakes with only a 'daily' at her service – plus, of course, the occasional helping hand from William...

Richmal Does Her Bit

X

Having reflected the threat of war in his previous title, William launched himself into wartime proper with a title inspired by early activity on the Home Front: *William and the Evacuees*. With this book's publication in April 1940, William himself became an evacuee. The title story marked the end of his long and mutually advantageous partnership with *Happy Mag*: the office building that housed the magazine was an early casualty of the war, and the new series Newnes started in the early spring of 1940 ran to only two issues. *William and the Evacuees* contains only eight stories; though few fans would cavil at the quantity when the quality is so high. 'William and the Bird Man', 'William and the Man From Africa', 'William and the Blackout' and especially 'William and the Unfair Sex' are all top-grade William.

From very early in the war, Richmal had her 'own' evacuees: a group of Liverpool schoolchildren, evacuated to a village near Caernarvon in the charge of a schoolmaster, Bryan Blades. Mr Blades had nobly contributed his own almost complete set of William books to the founding of the new school library; and when they proved not only popular but inspirational, he collected the children's own 'William' stories and illustrations and sent them to Richmal, who responded appreciatively. She appreciated, too, Mr Blades' account of his brother's introduction to William. The brother, a farmer who had never before been known to read for pleasure, one day asked for 'an interesting book' to fill the hours of a stay in hospital. Mr Blades, startled but pleased by this unprecedented request, gave him *Just – William*. Having read it 'from cover to cover and, like Oliver, asked for more', the farmer went on to devour the rest of his brother's William collection. Mr Blades, meanwhile, his professional instincts no less excited than his fraternal pleasure, had carefully assembled a range of books guaranteed to nurture the newfound interest. But the farmer, having regretfully closed the last of the William books, never read again: his sole acquaintance with the world of literature was to remain William. On hearing this, Richmal 'roared with laughter' and declared it the greatest compliment she had ever been paid.

In July 1940, *Steffan Green* was published by Macmillan, who reprinted it within the month. With this novel, Richmal broke new ground by making her central character, Lettice Helston, a divorcée. Instrumental in restoring Lettice's confidence and self-respect is the wise and understanding Mrs Fanshaw, the Steffan Green vicar's wife: a character Richmal clearly intended to be sympathetic. As yet another recanting suffragette, however, Mrs Fanshaw is ultimately more tiresome than delightful:

> 'I hated doing it. I was literally sick before the – demonstration, as they called it, but I felt I was doing it for posterity. Well, we got the vote and I took a doctor's degree and then I married and had a daughter, and I thought, She shall have everything that I fought for. She shall have freedom and a career. And the amusing part is that she didn't want it. All she wanted in life was what I'd fought against. She wanted to live at home and potter about the house and do the flowers and help in the parish, and she's tremendously interested in nice young men. It's funny to think that I killed my mother because I wanted to save my children from that fate. My mother literally died of shock when I went to prison and was in the headlines... And really all for nothing...'

Lettice Helston, recipient of this cosy philosophical exposition, might have pointed out that at least the daughter enjoyed a choice, where Mrs Fanshaw's generation had not; but Mrs Fanshaw, unchallenged, goes on to conclude, with an 'almost imperceptible smile':

> 'It was all rather futile. We were fanatics. We thought that the vote would bring the millennium and it didn't. Except for a few women doctors and M.P.'s we're pretty much as we were. And I've come to the conclusion that we're all right as we were...'

The wartime flavour of *William Does His Bit*, published in April 1941, was much stronger than that of its predecessor. Despite its topicality, however, this collection constitutes a relatively undistinguished volume, with only 'William – the

Salvage Collector' and 'Claude Finds a Companion' worthy of note. The story 'William the Highwayman' suggests a rare slip in liaison between publisher and artist: in the text, General Moult is sporting 'his tin hat and Civil Defence armlet'; in the illustration, he is wearing a trilby and no armlet.

Also published in 1941 was *Narcissa*, the story of a woman's obsession with her own image. There is much that is perceptive in this attempt at the depiction of remorseless self-absorption; but in the end, the portrait of Stella and her narrowing world fails to convince. Richmal's descriptions of the Carlswell family, into which Stella at first hopes to marry, are startlingly inconsistent. Early in the story, she introduces them thus:

> Hugh Carlswell... carried his slender figure with a careless air of breeding, almost of arrogance, as though the spirit of his forebears, who had exercised lordship over Runeham and the surrounding villages for so many generations, still lived in him. Many of them had held high offices of State, but the present baronet, Sir Miles Carlswell, though a staunch Tory, contented himself with the life of landlord and sportsman and the leadership of local affairs. He and Lady Carlswell still reigned in almost feudal fashion at Runeham, dispensing charity with open hands, fulfilling every obligation of their position punctiliously according to their lights – kind-hearted, generous, intolerant.

Primed with that very clear picture of the family, one is almost prepared for such utterances as:

> 'The gel's a ravin' beauty,' said a tiaraed dowager to Lady Carlswell. 'The boy's got taste.'

Having swallowed all that, however, one is taken aback to find the Carlswell circle later presented as tolerant, open-minded, even avant garde:

> ... the Carlswell women, many of them quite plain and dowdily dressed, displayed a knowledge of politics and art that seemed to Stella little short of an insult. At first she tried to despise this knowledge as unwomanly, to see herself set on a height far above this futile chatter. These ridiculous discussions about politics did not belong to a woman's sphere at all. The discussion veered to Woman Suffrage, and there again she was irritated to find that the majority of the guests sympathised with the movement, of which she had always disapproved.

A minor point of interest is the recurrence of a remark credited sixteen years earlier, in *Anne Morrison*, to the heroine's father; and in 1932 to the heroine of *Marriage of Hermione*. In this twenty-seventh novel, it comes from a local headmistress:

> 'Officially I am supposed to frown upon the movement as unwomanly, whatever that may mean. Privately it has my deepest sympathy. Even the militants. After all, men got the vote by rioting.'

Drawn reluctantly into a rare discussion of her work, Richmal said that Henry James's expression 'sincere imposter' described Stella. As a psychological study, however, *Narcissa* is seriously flawed; and as a novel, it falls far short of the tragedy it was surely meant to be.

Richmal's 1942 novel, *Mrs Frensham Describes a Circle*, begins with a tragedy – the death of a mentally ill husband – but swiftly proceeds to a much lighter mood. Swept from the scene of bereavement by her married daughter, Mrs Frensham is very soon waist-high in difficult relationships, but manages eventually to engineer a happy ending for all. *William Carries On*, which carries the imprint 'May 1942', was not in fact published until the July of that year. After two years of austerity, life is noticeably less comfortable for the adult Browns, and even William is feeling the strain:

> Gamekeepers had been called up and he could trespass in woods and fields with comparative impunity, but, on the other hand, sweets were scarce and cream buns unprocurable. Discipline was relaxed – at school as the result of a gradual infiltration of women teachers and at home because his father worked overtime at the office and his mother was 'managing' without a cook – but these advantages were offset by a lack of entertainments in general. There were no parties, summer holidays were out of the question because of something called the Income Tax, and for the same reason pocket money, inadequate at the best of times, had faded almost to vanishing point.

That he has nevertheless retained his ingenuity and insatiable curiosity is amply demonstrated by the first story, 'Too Many Cooks', perhaps the best of this collection steeped in the essence of wartime rural England. It is, however, another of these ten stories – 'Guy Fawkes–with Variations' – that exposes the secret of his enduring magnetism.

One suspects that William's most devoted readers have always been those who in childhood were – as the young Richmal had been – generally well behaved, quiet, even studious. (Boisterous, rebellious, adventurous souls were out doing the sort of thing William did, not sitting at home reading about it.) The academically inclined could regard with indulgence his condemnation of all who took an interest in Latin, French or maths; the cat-lovers could tolerate his contempt for the breed; those who were female could even forgive his despising their sex; in fact, every real William fan would have excused him *anything* in return for his frequent glorious triumphs over Authority. In 'Guy Fawkes – with Variations', Authority is represented by a headmistress, a Miss Cummins, who has just visited Joan's mother and offered to accept Joan at reduced fees at her boarding school. Joan is out playing with the Outlaws but her mother explains where she can be found and what she is wearing, and Miss Cummins decides to introduce herself on the way back to the station. William, meanwhile, wholly absorbed in his temporary role of Guy Fawkes, is fleeing from 'prison' disguised as Mrs Fawkes; and thus it is William, clad in Joan's best green coat and hat, that Miss Cummins encounters:

> Miss Cummins started. As headmistress of a large girls' school she was familiar with various degrees of plainness in her pupils, but she thought she had never come across such an uncompromisingly ugly little girl in all her life before. And not only ugly – but hard, brazen, tough. Yes, tough was the word. A tough little girl. Miss Cummins shuddered at the combination. Scowling aggressively, William returned her gaze.
>
> 'D'you want anything?' he said impolitely.
>
> 'Are you Joan Parfitt?' said Miss Cummins.
>
> 'Yeah,' said William, determined to sustain his disguise. How did he know who the woman was? A spy probably. Ginger's family had a schoolmistress billeted on them, whom William had not yet seen and who, Ginger said, was one of those sickening people who were always trying to "enter into the children's games"... For all he, William, knew, she had found out about this game and was "entering into it"...
>
> Miss Cummins glanced with increasing disapproval at the short stocky figure... The child, of course, could not help her looks, but her manners seemed to be as ungainly as her appearance. It would certainly be one of the hardest cases her

school had ever tackled...

'And where are you off to?' said Miss Cummins.

William's suspicion that the unknown was Ginger's family's evacuee "butting into the game" deepened. He decided to nip it in the bud.

'You mind you own business,' he said brusquely.

Miss Cummins blenched. Never in all her life had a child spoken to her like that before.

'You'll have to learn to be more polite than that if you come to my school,' she said grimly.

'I'm not coming to your rotten ole school,' said William.

There, surely, is crystallized the essence of William's appeal: the vicarious satisfaction to be derived from his rudeness, his rowdyism, his refusal to be put down. 'You mind you own business': pure, timeless delight for the civilized, child or adult.

The following year, 1943, was the first since 1921 to see no new William book published; and the first since 1922 not to bring forth a new novel by Richmal Crompton. There had been less time for writing since Gwen and her younger daughter, Richmal, had moved into The Glebe on the outbreak of war. It had been an arrangement destined to suit only one of the participants: 'Mother was worried about her sister being alone in the fearful air raids that were anticipated and felt she should look after her – and Auntie couldn't say "no" firmly. As they were both independent characters, neither was happy sharing a home, but it took Mother four years to believe that Auntie could manage perfectly well. I was the one who benefitted!'

There was also voluntary service to be fitted into the working week. Since the beginning of the war, Richmal had worked at the telephone switchboard of the Bromley Auxiliary Fire Service, and (first at Bromley Common, later at nearby Keston) at the Toc H canteen, where, 'small, smiling, self-effacing', she attended 'with a nervous eagerness' to her customers' needs. She said she didn't dare attempt anything in the cooking line more complicated than tomatoes on toast. When everyone had been served, she would sit quietly behind the counter 'and try to look part of the furniture'. Former WAAF Nancy Bowden's first impression was of 'extraordinary eyes, mobile, slightly protruding. They were blue, often seeming very blue, and flashing intermittently with white light. She was, of course, watching every one – catching us all in turn in her beam.'

Richmal's desire for anonymity was genuine and heartfelt; but the childlike initial shyness dissolved quickly enough in the warmth of kindred interests, and she was soon deep in conversation with Nancy and her WAAF friends, on the subject of Dr Johnson. Rarely, however, was anyone able to draw her out on the subject of her own work. The novels belonged in that innermost room, where defence, devious if need be, was paramount. Her protective instinct was constantly on the alert, ready to be summoned on behalf of not only the foetal work but also the offspring of earlier years. A measure of its strength – and of its effectiveness – is provided by the percentage of friends who refer to Richmal's having 'started writing after being crippled'; whereas in fact, by the time she contracted polio, she had already written at least four novels, published one, and was some way along the road to fame as the creator of William. Years of practice had ensured facility in diverting the threat while appearing not to recognize it; in this, humour was a powerful ally. (One acquaintance, having expressed at length her admiration of William and the novels, remarked that Richmal must be sick to death of praise. 'My dear,' said Richmal drily, 'you can't lay it on too thick.') But the whole area, however skilful her redirection of invaders, would remain painful territory. Shortly after publication of her next book, *Weatherley Parade*, in April 1944, she was to write to a friend: 'Every book I write comes so far short of the "idea" of it in my mind that I feel a little ashamed. I can never bear to read them once they're printed. I do, of course, when I get the complimentary copies, but they always give me a nasty shock!'

In *Weatherley Parade*, Richmal again presented both points of view of the struggle for women's rights. The novel charts the Weatherley family's experiences from 1902 to 1940; and in 1908, the head of the family reacts violently to mention of the Movement:

> 'Unsexed hooligans!' he said angrily. 'The whole thing's outrageous. They've lost their influence over men as decent women and they've nothing to put in its place. This modern tendency to anarchy – strikers, Ulster volunteers, and now, Heaven help us! rebels in the House of Lords itself – is undermining the entire fabric of democracy... As for these women, they don't even stand by their own friends. They try to break up Grey's and Lloyd George's meetings as well as McKenna's and Asquith's. That fellow Keir Hardie ought to be jailed for encouraging them.'

(A subtle piece of writing: only the most bigoted could have regarded Grey and Lloyd George as champions of women's suffrage.)

> 'I do so agree with you, Major,' said Lady Evesham from her son's arm. 'A woman's sphere is the home.'
>
> 'But what about the women who have no home?' said Miss Clorinda, joining the fray with a warlike rattle of beads and rustle of hand-woven materials. 'What about the thousands upon thousands of sweated women workers, whose lot no one troubles to ameliorate because they have no vote?'
>
> 'Violence never won anything worth having.'

And then, amongst the clamour of comment, again that justification uttered in three of the earlier novels:

> 'After all, men got the vote by rioting.'
>
> 'Surely an educated woman has as much right to a voice in her country's affairs as a man who can't write or read and is in any case willing to sell his vote for a pint of beer?'
>
> 'They'll outvote the men, and then where shall we be?'
>
> 'Petticoats at Westminster! Good Lord, can you imagine it?'
>
> Helena shrugged helplessly. The familar argument was well under way, and nothing could stop it.

A very readable and often moving story, *Weatherley Parade* was reprinted within a month of publication. Before the war, Richmal's novels had sold, on average, between two and three thousand copies in the first year and a few hundred during the second year, with only occasional sales over the next eight to ten years. During the war years, however, there was – presumably owing to the disappearance or curtailment of other forms of escapism – a small but significant revival in sales, particularly of the more romantic of her books, such as *Millicent Dorrington* (1927), *Blue Flames* and *Naomi Godstone* (both 1930).

BOOK PRODUCTION WAR ECONOMY STANDARD

The gem of the *William and the Brains Trust* collection, published in April 1945 and reprinted during the same year, is 'Entertainment Provided', which has William resorting for inspiration (in an altruistic attempt to find an escort for Ethel) to a book entitled *Court Letter Writer*; but with the title story, 'William's War-Time Fun Fair', 'William and the Tea-Cake' and 'Soldiers For Sale', it is altogether an appropriately triumphant volume. Eleven years later, Newnes were to change two of the five war-time titles: *William and A.R.P.* became *William's Bad Resolution* and *William and the Evacuees* became *William – the Film Star*; and in 1972 Collins changed *William and the Brains Trust* to *William – the Hero*. The retitling seems in retrospect an unnecessary act. Mystification was certainly no bar to pleasure for those of us who came to William in the 1950s; rather, our enjoyment was enhanced by the esoteric glamour of 'the blackout', by the thought of a Britain bereft of signposts, by the novel and intriguing idea of children leaving their homes to live with total strangers, by the sinister prevalence of such mysterious beings as black marketeers, Fifth Columnists and spies.

According to Richmal, Bromley took the long-awaited peace 'very quietly'; she added, darkly, 'in some ways, of course, it's going to be worse than war'. Life and work gradually returned to normal; though, with the demise of *Happy Mag*, she no longer had to produce William stories on a regular, one-a-month basis. He was leading/dragging her into new paths; from now on, broadcasting and films would demand much of her time. By the autumn of 1945, she was travelling up to the BBC every Tuesday to spend the day 'evolving William "layouts" (as they're called) with a producer and a script writer' for William's first radio series. Richmal wrote the scripts; but 'the professional script writer edits them – in other words, chops them to pieces!' She was not consulted on casting: 'I think they have chosen quite the wrong type for William . . . but only heard the boy [John Clark] for the first time at a final rehearsal.' The search was to continue for more than thirty years, throughout four more radio series, two more films and four television series; but the right 'type for William' would never be found among young professional actors, however gifted.

On leaving the BBC one day, Richmal shared a taxi with a woman accompanied by her young son, who chattered excitedly and unceasingly about William and the current radio series. She had, of course, revealed her identity? What joy for the child, to meet the creator of his hero! But no: 'He would not have believed me: or else he would have believed, and I would know I had shattered his dream.'

In March 1946, she went to see the 'much-talked-of film' *Brief Encounter*. Her stringent comment on it nicely reaffirms her unerring critical faculty: 'I was much disappointed. Somehow it didn't ring true and I couldn't feel any sympathy with the love-lorn couple.' She had, one friend remembers, 'little taste for frivolous theatre or cinema fare'. Her reading matter, too, remained infinitely more literary than the novels she wrote. She had by now discovered Proust and Henry James, and the formidable trio of Proust, James and Compton-Burnett ('the one contemporary writer who's sure of immortality . . . so concise and witty and pointed that you can read the stories again and again') remained to the end of her life the post-Victorian novelists Richmal most admired.

Her own next adult offering was *Westover*, which covers three months in the life of an 18th-century manor house, turned into flats for superior tenants just after World War II. Relationships between the new residents and the family that owns the house are detailed with Richmal's customary competence; though there are a few inconsistencies, as when Cynthia, who has taken an instant dislike to her brother-in-law Hubert's new wife, comes in for some bracing criticism from husband Godfrey:

> 'I know what's in your mind, you hard-boiled little snob! She talks about Hubert as Mr Fielding and she puts Westover in inverted commas and she says "That's right" and she holds her knife as if it were a pen and eats her sweet with a spoon instead of

a fork and does a hundred other little things, I daresay, that were supposed to "class" people in the old days. My dear, they're words in a dead language. They don't mean anything any more.'

Admirable sentiments; but they sound uncharacteristically liberal for Godfrey, whose

scale of values was rigid and undeviating. Men with the right background and standards were 'decent chaps', the others did not exist for him, though he was uniformly courteous when contact with them was forced on him.

Two days before the Christmas of 1946, the BBC cameras paid a visit to the Granville Theatre, Walham Green, where the play 'Just William' (adapted and produced by Alick Hayes, producer of the first and second radio series) was being enacted before enthusiastic audiences. Richmal noted that William seemed 'very busy these days'. He kept her busy, too; there was considerable feeling in her recommendation of Ruth Pitter's poems: 'I say the one beginning "Cure me with quietness" to myself whenever I'm beginning to get "het up" and it restores my tranquility.'

In March 1947, the novel *The Ridleys* appeared. A Universal Book Club edition was published in May of the following year, and a Howard Baker reprint in 1970. One friend believes *The Ridleys* was Richmal's own favourite among her novels. It was certainly based on a favourite theme (the charting of one family's life over about forty years, from a usually unspecified point in the late-Victorian era); and the writing is perhaps tauter than usual. The five Ridley children are typically well drawn. As in *Millicent Dorrington* (1927), Janet is the strong-willed, bold, basically selfish sister; while Rosa, tiresomely intense, touchy and unknowingly sensual, is a near-replica of Millicent Dorrington's sister Doris.

By May of that year, Richmal had produced twenty-one very short stories about a new *enfant terrible*, Jimmy Manning, for the London Star newspaper. But Jimmy, though at 'seven and three quarters' indisputably more *enfant* than William, was not half so *terrible*, and attempts to interest the provincial papers in these stories (illustrated by Lunt Roberts) were largely unsuccessful; only the Liverpool Post responded and they 'evidently soon had enough!' They proved more popular 'down here', Richmal reported, being 'read aloud in many schools'; and 62 of the stories were later brought out by Newnes in two hardback collections, *Jimmy* (1949) and *Jimmy Again* (1951).

A holiday in Sweden (whose border William had crossed more than twenty years earlier) at the end of May, with her niece Richmal and a friend, brought a brief respite from the heavy work schedule. In July, back at work and with a second film ('Just William's Luck', issued in December 1947) under way, Richmal wrote: 'I now move among the denizens of the film world and am gradually learning the language.' By September, she was fully occupied with meeting deadlines: 'I haven't seen or done anything since I started the film book . . .[38] Next week, too, the shades of the BBC close round me. Sometimes I wonder why I ever thought of William!' October saw her 'horribly busy, coping with broadcasts, film, etc. – and now Television has cropped up. They want me to interview the new BBC William[39] on Wednesday (Picture Page) and I have to go up tomorrow to arrange details of the interview.' Her first television interview Richmal regarded with mingled apprehension and amusement: '. . . it's only six minutes so will soon be over. I've been told to wear something *light* as dark colours don't register, so see myself arriving in white muslin through a blizzard!'

Early in November, she wrote of the penalties of local celebrity: 'I opened a little sale of work here in aid of the Restoration of the Church Clock yesterday. They all fell upon the stalls as soon as I'd finished, but the man who had been told to propose a vote of thanks went on proposing it from behind his stall for about five minutes. You could see his mouth moving and that was all!' Of the film, which was now being edited, she reported: 'I've not seen it except for one very short visit to the studio, so I don't know whether it's good or not. The film people say it's "terrific" – but as that's their usual description of anything they're concerned in, I'll reserve judgement till I see it properly.' On 28th December, on 'The Week's Good Cause', she made the first radio appeal on behalf of The British Polio Fellowship, to which she belonged. The broadcast proved less of an ordeal than she'd feared ('after television, it was quite easy') and her appeal raised a gratifying £4,070, plus 'a spate of correspondence'.

The following year, 1948, began busily, with scripts for the fourth radio series to be written to deadline and a new novel in incubation. The film 'Just William's Luck' had been released in time for the end of the Christmas school holidays; the January issue of *Bandwagon* magazine reviewed it ('an unpretentious film that will delight the whole family') and also published an interview with its star. Though William Graham lacked the stocky build and just about every other physical characteristic essential to his role, the interviewer did his best to establish the young actor's affinity with William:

> 'Once, one of my school-mates told me how to make fireworks. After I'd made some, I lit one in an old cocoa tin. It blew up and set fire to my chemistry set. I had to drench it with water and this and the chemicals ruined the carpet.'

The studio intended 'Just William's Luck' to be the first of a series of ten films; but only one more, 'William Comes To Town' (also issued as 'William Goes to the Circus'), was in fact produced. Val Guest directed both films. *Just William's Luck*, the story of the film and the only William book written in novel form, contains much material taken from earlier stories. William was undoubtedly more at home in the short story, but the novel does contain some very funny passages.

Richmal was soon regarding her latest BBC commitment as something of a chore. For the third radio series she had written only one in four episodes. For the 1948 series, she was required to complete all twelve of the episodes by the end of July. She wrote in March: 'I go "all of a panic" when I think of it, as I'm not a quick worker. I meet the new producer [Audrey Cameron] tomorrow and will then get down to work.' Her daily domestic help was in hospital, which meant that Richmal had to cope single-handed except on Wednesdays and Saturdays, when her twice-weekly help came. Cleaning and cooking had never ranked among her favourite occupations, and The Glebe was a large house to manage, especially for someone with a physical handicap. In May, however, she wrote with relief: 'My domestic troubles seem to be over, as I have secured what seems to be a Treasure. She's only been with me two days, but there seem to be no snags!'

The pace of working life had not slackened by June: 'I've had a hectic week with BBC auditions and scripts... I'm getting dug into my William scripts and have now done 6½.' There was little time to read or to indulge her other great love, theatre-going; though she did manage a visit to the local repertory company's performance of Priestley's 'Dangerous Corner', at which, she reported, the audience, 'not quite knowing how to take it, giggled foolishly'. In July, she wrote of the new radio William: 'David [Spencer] is a very good little actor and most intelligent – but he has a somewhat precise little voice that certainly does not suggest William.' She added: 'I have come to the conclusion that it is impossible to find a real William among the ranks of child actors, though he exists in his thousands in real life.' A July issue of *Radio Times* carried a photograph of William's creator. The camera-shy Richmal noted ruefully: 'I look thoroughly debauched!'

Attention of an even more unwelcome kind had been centred on her in the previous week: 'I knocked a girl off a bicycle last week in Bromley with my car and took her along to hospital, where they said she was only bruised. Everyone (including the police) was quite kind about it – much to my relief!' Opinion is sharply divided as to Richmal's driving ability. Some – perhaps significantly, chiefly non-drivers – agree with the (non-driving) friend who says: 'She drove with a deceptive casualness, but I am sure she was a master of the art. I always felt completely safe with her.' Others share the opinion of another friend, a wartime motor-patrol police driver: 'Her driving really worried me. On one occasion, after a very pleasant lunch in Rottingdean, she drove off, waving frantically out of the window (to the mystification of following motorists attempting to interpret this new hand signal). As she went on her way, I noticed her car door was flapping, so leapt into my car and had to chase her halfway to Brighton before I was able to wave her down.'

Unperturbed by such experiences, Richmal claimed she enjoyed the protection of a guardian angel; and perhaps she did. Lunching at an hotel with a friend one day, she was urged by the head waiter – anxious to demonstrate his gratitude for the generous tip Richmal had already bestowed, it being the last day of her stay in the hotel – to move to the nice table by the window; the table waiter, meanwhile, equally appreciative of her generosity, begged her to remain. Eventually, the head waiter, having either proved the superiority of his powers of persuasion or pulled rank, prevailed and Richmal and her companion gathered up their belongings and moved to the other table. As they settled themselves in at the window seat, a heavy light-fitting crashed down onto the table they had just left. The guardian angel certainly had his work cut out. On another occasion, Richmal failed to set her car handbrake properly when parking on a slope. She got out of the car to post a letter, slipped, and fell flat. Unable to raise herself quickly, she lay prone and helpless as the car rolled backwards towards her. Then, miraculously, it stopped, inches away: her special walking stick had fallen in the path of one of the rear wheels – and the stick's big rubber foot had providentially become a chock.

September brought a short break from such experiences and from work. She wrote from the Roxburghe Hotel, Edinburgh: '... it's nice to be completely lazy ... It would pal (or are there two l's?) after a time, but it's nice for a bit!' And December brought publication of her latest novel, *Family Roundabout*. Richmal sent a copy to a friend, with the brief, typically detracting comment: 'It's very much like all the others!' It is, of course, covering as it does (in flashback, this time) a family's story from about the time of Richmal's own birth to just before World War II. But it is very readable; and its charm is immeasurably enhanced by the early demise of that ubiquitous bore of a husband, whom Richmal had this time sensibly killed off six years before the story begins:

> He had been ten years her senior, and she had fallen in love with him at their first meeting, realizing even then how unlike she was to the wife he wanted. He wanted, she knew, a "little woman", clinging, adoring, self-effacing, ready to accept and defer to his judgment – a replica, in short, of his mother. And deliberately, determinedly, she had set to work to make herself that woman, becoming, for love of him, stupid and docile, hiding her intelligence as though it were some secret vice. Stupidity is not an easy quality to assume, and there had been times when her real self had broken through the barricade, and she had startled and hurt him by which (sic) he called her "oddness", but on the whole they had been happy. She had known the price she must pay for his love and she had been willing to pay it.

Since the reminiscence of one of this novel's characters echoes an incident in the story 'William Goes Shopping' (*William's Happy Days*), one suspects that the young Richmal, too, had gazed fearfully and wondered ...:

> '... I believed that those wax figures in the window of Crofton's Juvenile outfitting department were dead children that old Crofton caught and killed himself. A boy told me that and I never for a moment doubted it. I always used to run past the shop in case he came out and grabbed me.'

'I'm trying to get down to another novel,' she wrote in December, 'but other things keep coming in the way!' Her strong regard for family ties was never more clearly demonstrated than at Christmas time. On the 27th she reported: 'I had... Christmas Day with my sister and yesterday with my brother. I'm going down to my sister's again this evening as she's having a small cocktail party. My youngest niece Sarah (aged four) [Jack's daughter] is just at an age to enjoy Christmas and was bubbling over with excitement all the time... I'm just getting into my holiday-auntish swing. I've taken them all to "Blithe Spirit" at the Bromley Rep. The next item is taking Richmal and another goddaughter and parents to "Miss Mabel" and David [Jack's son] and his parents to, I think, "Happiest Days Of Your Life". Then I'm going to help David with his Greek (he's had a double move up at school and finds it difficult), have Richmal up for a day, and a few oddments of "coming to tea"... I'm reading Balzac's *Cousin Bette* and finding it rather depressing. The other book I've got from the library is *Life of Rabelais*, which should be merrier!'

No new novel and no new William collection appeared in the following year; she seems to have spent much of 1949 in recovery from the hectic pace of the three preceding years. In March, she wrote: 'I've got a book of Sansom's short stories from the library – some of them quite terrifying! I'm also reading Defoe's *Moll Flanders* & have just finished Cecil's *Two Quiet Lives*, which I liked very much – the lives being those of Dorothy Osborne & Gray... I had got tickets for the Antigone yesterday but the programme was changed and they did the School for Scandal instead. It was a lovely production with all the mannered elegance and artificiality of the XVIII century – almost ballet-like in parts. I saw "The Heiress" with a friend about a fortnight ago & enjoyed that very much.' It was a luxury to be free of the pressures of writing to deadlines, to be able to take the next novel at a comfortable pace, to have time to visit galleries and exhibitions and plays to her own taste, to visit congenial friends and 'sit about in the garden reading books – the sort of holiday I like'. Despite a relatively peaceful year, however, she confessed herself at the end of December 1949 'still a little dazed' with Christmas fare and 'not quite equal to facing the audience of the Granada Cinema, Sydenham, where I have to appear this evening to present prizes to the writers of the best poem under the title "When William Came to Sydenham

Town" recited in the most William-like voice!'

For several years now, since 1943, Richmal had lived alone at The Glebe. Though the frequent visits from family were always welcome, she had long desired and now greatly treasured the privacy afforded by living alone. In March 1950, however, Jack, having sold his house but not yet found another, came to stay at The Glebe with his wife and two children until the end of May. Ten days after their arrival, Richmal wrote conscientiously: '... I think it very good for me to be invaded for a time and jerked out of my rut!' But she had never found her sister-in-law congenial, and was much relieved to get back to her rut in June: 'I'm just beginning to get back to normal and lose that chewed-up feeling...'

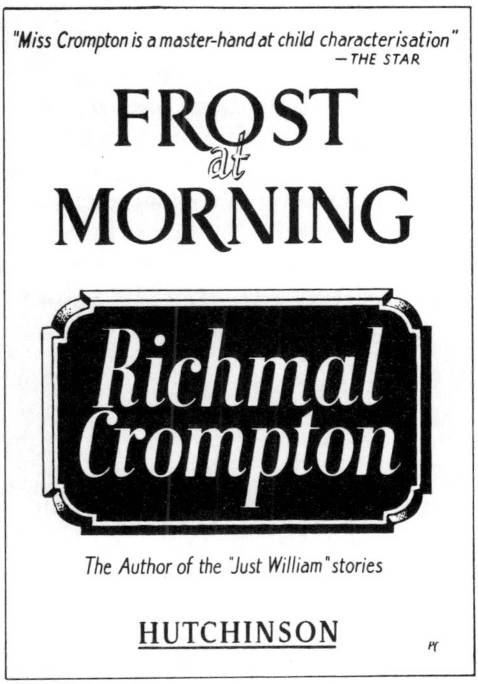

To a friend who enquired in October about the progress of her latest novel (*Frost at Morning*), she admitted it had just been published. She added: 'I could let you have a copy if you like, but it's just like all my others... It's "the mixture as before", I'm afraid!'; and hastily moved on to less painful comment on Proust, on a recent visit to the Tate Gallery (where she had observed 'a slightly oppressive note' in the 'exotic aristocracy of

Sargent's portraits, as if they foresaw that their world was coming to an end'), on a proposed theatre visit ('Emlyn Williams should be worth seeing, even in what the reviewers call an "unpleasant situation"!').

Frost At Morning is, in fact, an enjoyable book. A delicate power pervades her portrait of the mother who dislikes one of her children (in this case, an adopted child; but the rejecting 'natural' mother had been drawn, in several of the earlier novels, with equal sympathy and perception); and the reader is made painfully aware of the vulnerability of another child, Monica, whose only anchor in life is an alcoholic mother. Nevertheless, Richmal had handled these themes before. What redeems this novel, the additive that precludes its being justly described as 'the mixture as before', is the comic genius that Richmal allowed to peep through. The light of her humour – so effulgent in the William stories, so fleetingly apparent in the novels – shines particularly strongly in *Frost At Morning* on Mrs. Sanders, the vicar's dreadful wife, who, sublimely indifferent to parish duties, spends all her time writing 'novelettes' and gloriously confusing her characters with reality. Her husband, long resigned to her vagueness and deep immersion in her plots, merely attempts to ensure that his wife and his bishop meet as infrequently as possible. Mrs Sanders, however, is not the retiring type:

> 'You'll be taking the chair at the meeting, I suppose?' said the Bishop.
>
> 'Oh, yes, my lord,' said the Vicar. 'I went over the agenda with the secretary last night.'
>
> Suddenly a shrill and passionate voice rang out from the closed door behind the Bishop.
>
> 'Give me back the letters. I wrote them when I was little more than a child. Are they to darken my whole life? I have paid for my sin a thousandfold. I will sell my last jewel, pour out the last drop of my heart's blood, to get those proofs of my guilt back into my hands and destroy them, as I wish to God I could destroy you.'
>
> The speaker stopped abruptly and cleared her throat. The Bishop threw a glance of startled enquiry at his host.
>
> 'My wife,' said the Vicar with a somewhat constrained smile. 'She writes, you know. She has recently acquired a dictaphone and she is apt to raise her voice, I think, more than the instrument actually requires. She is not, as yet, quite accustomed to it.'

'I see,' said the Bishop, his fascinated gaze still fixed on the door. No further sound came from it but the rustling of papers.

'Well . . . ' said the Vicar, turning to the front door.

But the Bishop still lingered hopefully. The rustling of papers stopped and was replaced by the sound of the opening and shutting of several drawers in succession.

'Did she – get the letters?' said the Bishop, turning to follow his host.

'I'm not sure, my lord,' said the Vicar. 'My wife has not discussed that particular story with me.'

They walked together down the drive to the gate where the Bishop's car was waiting.

'Would you like me to send you a copy of the agenda, my lord?' said the Vicar.

'Yes', said the Bishop absently. 'What is it going to be called?'

'Called, my lord?'

'Your wife's story.'

'Oh . . . I believe that particular story is to be called *Gilded Pinnacles.*'

The Bishop stopped and took a note-book and pencil from his pocket.

'I'll just make a note of it,' he said. 'I should rather like to read it when it comes out.'

The William book published in July 1950, *William – the Bold*, was the first to appear since 1945. It contained only eight stories, and at least one of them, 'The Battle of the Flowers', had clearly been written immediately after the war. The title story, the best of this collection, makes successful play on William's ignorance of historical fact (a theme used to great effect in many of the early stories), which proves a considerable handicap in deciding on a protagonist for his historical play:

'I dunno that I want to have Queen Elizabeth at all,' said William. 'She wasn't very int'restin'. She didn't do anythin' but go trampin' about in puddles over people's coats. Gosh! I bet they got into rows when they got home.'

'She beat the Armada,' said Henry.

'No, she didn't,' said William, 'Nelson did that.'

'Drake.'

'Well, Drake, then. But *she* didn't. I 'spect she jus' swanked about in an A.T.S. uniform, same as Ethel did in our war, but she didn't do any fightin' . . . '

The adult Browns still add the occasional touch of spice; Miss Milton continues to represent outraged spinsterhood, General Moult to stump about the village parading his memories of the Boer War; Joan persists in quietly and shyly adoring William, Violet Elizabeth in noisily and brazenly annoying him; 'Hubie' and the odious Mrs Lane remain beyond the pale. There are, undeniably, patches of 'good' William in this twenty-seventh volume; but it nevertheless marks the onset of a decline. The stories from now on would become increasingly mechanical as the once copious flow of inspiration gradually narrowed to a trickle. But Richmal, sixty years old in the November of 1950, was not yet to be granted her release from William's domination.

Richmal Carries On

XI

Early in the New Year, on 24 January 1951, BBC Television broadcast its own version (produced by Joy Harrington) of the play 'Just William'. Richmal, who watched the play on a neighbour's set, afterwards paid tribute to the efforts of the protagonist: 'The boy [Robert Sandford] was excellent.' Her conviction that the essence of William could not be captured on screen was nevertheless unshaken.

The novel in incubation at the beginning of this year was, she reported, 'taking more time than it should'. Distractions – some pleasurable, some tedious – were legion. Though she found the current revival of 'The Three Sisters' 'not so moving as the last revival with John Gielgud and Peggy Ashcroft', she still attended two performances within the space of three weeks. Before the 'annual job of Spring Cleaning' could be delegated, there was the chore of 'going through every cupboard and drawer in the house with duster and clean paper and also dusting all my books – an exceedingly lengthy job as one keeps dipping into books and remaining submerged indefinitely!' Social and public commitments, too, though carefully limited, impinged occasionally on Richmal's working time. She contrived generally to avoid uncongenial people and occasions; but a few could not be avoided, and one 'frightful' engagement in late spring provoked a rare note of irritation: 'I . . . was bored beyond description.'

A grateful Australian called unexpectedly at The Glebe one afternoon towards the end of May. William had established an antipodean foothold some years earlier, and the visitor had subsequently written for, received and successfully acted upon Richmal's advice to the aspiring writer: 'Go on writing!' Her reluctance to wound ensured a consistently generous response to the many hopeful authors who appealed for advice or encouragement. That reluctance led also to a most improbable friendship, with the late Fred Bason – Richmal's opposite in almost every respect. She stipulated at the beginning of their acquaintance that he must never write about her; and, much though it must have grieved him, he kept faithfully to the agreement. Although they had little in common, they did share a love of books; and Richmal maintained that 'little Freddie' could affect a 'very good prose style' when it suited him to do so. She noted, with indulgent amusement: 'I'm so very different from him that he can't quite make me out and is trying to infuse more "push" and "go" into me – quite without success. He's a great believer in self-advertisement and simply can't understand people letting go any chance of it!'

Early in June, a friend pressed on her a manuscript dealing with the friend's conversion to 'some vague occultism that she calls "the new knowledge"'. After ploughing dutifully through the manuscript, Richmal remarked dryly: 'I find the old knowledge so much simpler and more comforting.' Half the year gone already and still the distractions from work abounded: July brought discovery of a bees' nest under the eaves of The Glebe. Richmal, aware that a swarm in July 'isn't worth a fly', was anxious for their prospects of survival. With a vague idea of taking their minds off their probable fate, she did her best to keep their spirits up: 'I wanted to tell them something but couldn't think what to tell them till I heard that Richmal had passed her Finals, then I went out and told them that!'

Some years earlier, she had acquired her first pet, a Peke named Ming. With the exception of Jack, who had devoted much time and care to the doves and insects he kept in the Malvern Villas garden, none of the Lamburns had been fervent animal-lovers; Clara had disliked cats, especially, to the point of not being able to bear them near her. Richmal herself, while not antipathetic to any particular type of animal, held stringent views on those who tend to obsession in their regard for four-legged creatures: 'Yes, I know those animal-lovers. They watch a human-being being boiled alive in oil without turning a hair but if a dog gets a cold in the head, they break their hearts over it!' She had briskly dispelled the mists of animal-loving sentiment many years before, in the novel *Journeying Wave* (1938) as well as in the story 'William and the Black Cat' (1924):

> Bunker was very old and very mangy. He employed habitually an ear-splitting and horrible yell, long drawn out and increasing

in volume as it neared its nightmare climax – a yell which William loved to imitate . . .

Ethel, who had hardly looked at Bunker for months without disgust, began, now that his dissolution was imminent, to dwell upon his engaging kittenhood . . . to experience all the feeling that one ought to experience when one's beloved pet is torn from one by Death. She would even have fondled him if he hadn't been so mangy . . .[37]

Ming had come to The Glebe from Jack's house, where, following the arrival of Richmal's youngest niece, she had found herself *animal non gratum*. Despite the Peke's having come to her by circumstance rather than by choice, however, Richmal had become quite attached to 'Mingie'; and spent much time 'comforting her & tempting her to eat' when the dog was ill that year.

Reading, of course, was a permanent distraction from writing. Richmal noted in July that her 'vice of reading about a dozen books at a time' was growing on her; the current list included *The Captive* (Proust), Fielding's *Amelia*, Berdyayev's *Dream and Reality*, 'a book on Philosophy (which ties my brain into hopeless knots)' and Enid Bagnold's *The Loved and the Envied* ('but couldn't get on terms with the people so gave it up'). By the 28th, however, her own novel was again to the fore: 'Tomorrow I'm going up to the editorial office of "The Lady" to consult their files and see how people dressed in 1892.'

Gardening was another time-consuming interest, though Richmal's disability precluded her coping with much of the practical work. The acre of garden at The Glebe was therefore tended mainly by a professional; a man who combined a silent contempt for the knowledgeable amateur with a fiercely possessive attitude to Richmal's garden. In November of that year, she reported with decorous sympathy that the gardener had broken his ankle and would be away for several weeks; and concluded with irrepressible glee: 'I'm running amock (sic) in the garden, putting the wrong bulbs in the wrong places and enjoying the feeling of being able to do just what I want.' She often (in the gardener's absence) culled vegetables from her kitchen garden to take on family visits: 'I generally arrive there in a bower of greenery – a sort of animated Harvest Festival!'

December brought its usual round of commitments. On the 7th, she wrote: 'I treck (sic) out to Stanmore on Friday to a children's party at a convalescent home at which a Games Library is to be inaugurated. I'm supposed to explain to the children how to play the games and as I haven't a games mind the result will probably be a wild confusion!' At one function attended in her capacity of William's creator, Richmal's tiny-boned frame was knocked to the ground by a stampede of excited children. The experience must have been terrifying, but she only said, wryly, afterwards: 'I thought to myself that it would be poetic justice if I, who had *battened* on children for years, were killed by them.'

In February 1952, she wrote: 'Life's been in a curious state of suspension since the King's death, hasn't it? It seems to have stopped completely.' She added, with a nice touch of bathos: 'I suppose it will begin again next week.' Another William radio series, the first since 1948, had been tentatively planned for the autumn, and Richmal viewed without apparent pleasure the prospect of scripts and deadlines. In early March, she wrote wistfully: 'I've had rather a full and non-reading time . . . ' She nevertheless launched into an enthusiastic dissertation on Proust's *The Sweet Cheat Gone*:

> I was glad when Albertine vanished (the telegram apparently announcing her return to life filled me with dismay at first!). She gives me an oddly frustrated feeling because I can't see her as a real person of flesh and bood. She's just a vague figure of charm and 'infinite variety'. Sometimes I feel that Proust just used her as a peg on which to hang his knowledge of woman's love for woman & his analyses of love and jealousy. But then I suspect it's my own lack of subtlety that's at fault. Still – I feel I know all the other characters so well – Albertine eludes me. I have enjoyed the book so much. I think I love the Duke and Duchess of Guermantes the best . . .

A casual reference to her latest novel, which had reached completion in spite of the previous year's distractions, followed: 'I was interested to hear that Hutchinsons really are going to bring out *Linden Rise* in May. I wonder what it's like (which sounds an odd thing to say but is just what I feel about it).'

She heard later in March 'that the BBC may not be able to fit in the William programme – at which my heart leaps for joy! I hate script-writing and I hate being chivied and harassed and driven. I like to write my own slow stories in my own slow way.' Much relieved by the news, she set off light of heart on an April visit with her niece Richmal to Rome. Two incidents observed in the Italian capital were to find their way into her travel notebook:

> Thursday morning – Bank gave me £20 for travellers cheque instead of £2. Terrific scenes when returned. Crowds of Bank officials expressing gratitude & general satisfaction.

The second incident underlined even more strongly the differences between the British and the Italian temperament:

> Saw . . . slight accident between car & motorcycle – large gathering – two drivers fought it out in middle ferociously while police stood idly by.

The euphoric sense of reprieve with which she had embarked on the holiday quickly evaporated on her return: the BBC, despite their indecision on the autumn schedule, still required the radio scripts.

Linden Rise did appear as planned, in May, and Hutchinsons also brought out a Universal Book Club edition a year later (May 1953). This was the novel for which Richmal had conscientiously searched the files of *The Lady*, to 'see how people dressed in 1892'; though she might equally fruitfully have searched the dozen or so earlier Richmal Crompton novels that begin in the same period. *Linden Rise* is quite enjoyable, however, and particularly so in its unsentimental presentation of Miss Maple's aged mother. Richmal clearly was aware that extreme age is not necessarily synonymous with charm; that nasty young people grew into nasty old people:

> Mrs Maple sat in an arm-chair by the fireplace, huddled in a black shawl, wearing a lace cap trimmed with imitation violets. A pair of small dark malevolent eyes looked out from a maze of wrinkles, and the shrunken mouth was ominously set.
>
> 'What are all these children doing here?' she said as the party entered. 'Send 'em away.'
>
> Miss Maple gave a gay little laugh in which could be discerned a faint note of apprehension.
>
> 'They're the young Culvertons, Mother,' she said, bending down to speak loudly into the old lady's ear. 'My pupils.'
>
> 'Your what?' said the old lady grimly.
>
> 'Pupils, darling,' shouted Miss Maple. 'I teach them.'
>
> The old lady gave a sudden croaking laugh.
>
> 'How can you teach them when you don't know anything?' she said.
>
> 'There!' said Miss Maple, turning to the children. 'I told you how witty she was, didn't I! Come right in and sit down. She wants to see you all. She loves children.'
>
> She planted the children on various small seats among the forest of furniture, and the Vicar took the arm-chair opposite Mrs Maple . . .
>
> 'Ninety next year,' said Mrs Maple. 'Not much longer for this world.' . . .
>
> 'Oh, you mustn't talk like that, Mrs Maple,' said the Vicar. 'You're wonderful for your age, you know.'
>
> 'Oh, well . . . ' said Mrs Maple. Elated by her small triumph, she drew her shawl about her coquettishly. 'There's not many can get to ninety and keep their wits about them. I've always kept my own.'
>
> She gave her croaking laugh.

'Charming, isn't she?' whispered Miss Maple to Edmund. 'I told you she was.'

Althea remained kneeling on the floor, looking at the curios and making little exclamations of interest and delight. Mrs Maple threw her another malevolent glance. Children . . . They were all the same. Stealing the limelight that belonged by right to old age. They ought to be put in their places . . .

'Stop that child breathing on the glass,' she said sharply, putting Althea in her place.

One of the 'young Culvertons' of *Linden Rise*, Richard, shares Richmal's knowledge of and enthusiasm for gardening:

Richard was a good gardener. He felt an affection – even a respect – for all growing things and took a deep delight in tending them.

'You'd think they were alive, the way he goes on with them,' said Polly. 'I hear him talking to them sometimes.'

'They are alive,' said Richard, his eyes twinkling. 'Plotinus tells us that they each have a share of the Universal Soul. They respond to love and reach up after the Divine, which is more than some humans do.'

And here he enlarges on an opinion several times expressed in Richmal's letters:

'The eighteenth century . . .' said Richard slowly. 'It's the only age of civilization that England's ever known. It had elegance and graciousness and taste and culture. Look at their furniture, their houses, their poets, their philosophers. It's the only age when the English knew how to live. They had wit and culture – as well as money. Wit and culture don't exist any more and we don't know how to use money when we've got it . . . I was reading *Lady Holland's Journal* the other day and her reading in six months would simply astound you – *Juvenal*, *Arioso*, *Tasso*, *Ovid*, *Montaigne*, *Burnet's History*, *Hearn's Travels*, *Lazaritto de Tormes*, *Let's Life of Sextus the Fifth*, *Cook's Voyages*, *Wolf's Ceylon*, *Bayle*, and a dozen more I've forgotten together with innumerable French and German novels. And she was a busy Society hostess, not a recluse.'

Three months later, in August, Richmal wrote: 'The BBC have now drawn up their final autumn programme and decided not to have the William. I should feel outraged and affronted but actually feel much relieved. They say they'll pay me for the work I've done – and it will be lovely not to have to treck (sic) up there every week for 3 months. It's only one day a week, of course, but it seems to spill over and fill the week!' The lightheartedness engendered by the news was apparent as she went on to confide: 'I had some people to tea yesterday and their dog went into the kitchen and ate 12 iced cakes from a plate on the table, ending by knocking the plate onto the floor and breaking it. Fortunately, they didn't know – it remained a secret between the dog and me!' And thence to the more absorbing subject of her current reading: 'I'm halfway through *De Profundis*. Poor Wilde seems to have been *fated* from the beginning. It has all the inevitability of a Greek Tragedy. He tried to get out of it (or did he, really?) but the net closed slowly round him. I've been reading a book about James I (who was addicted to "minions") and there's a letter in which he blames one of them for his "moods and sulkiness" and for his trying to rule him "by feare instead of love". They seem to run to type!'

William was, in fact, finally reinstated by the BBC and the fifth radio series, consisting of thirteen programmes (produced by Peter Eton), began early in the October. Richmal glumly reported on the 5th that 'BBC work' had lately demanded much of her reading time. She nevertheless went on to mention that she was 'in the middle of Gide's *The Counterfeiters* and *Survivors of Famous Trials* (by someone else!)'; though, for Richmal, having 'only' two books on the go probably *was* something of a deprivation. Andrew Ray, the latest William, was, she noted, 'a very keen and intelligent boy'; 'as good as we're likely to get'. She was making a conscientious effort 'to give the young listener as many sound effects as possible; but too many of them irritate the older listener. I'm trying to keep an even keel between the two!' The BBC had hired 'at vast expense' a performing dog, 'guaranteed to bark on the word of command', to play the part of Jumble. Unfortunately, at the last moment the dog revealed himself possessed of the traditionally unpredictable temperament of the true artiste. 'He refused to utter a sound,' Richmal reported with delight, 'and the sound-effects man had to do the barking and growling as well as everything else!'

It was shortly after publication of *William and the Tramp*, in September 1952, that Richmal wrote to a friend who had feelingly described a harrowing journey home from The Glebe:

'I can't really deplore the gang of young hooligans who shattered the peace of your railway carriage, as I make my living out of them!' The new volume contained eight stories, six of which were unusually long. All are entertaining; and two, the title story and 'William and the Professor', briefly recapture the essence of William. In the first, the Outlaws are hoping that the tramp they have temporarily adopted will pass as the lecturer awaited by the Literary Society:

> 'No one would think he was a real lecturer – not with those clothes,' objected Ginger.
>
> 'Why shouldn't people with holes in their clothes give lectures?' said William.
>
> 'I don't know,' said Ginger, 'but they don't.'

In the second story, the Outlaws' headmaster has urged his pupils to enter for an historical-essay competition, to be judged by a visiting university professor of history:

> 'Professor Golightly,' he had said, addressing the school on the subject, 'is one of the most distinguished scholars of the age. We cannot let him go away with the impression that our children are devoid of intellectual interests.'
>
> 'I don't see why we shouldn't,' said William. 'I'm jolly well devoid of 'em an' I don't know anyone that isn't.'

One feels, nevertheless, slightly deprived. Had those stories been written in the twenties or thirties, 'lecturer' and 'shouldn't' would have been 'leckcherer' and 'shun't'; and 'I don't know anyone that isn't' is somehow much less satisfying than 'I don't know anyone wot isn't'. The counterpoint of adult circumlocution – an intrinsic part of the best of William – was undoubtedly at its most effective when played against the strong melody of fractured phonology and syntax provided by William and his contemporaries in the earlier stories.

Mrs Brown by 1952 was reduced to dependence on one 'daily'; and was obliged, the servant problem being what it was, to adopt an almost propitiatory manner toward her:

> 'I can't 'elp it, mum,' she was saying. 'Go through the wood again I couldn't – not if me life 'ung from it by a thread, as it were.'
>
> 'Oh dear!' said Mrs Brown, arrested in the act of cracking an egg into a basin and gazing at Mrs Peters in dismay over two dripping half shells, 'But you could come by the main road instead, couldn't you, Mrs Peters, if you feel like that?'
>
> Mrs Peters heaved a long sibilant sigh.
>
> 'Well, I could an' I couldn't, mum,' she said. 'What I means is, the main road's there, all right. It's me feet that's the trouble. I'm 'eavy on me feet an' I'd be wore out before I got 'ere, comin' all that way round.'
>
> 'Oh dear!' said Mrs Brown again, absent-mindedly pouring the egg into the flour without beating it and adding yet another 'Oh dear!' when she saw what she had done. 'But what exactly is the trouble about the wood, Mrs Peters?'
>
> 'The 'aunted cottage, mum,' said Mrs Peters in a hollow voice.
>
> 'You mean the keeper's cottage?' said Mrs Brown, who had decided to cut her losses on the egg and the flour and start again.

'Oh, but it's not haunted, Mrs Peters. It was blitzed by that rocket in the war and it's practically in ruins, but it's not haunted.'

'That's all you know, mum,' said Mrs Peters, setting her lips grimly. 'I seed what I seed.'

'What have you seed, Mrs Peters?' said Mrs Brown distractedly. 'I mean seen... there aren't any such things as ghosts.'

'It's all right comin' 'ere first thing in the mornin',' said Mrs Peters. 'It's not 'aunted then. But when I goes back with the dusk a-comin' on an' that there chimbley a-pullin' faces at me through the trees an' that there white thing a-movin' about in the downstairs room – well, I'm only yuman an' it's more'n flesh an' blood can stand.'

'Oh, Mrs Peters, I do hope it doesn't mean that you're going to leave us,' said Mrs Brown.[40]

Richmal's next novel, *The Gypsy's Baby*, had been with Hutchinsons since the beginning of the year; so she was not unreasonably put out in November, when the typescript was returned 'with a note that it was too short & must have another 10,000 words added – & that in only four weeks' time or it couldn't be published this year'. Despite her annoyance, she set to work determinedly, drastically pruning her reading time and yielding only to the temptation of a dramatized radio version of the Compton-Burnett novel *A Family and Its Fortune*. She had intended 'just to hear the beginning'; but 'needless to say, sat spellbound to the end'. Unrepentant, she added: 'It was a *wonderful* performance and the casting was miraculous... I buried myself in *Men and Wives* for the whole of the next evening!... I have a prejudice, as a rule, against BBC "dramatisation" of books, but this has overcome it.' The 10,000-word addition was to take much longer than the requested four weeks. Six months later, in the middle of May 1953, she sent a friend a harassed progress report: 'I'm just putting in lines here and there and altering them wildly when I've done it and shall just send the whole wretched mess back to them as it is and let them sort it out! I'm hoping to finish it by the end of next week. I keep putting things in and then finding that they come in anyway, later on in the chapter.' She went on to recommend the radio programme 'In All Directions' ('*really* funny, not just BBC funny'); and ended the letter on a desperate note: 'My writing seems to get more illiterate day by day. Words have demoralised me.'

By July, the chore was completed and Richmal was able to relax again. She took Fred Bason to lunch one day at her brother's house in Sandhurst. True to Clara Lamburn's training, she allowed 'heaps of time' for the journey. But they had to pass '*five* second-hand bookshops', into which 'little Freddie' insisted on disappearing for long periods, and the two eventually arrived to find Jack and his wife 'in a state of wild anxiety'. 'That's the worst of having a reputation for punctuality,' Richmal wrote; 'when you're a few minutes late everyone takes for granted that you've had an accident!' The reputation was well founded. Whatever her destination, Richmal invariably arrived early; she would immerse herself in the current 'car book' for a while, and then present herself at precisely the appointed time.

On November 15th, her 63rd birthday, she wrote in delighted gratitude: 'It's lovely to have this gorgeous Proust banquet outspread before me...' She enjoyed the later volumes of *Remembrance of Things Past*, 'but I think I like the earlier ones best – partly because they seem to lead one into a new enchanted world, while the background to the later ones is the background of the 1914–1918 war, with which I (at any rate!) was all too wearily familiar ... I felt the magic vanishing in the last books but I didn't know how or why.' She added: 'I've just read *The Go-Between*, *The Year Of The Lion* and *The Victorian Chaise-Longue* – all very good – and been dipping into Horace Walpole's letters. The eighteenth century has a great fascination for me ...'

The day after that birthday, Richmal was due to judge a short-story competition and give a short talk to the members of the new writers' class at Maidstone Prison. The prison's director of education, an old friend of Richmal, had obtained the governor's permission on the condition that no mention of the visit was made in print ('... the Prison Commissioners might think he was going in for too many amenities!'). In the course of introducing Richmal to the assembled writers' class, the friend brightly enquired how many of them had been brought up on William. 'Nearly all their hands shot up,' said Richmal, afterwards, 'and I thought to myself, am *I* responsible for all this?'

The Gypsy's Baby eventually made its appearance in February 1954, fifteen months after Hutchinsons had returned it for the 10,000-word addition. Though refreshingly deficient in the airs of breeding and other symbols of Quality that pepper the earlier novels, *The Gypsy's Baby* is nonetheless strikingly anachronistic. The story begins with the vicar's wife's discovery of the vicarage maid's pregnancy. One assumes that the first reaction of the 1954 reader to this early passage was to look askance at the vicar:

> Mrs Medway rested her elbows on the table. Her brows were drawn into a thoughtful frown. The situation was not new to her, of course. During the twenty years that she had inhabited the Vicarage, other maids had found themselves in the same predicament, and Mrs Medway had early evolved a method of dealing with the situation. They were given a month's wages and despatched home within a day of the discovery. Careful arrangements were made for the journey. Mrs Medway herself looked out the trains, prepared a packed tea or luncheon of sandwiches, currant cake and an apple, and saw the culprit off at the station, with instructions where to change, a solemn warning on the wages of sin and a caution never to apply to the Vicarage for a reference.

The vicar's equally Victorian response to the news immediately absolves him from any such unworthy suspicion on the reader's part; but the story thereafter proceeds as unconvincingly as it began. Only in the minutiae of the Hammertons' family life, warm and chaotic, does the novel satisfy. The vaguely wholesome Jane Burden and her satellites (companion, brother and sister-in-law) fail even briefly to come to life; one suspects that they account for most of the 10,000 words added. Certainly, the novel would be complete, if very short, without these four characters.

Richmal left The Glebe during that February and moved to a smaller residence, a cottage-style bungalow named Beechworth, on the Petts Wood side of Chislehurst. She understood the place, which had once been more grandly known as Wick's Folly, to have been built for Henry Wickham Steed, a former editor of *The Times*; and duly retailed this intelligence to the *British Digest* interviewer who arrived early in March to gather facts for a short article ('For the Woman Reader') to be entitled 'The Woman Who Writes About William'. Soon after publication of the article, however, it transpired that the bungalow's first owner had been not Wickham Steed but 'Wick Steed of the *Daily Express*'. Henry Wickham Steed, perhaps incensed by the idea that anyone could believe him to have resided in a bungalow named Wick's Folly, was not mollified by the innocence of the misunderstanding; he took, Richmal reported, 'great umbrage and needed a good deal of pacifying!'

It was during this year that Richmal first met Thomas Henry, who had now been illustrating the William stories for thirty-five years. They met in Nottingham, at the Book Fair. Henry's wife, Mrs Anne Fisher, thereafter kept in touch with Richmal by letter, and sent her beautifully embroidered small gifts at Christmas. The 1954 volume, *William and the Moon Rocket*, saw William in reasonably good form, particularly in the second story, 'William and the New Game'. Shortly after the book appeared in September, Richmal reported the receipt of a letter 'from an old lady of 85, saying that she had 18 William books and reads them over and over again!'

Christmas was always an important family occasion for Richmal; but the Christmas of 1954 brought her especial pleasure. On 27th December, her first great-nephew, Edward Ashbee, was born; and few of the letters she wrote thereafter failed to reveal the delight she took in him. There seems to have been, almost from his birth, a particular understanding between them. At ten weeks, he was 'still a great joy'; and in May 1955, Richmal described 'a very quiet and pleasant fortnight at Westgate – spent mostly on the beach or playing with Edward indoors'. She added, as proudly as a first-time parent: 'He really is a pet – with a great sense of humour.' May also brought publication, two months earlier than she had expected, of *Four in Exile*. This thirty-fifth novel echoed without spirit the characters and situations of a dozen of the earlier novels; although the *Manchester Evening News* reviewer seems to have liked it: '*Just William's* creator has added another tender story to many which have established her as one of the leading writers about children... An amusing novel, this – especially to parents.'

With the passage of years, Richmal's wasted leg had become more troublesome. In September, she wrote: 'I've been going down to the Bromley Hospital lately to have sunlight treatment for my leg and I'm amazed at the efficiency and kindness of everyone.' It was very rare for her to make any such reference; indeed, so little did Richmal's lameness appear to matter to herself that friends, too, were hardly aware of it. Occasionally, though, it refused to be ignored, as one friend remembers: '... as we were walking from the Opera House, Richmal leaning upon my arm, I stumbled and half fell and, being unable to steady either myself or her, caused her to fall heavily – or as heavily as such a slight and tiny-boned person *could* fall. When I looked down, horrified, she laughed up at me and reassured me as I helped her to her feet; then she returned to our conversation about the performance we had just seen.'

At the end of an exhaustive contemplation of the Diaghilev exhibition at Forbes House, her able-bodied companions were wilting, mentally and physically; Richmal's vitality was undiminished. Stairs and steps she managed by swinging herself up or down on the handrail; she refused absolutely to allow her disability to deny her access to shop, theatre or gallery. Towards the end of 1955, she reported with satisfaction: 'I managed to get to the Stanley Spencer exhibition and enjoyed it tremendously – especially Christ Carrying The Cross. It's beauty gives you a sort of shock, as if you'd seen a vision! I love the Blakes at the Tate. I feel that, although they're so different, Blake and Spencer have a lot in common. Both live in another world and bring their vision from that world to this and there's something terribly compelling about them both – and in the same way.' Her interest in art was lively and extensive: she 'felt' paintings as she 'felt' books. (Of the recently cleaned 'Virgin of the Rocks' in the National Gallery, she said regretfully: 'I liked it better before.' The figures had looked mysteriously beautiful, she said, behind the old varnish, and some of the beauty had now vanished.) Her acquaintance with music was much more limited, and her lack of knowledge in this area is now and again apparent in the novels. She enjoyed listening to concerts on the radio, but her musical taste remained unsophisticated.

The tiresome inevitability of waiting for hospital appointments was mitigated by the opportunity it afforded for extra reading. In October, she wrote: 'I've been reading odds and ends – 'Measure for Measure' and a sonnet anthology (there's something *most* satisfying about sonnets) and a book on the Antarctic . . . went to see "Waiting for Godot" . . . didn't really understand it but things one doesn't understand are often so much more stimulating than things one does!' Christmas 1955 proved as hectically family-centred as ever: 'I collected Richmal, Paul and Edward on Christmas morning, took them to Gwen's, returned them home after tea and went back to Gwen's for the evening. On Boxing Day I went to my brother's, stayed the night there and got back to Richmal's next afternoon for Edward's birthday party, finally reaching home near midnight!'

Her 1956 novel, *Matty and the Dearingroydes*, was, according to the *Glasgow Evening Times*, a 'warm-hearted and absorbing tale which in its own quietly humorous way cleverly mirrors many human weaknesses'. The quiet humour is certainly there; as are many narrative weaknesses. But one feels there is much of Richmal in Matty: 'She was over sixty but there were times when she felt like a young girl.' Through another of the characters, Richmal made gentle fun of her own weakness for crime fiction:

> . . . Flora had put the kettle on and arranged the tea-tray and was sitting at the kitchen table reading a detective story.
>
> 'See to things, won't you, Matty?' she said, raising her eyes dreamily from the page. 'I want to have my tea here in peace. Tell them I'm busy with the dinner . . . ' She lowered her eyes to the book again. 'I feel certain that the butler did it in spite of his alibi. If it wasn't the butler it was the secretary. Or it *might* have been the uncle. He's an invalid in a wheeled chair and they always pay for watching . . . Anyway, I shan't have a moment's

peace till I know, so don't disturb me.'

'Why not look at the end?' said Matty.

'Good heavens, no!' said Flora. 'I've done some pretty shady things in my time, but I've never looked at the end of a detective story yet.'

In August, she reported the arrival of a sister, Catherine Richmal (to be known as Kate), for little Edward. Great-aunt Richmal was mischievously amused by Edward's account of the delivery: 'His mother had been at great pains to give him an up-to-date and scientific account of the coming of the baby and he has reverted, of his own accord, to the old Victorian explanation of the baby's being brought in the doctor's bag!! After all, it's much simpler!' Going over to the Ashbees' house, three miles away at Chelsfield, every day 'for the next week or so to take Edward off their hands' was clearly not a necessary chore (Edward being already surrounded by parents, grandmother and an au pair) but a great delight: 'He's quite adorable and really very good.'

The gem of *William and the Space Animal*, published in the September and dedicated to Edward, is 'A Helping Hand For Ethel', in which the Outlaws do their best to find gainful employment for William's sister. Armed with newspapers and journals, they first eliminate the available jobs to which she is definitely not suited:

'... *Review of Public Affairs* ... What's that about?'

'Politics,' said Henry.

'Well, that's no good either, then. She doesn't like pol'tics. She once met a Member of Parliament that was so ign'rant he didn't know Stewart Granger from Clark Gable, an' she said it put her off pol'tics for the rest of her life.'

He was left finally with a copy of the *Hadley Advertiser* ...

'"Good plain cook wanted",' read William. 'Well, I dunno about that ... '

'Is she a good cook?' said Ginger.

'Yes, she is. She made a cake las' Saturday an' it was only a bit burnt at the bottom an' a bit sort of sunk in at the top. They gave it to me an' it was jolly good, but she's not plain, so that one won't do ... Here's another for a cook ... No, that's got to be plain, too ... '

'Why do they all want cooks plain?' said Douglas with a mystified expression.

'Dunno,' said William. '... This one might do. "Wanted companion-help. Able to drive a car." I bet she wouldn't be much help, but she can drive a car ... No. Look! It goes on, "Must be careful driver". She wouldn't do for that. She's an awful driver. She nearly ran over a p'liceman las' week. He was mad at first, then she started smilin' at him an' he stopped bein' mad ... '

'Could you get her a job smilin' at p'licemen for people that have car accidents?' suggested Ginger tentatively.

'Sort of hire her out to criminals at so much a time,' said Douglas, developing the theme ...

'Look! Here's another,' said Ginger. '"Gentle-woman wanted as companion-help to elderly lady. No rough work. Every comfort".'

'Yes, that sounds all right,' said William, interested. 'She's jolly good at havin' every comfort ... No, it won't do ... It says "Pleasant disposition essential" an' she's jolly well not got one. I bet she'd snap this elderly lady's head off the minute she started crackin' nuts or chewin' chewin' gum or borrowing her things ... '

'Here's another,' said Henry. 'It's for a cook-housekeeper an' they don't seem to mind about her bein' pretty. It doesn't say "plain", anyway. It says, "Quiet family. No late hours".'

'Gosh, that wouldn't suit her,' said William. 'She doesn't like quiet fam'lies an' she likes late hours . . . '

They finally settle for 'companion help under thirty, devoted to animals, especially cats'. Ethel dislikes cats; but William, armed with his customary unjustified faith in the persuasive power of his 'p'lite manner', sets out to convince the advertiser that she'd be better off with dogs, anyway. The resulting encounter is Richmal Crompton at her best; and the story is vintage William.

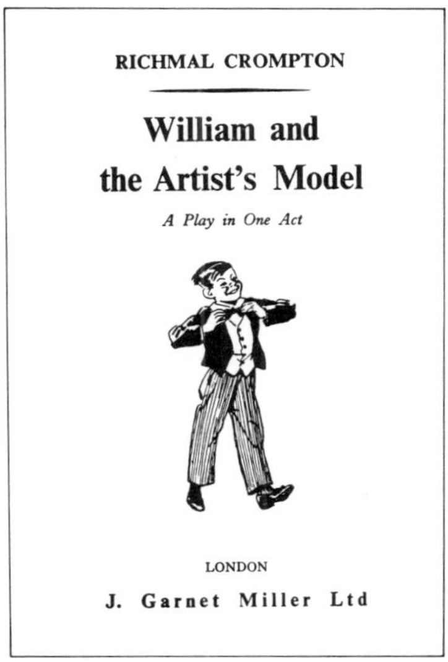
RICHMAL CROMPTON

William and the Artist's Model

A Play in One Act

LONDON

J. Garnet Miller Ltd

A new, one-act play, 'William and the Artist's Model', appeared during 1956. Published by J. Garnet Miller Ltd., it was adapted by Richmal herself from 'Violet Elizabeth Wins', the first story in *William – the Bold* (1950). The year also brought a suggestion that William could be held responsible for the outlook of Britain's Angry Young Men; a theory that very much amused Richmal.

William continued to disregard his creator's preference for peace and privacy. Richmal wrote in mid-October: 'I had a photographer and reporter from the Observer Coloured Supplement yesterday (they're "doing" children's authors in a number around Christmas) & next week the Swedish Television are coming over. I find these Occasions rather trying and am always *most* relieved to get them over. (I find the BBC television too much for me and said "No" very firmly the last time they asked me.) I think that William takes an impish delight in involving me in them!' Though she sensibly rejected potentially exhausting undertakings, and had slowed her working pace considerably (William now appeared every other year, and the novels were shorter), life was still very full. Her strong sense of commitment to family was unimpaired, and local good causes continued to depend on her personal or financial support. To one assembled audience to whom she was about to deliver a talk, she was introduced by the chairman as 'one of our borrowers'. Said Richmal afterwards, 'I felt about three inches tall!' (Mary Norton's books about 'The Borrowers', a tiny humanoid species, were among the very few contemporary children's books Richmal enjoyed.)

Early in December, she received a letter – 'out of the blue' – from another best-selling children's writer, Enid Blyton, who suggested it was time they met. Richmal reported after the meeting: 'I . . . found her most pleasant and quite un-bumptious – rather apologetic for her vast success!' Richmal's own vast success had brought about several encounters with the famous, usually at such functions as literary luncheons. Fellow-Lancastrian Gracie Fields she had liked for her unaffected warmth, and the cheerful resignation with which she had said: 'Isn't it a pity, love: both of us crazy about kids and neither of us has got any!' Rose ('There Are Fairies At The Bottom Of Our Garden') Fyleman, who also had begun a teaching career before concentrating on writing, became a good friend.

On 9 August 1957, Richmal wrote diffidently: 'My "next" is to be published next week. I'm afraid it's rather the "mixture as before".' The London *Star* reviewer waxed enthusiastic about *Blind Man's Buff*: 'From the vicar to the pub "regulars" the characters are straight from life.' Since the novel contained no pub 'regulars', however, Richmal was less than delighted with this review.

Great-nephew Edward remained a source of fascination. She had long collected from within the family amusing snippets of childhood comment (such as the warning from one young niece: 'I'm busy. Don't intersturb me.'; and another's response to being told to say 'sorry': 'All right, but I'll only whisper it.'). Going on three now, Edward was 'tremendously interested in electric cleaners and fanatically partisan for the Electrolux. The first thing he wants to know about a new acquaintance is what sort of domestic cleaner they have. If it's a Hoover, their stock goes down at once.'

On November 17th, two days after her sixty-seventh birthday, the *Sunday Dispatch* published an embarrassing article on 'Miss Richmal Crompton Lamburn... "mother" of a golden boy'. Richmal had long been resigned to errors of fact in articles about her, but the *Sunday Dispatch* article plumbed new depths of archness and inaccuracy. The writer attributed Richmal herself, as well as her unusual Christian name, to Yorkshire instead of to Lancashire; referred to her having 'hesitantly launched William in 1923' and having written serious novels 'under a different name'; and ascribed to her several wholly uncharacteristic utterances, such as: 'Even then I didn't realise what a little goldmine I had.' The opening paragraph bestowed upon this article a spurious appearance of authenticity:

> 'Little Miss Lamburn celebrated her 67th birthday with me on Friday – and agreed that she was going to have another very happy Christmas. *Thanks to William.*'

In fact, Richmal had spent her birthday at Chelsfield, with her niece Richmal and family. Arriving home at nine in the evening, she had 'found the press on my doorstep and learnt that they had been waiting there since 2 o'clock – so couldn't turn them away'. After commenting on how distasteful she found that kind of article, she added: 'Most of the interview was an invention of their own!'

By mid-January 1958, she was 'still a little shaky' after a fall at Christmas; but 'able to carry on normally'. She was still driving; though the days of her 'little blue horror', an adapted 1938 Rover saloon, were numbered: 'The engine needs re-boring (it's pouring oil in all directions) & it would cost more than the whole car's worth.' The prospect of accustoming herself to the new car, a Standard with hand-operated clutch lever, saw her 'paralysed by fear'. The poorly designed Standrive gear-change mechanism made smooth operation virtually impossible. By May, however, she was able to report cheerfully: 'I'm beginning to get on better terms with my new car and am less of a menace to the community.' May also brought a visit to the Hutchinsons editor who had 'suggested (tentatively) that I altered the beginning of my new novel and got the story going sooner. (I'd almost filled all the first chapter with a description of a town and the ramifications of a family)'. Richmal added: 'I think she's right and I'm knee-deep in it now, but somehow it gives one a dreadful feeling of nausea to go back to a piece of work one thought one had finished. Like having to eat up the cold congealed remains of a meal!' At some time during the late 50s, she had a novel rejected; a humiliation she had not suffered since William had thrust her to fame, nearly forty years before. There is no mention, even of the title, of the rejected novel in any surviving letters; but Mrs Ashbee remembers that her aunt was very much depressed about it.

There is not much in *William's Television Show*, Richmal's only 1958 publication, to excite the longstanding William fan – apart from a suggestion that Mrs Brown was not, after all, beyond hope of reclamation by feminists. Scratch the surface of the most domesticated of women and you find depths of regret and longing . . . :

> Then Mrs Brown entered.
>
> She looked coy and bashful and radiantly pretty. Her cheeks were delicately tinted, her eyelashes darkened, 'eye-shadow' enhanced the blue of her eyes and lipstick gave to her lips an allure with which nature had never endowed them.
>
> 'I've been made-up,' she said simply. 'The woman used me as a model.'
>
> 'Heavens above!' said Robert helplessly.
>
> 'You're a menace,' said Ethel. 'I shall never dare invite a boy-friend to the house again.'

'Oh, I'll wash it off,' Mrs Brown reassured her, 'but' – she glanced at the mirror over the fireplace – 'it does look rather nice, doesn't it? What do you think of it, William?'

'I like you better old,' said William politely.

Then Mr Brown came in and stood in the doorway, open-mouthed with amazement.

'I've been made-up,' said Mrs Brown again. 'She used me as a model.'

'It's positively staggering, my dear,' said Mr Brown, partly gratified, partly outraged by the sight of his glamorised wife. 'I've never seen you look like this in all my life before.'

'And you never will again,' said Mrs Brown, 'so make the most of it.'

'What do you feel like?' said Robert.

Mrs Brown glanced again at her reflection in the mirror.

'It makes me think I've wasted my life,' she said. 'It makes me think of all the things I haven't done . . .'[41]

Another unwelcome encounter with the television cameras at around this period proved 'a bit of a muddle!' The crew spent half an hour setting up their equipment outside a house called Beech*croft* before realizing their mistake. After a frantic telephone appeal for directions, they finally arrived at Beechworth and the interview duly took place in the garden. 'I felt idiotic all the time!' Richmal confessed. 'It's ghastly having to hold forth to complete strangers firing personal questions at you. I don't think I could bear to watch it!'

Her penultimate novel, *Wiseman's Folly*, was published by Hutchinsons in 1959 and generously hailed by the *Sketch* reviewer as 'quite one of her best'. But the plot is stale and the characterization wooden; one is only briefly reminded, in this novel, of Richmal's talent for witty observation. Her next William book, however, would contain an incident fresh from her own experience. At a recent literary luncheon, she had listened with disgust to the proudly recounted story of how a woman had been dishonestly induced to part with a valuable book. The victim was not named, of course; and there was little Richmal could do to demonstrate her disapproval, beyond make it clear that she would refuse invitations to future luncheons. She could, however, broadcast the contemptible deed in fictional form, and this she did – in *William–the Explorer*, published in September 1960. In 'Don William and the Sunbather', at least, she could prevent the cheat's prospering.

The title of her novel published in 1960, originally *The Radlett Memorial*, had been changed by Hutchinsons to *The Inheritor*. This fortieth novel, despite its contemporary setting, was so far out of touch with the modern age as to be virtually lifeless; though there were, as always, redeeming touches of humour, as in the young Janet's conscientious efforts to mould her baby brother's progress to the pattern outlined in a book on child development:

> 'I'm worried about him, Gran. He's backward . . . Look.' She pointed to the page she was holding open. 'He ought to be starting to walk and talk and he isn't.'
>
> 'But how should he know he ought, the poor poppet!' said Magda. 'He can't read.'
>
> 'Janet's looked after him beautifully,' said Lucy. 'She's devoted to him, aren't you, dear?'
>
> Janet considered the question.
>
> 'No, I don't think I am,' she said. 'He doesn't really attract me, but I'd like to get him normal before I give him up.'

In August, Richmal had written to a friend: 'I am still writing but I find that, as old age increases, one's pace slows down – or perhaps one gives in more readily to laziness!' It was not she, however, but Fate who decreed that *The Inheritor* should be her final novel. In September, two months before her seventieth birthday, she suffered a severe heart attack.

Still – Richmal

XII

The weeks of enforced bed-rest that followed her emergency admission to Farnborough Hospital sorely taxed Richmal. Soon after her arrival she was transferred, at her sister's request, to a private room. She would greatly have preferred to remain the unknown Miss Lamburn in a public ward; so many people 'popped their heads round the door' to see the famous Richmal Crompton that she began to feel 'like some weird animal' in a cage. Once again, William had frustrated her desire for anonymity.

The day before she left the hospital, in mid-October, the consultant told her sister that the heart had been so severely damaged that Richmal was unlikely to live another year; and would certainly not survive a second year. When, five years later, Richmal learned of this prognosis, she expressed gratitude for having been kept in the dark. She had always before thought it better that a patient should be told of such a verdict; but now realized that, had she been told, she would not have made so great an effort to regain a normal existence. In October 1960, however, the family was obliged to appear unreasonably unshakeable in the face of Richmal's determination: with all due gratitude for the concern that was being expressed, she didn't want to go to live with anyone and she didn't want anyone to come to live with her. Eventually, a compromise was reached: she would stay for six weeks with a friend (Eileen Phelps, a well qualified and experienced nurse) in Sidcup, and the situation would be reviewed at the end of that period.

Although the consultant had spared Richmal his estimate of the time remaining to her, he had painted a very clear picture of the restrictions she would have to impose upon herself in the future: she must lead the life of an invalid, and she certainly should not drive her car again. Richmal left the hospital for Sidcup in a state of deep depression. Her car had been a major symbol of independence. Youth had been an important ally in her battle against the crippling effects of polio; now, frail and in her seventieth year, she had come to depend on the car to keep her mobile. Without it, she would feel 'like a bird without wings'. One day during the second week of Richmal's stay at Sidcup, Mrs Phelps found her, sad and defeated, making a list of belongings she had decided to give away. At the top of the list was her car. Mrs Phelps, however, having herself suffered a coronary attack some years before and being therefore aware of how very low Richmal was feeling, decided that a little bullying was in order. Under her stern direction, Richmal tore up the list she had made and obediently repeated her friend's words: she *would* regain reasonably good health, and she *would* drive her car again.

Mrs Phelps' psychological approach proved almost too effective: three weeks after her arrival in Sidcup, Richmal decided she was so much better that there was no reason why she shouldn't go home. The family and Mrs Phelps did their best to dissuade her; but Richmal insisted on leaving. She arranged for Mrs Watts, her dependable domestic help, to stay at Beechworth all day; at night, she said firmly, she would not require help or supervision. Less than a week after she had regained her sanctuary, however, the local doctor delivered an ultimatum: return to Mrs Phelps' care – or return to Farnborough Hospital. During the second three-week stay at Sidcup, her general health improved further, the desperation receded and she could contemplate with something of her usual sense of proportion the 'very circumscribed' life ahead of her. She agreed, very reluctantly, to employ a temporary resident companion-housekeeper; and Miss Mary Richardson ('Ritchie'), kindly, capable and highly recommended, came to Beechworth on Richmal's return, early in the December.

The next two years were to prove a frustrating period for Richmal, whose frail energies were concentrated on regaining total independence. On Boxing Day 1960, three weeks after her return from Sidcup, she wrote: 'I'm better but it's a slow business & needs *months* of rest before you see much improvement. The idea of resting is lovely when you're busy but as a full-time occupation it has its drawbacks . . . ' She was nevertheless almost alarmingly soon back at the wheel of her car. Every visit made, every country drive taken, was a further small triumph of progress towards normal life. New problems of health were met with the old determination to avoid 'fuss' by ignoring them as far as possible. Her wasted leg, now frequently swollen and affected with painful sores, became increasingly troublesome; and a severe attack of shingles early in the new year rendered her for a few weeks almost unrecognizable.

Summer brought a more serious setback to her plans for early independence. During a visit to her brother in Sandhurst, she tripped on a step, fell and broke a leg. Six weeks in the Tunbridge Wells hospital (Richmal made sure she was admitted, without fuss, to a public ward this time) were followed by five weeks in plaster at home; and a further four months on crutches (her 'veteran 1924' pair), with visits to the hospital physiotherapy department three times a week. At the end of November, she reported: 'I'm still on crutches but am "exercising" in a wildly energetic fashion – swinging my legs, moving my knee-caps up and down, etc., etc., – and hope eventually to get back to normal . . . I can still drive the car all right as it was adapted for one-legged driving and it was the non-driving leg that was broken.' In the same letter, she wrote: 'I'm very lazy about writing nowadays but I have written enough William stories for another book, which will probably appear next year. I haven't started another novel yet & I'm not sure that I'm ever going to. The idea somehow doesn't tempt me. Quite possibly I'm "written out"! Anyway, I think that anything else I did would be mainly repetitive. I've probably written all I have to write – & more?' To another friend, Richmal later said she had stopped writing the novels because she could no longer interpret the troubled world she saw around her. The market for her novels had in any case dwindled over the years; only for William did there remain a steady demand.

In mid-December, she faced the cameras again: 'The Southern Television is descending on me from Dover next Friday for a short interview for some programme called, I believe, "Day by Day". They wanted me to go to them and when I said I couldn't said they'd come to me. (They said that little boys would be thinking about William books for Christmas presents!!) I shall be glad when it's over. I always find these things so trying!' On Christmas Day 1961, BBC Television broadcast the 1947 film, *Just William's Luck*. Richmal herself had a very poor opinion of television, but had felt obliged to provide a set for her companion. Familiarity with the medium did not raise her estimation of its worth: in moments of musical rapture, she said, she would as soon not be granted a back view of Yehudi Menuhin's boots. (She did not, however, rid herself of the television set on Miss Richardson's eventual departure.)

William, as cheerfully indifferent to his creator's opinion as ever, was being prepared by the BBC for his first television series. This series, produced by Leonard Chase and transmitted weekly from the end of May 1962, comprised six original stories adapted by C. E. Webber. William was played by Dennis Waterman, who is about to recreate his role in what promises to be a startling new ITV series (William a minor civil servant, married and middle-aged; Henry his boss; Ginger a homosexual fabric-designer . . .). In the second BBC television series, transmitted the following year, William was played by Denis Gilmore.

Mrs Bott and William as portrayed by Diana Dors and Adrian Dannatt, in the 1977 London Weekend Television series

Earlier in the year, Richmal had written: 'The formidable length of the list of William books sometimes makes me feel that it is time he made a graceful exit, but there is at least one more in preparation (I sent the galley proofs back to the publishers yesterday). It will be called *William's Treasure Trove* & should be published later in the year. And after that – well, he will probably insist on making himself heard!' Of that collection published in September 1962, three stories held an echo of the best of William: 'William and the Holiday Cottage', 'William and Detective Journalism' and 'William Tackles the Job'. In the last-named story, William is once again trying to find a job for someone else, in this instance a pensioner, and as usual tries his own family first:

> 'I say, Dad,' began William.
>
> Mr Brown grunted.
>
> 'Didn't you say you were short-handed at the office?'
>
> 'I did, my boy. Very short-handed.'
>
> 'Well, would you like an old man?'
>
> 'A what?' said Mr. Brown, startled out of his study of the Financial Column. 'A what, did you say?'
>
> 'An old man,' repeated William patiently. 'I can let you have one. An old man in the prime of life with the strength of ten young men. You'd be jolly lucky to get him. I bet everyone'll be after him once they know about him. There's nothin' he can't do. He's felled trees over a hundred feet high. I bet he'd be jolly useful to you in the office.'
>
> 'In the event of our needing a tree felled in the office,' said Mr. Brown, 'I will certainly get in touch with your friend. But the occasion is unlikely to arise and in the meantime I'm afraid I have no opening.'

September brought also a holiday from Beechworth: 'I'm going away on Wed. for a fortnight – a week at Rottingdean . . . and then to my Worthing friend for a week. She's had her house made into 3 flats and occupies the bottom one, so that there are no stairs, though I'm becoming quite adept at stairs again!' An enquiry after her health was acknowledged in a brief postscript: 'I'm keeping *very* well, thanks – an occasional angina pain, mostly in the early morning, which yields at once to the tablets I take around with me, but otherwise I'm in the rudest of health.'

On 15th October, Thomas Henry died suddenly while at work on an illustration for the next William book. He was 83, and had been depicting William for more than forty-three years. A memento of his fruitful yet largely impersonal relationship with Richmal hung on the wall of her study: William in water-colour, by Thomas Henry. His successor, Henry Ford, was undoubtedly the most successful of the artists who attempted to portray William in one or another of the editions published in the 1960s.[42] (The six volumes in the William Collins 1972 abridged hardback edition were published without illustrations; but Macmillans, for their current edition, very properly reinstated the stories' original drawings and commissioned a long-time William fan, illustrator Gerry Haylock, to provide the new covers.) Henry Ford also took over the *Woman's Own* William strip, which ran from 1947 until 1969; ideas for the strip, at least in its later years, were supplied by the magazine's staff.

Reference to current political events was rare in Richmal's letters; generally, the most dramatic of events outside her own world prompted little more than passing comment. The Cuban crisis of October 1962, however, stimulated an unusually lengthy dissertation on the state of the world. After remarking that Khruschev's unscrupulousness was a more powerful weapon than his rockets, she continued:

> Men must have some ideal outside themselves to work for and make sacrifices for, and now that the ideal of religion is losing its grip on people they have to turn to something else and the Russians find it in Communism. It is their religion and they will make untold sacrifices for it. Our "never had it so good" ideal of materialism (fostered by politicians) can't stir the imagination or inspire loyalty. (It took Churchill's offer of "blood & tears & toil & sweat" to do that!)
>
> But we certainly live in thrilling days – with the upsurge of independence all over the world, and the mental stimulation of it and the tension of opposing forces everywhere (which makes for

life and movement. Heraclitus – Greek philosopher in 500 BC – said "It is the tension of opposing forces that makes the structure one"; "opposition is co-operation"; "everything happens through strife"). Anyway, it's odd that all this has happened (not to speak of the huge increase in population) just as people are adventuring into space. Maybe it's the second great adventure in evolution and just as large numbers of amphibians left the sea for land millions of years ago, so now large numbers of earth-dwellers (finding the globe growing too small for them) will leave the earth for other planets! Anyway, everything's in the melting pot and I'm sure that it's the beginning of a new age of some sort – it might be a wonderful and more spiritual (not necessarily more religious) age. Let's hope so!!

The thin vein of mysticism running through Richmal's deep religious faith had attracted her to group meditation some years before it became more generally popular. A few like-minded friends met regularly for prayer and meditation, and Richmal had joined them soon after the group's inception in 1960. In addition to her faith, she brought to the group her equally strongly founded commonsense: 'She hasn't thought it out,' she said gently, of a friend who was convinced her life had been saved by a miracle. 'Trolley buses don't work that way.' And when it was reported that two women had seen a ghost – a man in 18th-century wig – in the church: 'Yes,' said Richmal. 'I know. Wearing knee-breeches and white stockings.' The assembled friends were agog: had Richmal *seen* him? There was no reply; 'just the twinkle, hailed with unanimous pleasure'. That down-to-earth quality provided a rock for others, too. When an eloquent speaker deplored 'the darkness of our life here below', the group listened respectfully, 'hearts failing for fear'. Richmal restored their sense of proportion with a thoughtful 'I don't think it's all *that* bad . . . ' It was to a friend in the meditation group that she made one of her rare caustic comments, with reference to someone about to emigrate: 'Oh, dear, another rat to leave the sinking ship!' One doesn't *say* that, murmured the friend. 'But one thinks it,' said Richmal.

Politics again excited her comment in the summer of 1963. In her reference to the scandal that brought down the Tory government, there is a strong suggestion of the traditional attitude of women in the Victorian era: that it must be accepted, however much it is to be deplored, that the male creature is sexually corruptible; and manifestations, however unpleasant, of that fact should not be allowed to interfere with the running of the country:

> It was all horrible... It's fantastic to think of the British constitution being shaken to its depths by a trivial little trollop... It makes the Parnell and Kitty O'Shea case seem highly respectable.

'It was a good fight and revealed unsuspected resources of courage and prowess in the Hubert Laneites. It ended in a general mix-up of Outlaws and Laneites in a muddy ditch. There Outlaws and Laneites sat up panting and covered with mud, and looked at each other.'

William – the Conqueror by Richmal Crompton.
Cartoon by Nicholas Garland: *New Statesman*, 11 Feb. 1977

By the time Miss Richardson left, in September 1963, to live with her brother in Australia, Richmal had regained relatively good health. She would not agree to employ another companion: with 'Ritchie's' help, she had come through the health crises of the last two or three years; now, she considered herself fit enough to live alone again. In the midst of frantic preparations ('I'm knee deep in little parcels...') for the next day's visit to her sister, Richmal wrote on Christmas Eve to a friend who had sent the latest Compton-Burnett novel (*A God and His Gifts*): 'I haven't been able to keep it till Christmas Day. I've opened the parcel and *revelled* in it – in fact just let everything go till I'd finished it! Her marvellous wit and deep penetration are as wonderful as ever. The plot may be a little thinner than in some of her books – but the reaction of the characters to each situation as it arises is what grips and holds me so – and the humour is so rapier-like and penetrating.' She had evidently given up all thought of producing another novel of her own; there were by now few references even to William in her letters. The new Liverpudlian phenomenon, however, provoked an animated response:

> I simply can't understand the effect they have on the young. I suspect that one contributing element is the tom-tom rhythm of the music(?), that rouses a sort of primitive frenzy in the hearers. I suppose that the savage is quite near the surface of civilization! I've listened to them and tried to understand but feel only fury and horror. One can only hope the craze will be short-lived!

The Beatles' music may have been anathema to Richmal, but the young John Lennon was among her greatest fans.

There is no clear reason for the stodginess of the 1964 collection, published in September, *William and the Witch*; Richmal had, after all, given old plots a new twist before with indisputable success. But the five stories in this new volume were dated, repetitive and too long; passably entertaining, perhaps, to a ten-year-old coming to William for the first time; but a great disappointment to established fans. Thomas

Henry's final illustrations of William accompanied three of the stories; the remaining two were illustrated by Henry Ford.

At 74, Richmal was still driving her car, despite at least one harrowing experience. Early in February 1965, she drove home from her sister's house in Bromley through a fog that grew so thick that visibility, by the time she reached Petts Wood, was reduced almost to inches. Having followed the slow crawl of lights ahead ('I didn't know where I was half the time'), she eventually reached her road, but was unable to find the drive leading to her own gateway. Undaunted, she left the car and groped for the kerb on hands and knees; a venture that would have reduced many an able-bodied younger driver to a quivering state of nerves.

She continued to enjoy London theatre as often as possible. In June, she wrote with urgency: 'We simply *must* see the C. Burnett play – "Family and Its Heritage".'; and with heartfelt irritation three weeks later, when the play had folded: 'It had such wonderful reviews – and to think that plays like "The Mousetrap" and "Oblomov" and all the other rubbish flourish like green bay trees!'

Early in July, another fall resulted in a torn ligament in the 'good' foot and Richmal had again to resort to her 'veteran' crutches. She reported casually: '. . . with both feet out of action, I've been a bit put to it to get around . . .' With the cooperation of Mrs Watts, her domestic help, however, she managed to avoid the 'fuss' she hated and before the end of the school holiday was able to provide the usual family outings, to theatre, ballet and exhibitions. One holiday treat of a less cultural nature that summer proved dramatic. In the middle of a circus performance, a pony went out of control and jumped over the barrier, into the ringside area occupied by Richmal, Mrs Ashbee, Edward and Kate. Richmal was knocked to the ground: ringmaster, circus proprietor and a doctor rushed to her aid, while the horrified audience held its breath and nine-year-old Kate 'wept unconsolably'. Richmal, however, safely restored to her seat, claimed that the only damage was 'a few bruises'. She insisted on sitting out the performance and, later, on driving the party home. When a journalist present asked for the reluctant heroine's name, 'I couldn't resist saying "Richmal Crompton" because the whole thing seemed, like William, to belong to the world of the impossible'.

The 1965 volume, *William and the Pop Singers*, saw him rubbing shoulders with sandalled and bearded Bohemians as well as with the winkle-pickered, drape-jacketed youths of the title story. Inspiration seems nevertheless to have been sadly lacking: Miss Thompson, a minor character in the story 'William and the Protest Marchers', is a replica of Miss Maple, a minor character in the novel *Linden Rise*, published thirteen years earlier. Both reluctantly agree to found a local branch of an animal-lovers society; and both find it impossible to approach people to join. Miss Maple:

> '. . . I made a list of people to ask in Priors Green, but – I can't ask them. I just *can't*, Richard. I get as far as the gate and then I go back. Sometimes I get right inside the house, and then I pretend I've come about something quite different. I simply can't ask them for subscriptions. I haven't got the courage. I've tried and tried and I can't . . .'

Miss Thompson:

> 'But, William, I *couldn't*,' said Miss Thompson earnestly. 'I *tried*. I got as far as people's garden gates and I learnt by heart what I'd planned to say to them and I couldn't go in and say it. I just haven't the courage for that sort of thing. Then I thought I'd wait till people came to collect subscriptions from me for *their* societies. But somehow I couldn't do it even then . . .'

They find the same solution, too:

> '. . . I pretended that I'd got members for it and I invented their names and addresses and I sent up two and six a year from each of them just as if they'd been real people . . .'

Even the amount of the fictional subscription was the same in 1965 as it had been in 1952. It seems, however, that the two ladies' inability to drum up charitable business was drawn from life: from their creator's own experiences as secretary of a local branch of the United Society for Christian Literature in the 1940s.

Richmal went through that Christmas on crutches, after 'another of my little falls'. Four days later, however, she was writing with satisfaction: 'I'm back to a stick, though I haven't attempted the car yet!' Gale-force winds in the New Year did not deter the frail and lame 75-year-old from going down to Chelsfield 'to give a hand with things' when the Ashbee family succumbed to influenza. Unable to ascend their drive against the blustery wind, she 'hailed a passing milk cart and the milkman and I did the journey arm-in-arm!'

Reading continued to provide her deepest pleasure in life. She seems conscientiously to have sampled, during these later years, the work of almost every modern novelist and short-story writer, from Kingsley Amis to Angus Wilson. With much greater enthusiasm, she devoured poetry ('she seemed to borrow or buy every new poet who put pen to paper'), history and philosophy (with a special affection for Plotinus). She reread the classic 18th- and 19th-century writers (with the possible exception of Scott, never mentioned in the extensive accounts of her reading matter); Henry James, Proust and Compton-Burnett; Elizabeth Bowen and the early work of Elizabeth Taylor. Current reading in February 1966 included a 'life of Engles (sic)', a duty read ('written by a friend of mine') and evidently not much enjoyed: 'Both people and period are *so* dull and bleak... I think I'll give myself a respite with *Mansfield Park* and Mrs Norris before I go on with it.' She more than once expressed an antipathy to 'dishonest' biography; and was appalled by Fred Bason's view, that it was acceptable for a biographer to report as fact an incident that could or might have happened. To solve Richmal's problems of transport (one hand for her stick, the other for the small attaché case in which she carried her current reading matter), a friend made her an apron with a front pocket large enough to carry several books. Richmal took to her 'marsupial pinny' at once and the friend was very pleased with herself – until she saw Richmal using the pouch to transport sherry glasses to the sitting-room.

When, in February, young Edward presented his great-aunt with a tape-recorder, explained its operation and asked her to tape a radio programme that was to be broadcast during school hours, she was less than confident of success. Her mechanical aptitude being on a par with her enthusiasm for politics and mathematics, the undertaking was certain to be fraught with pitfalls: 'I sat over it in a fever of anxiety but I'd forgotten to push something up or down (I've forgotten which) and the thing didn't take. He was very kind about it! I have to try again next Friday but I have a horrible feeling that the thing will get the better of me again. It *knows* that I'm frightened of it!' A month later, she reported with pride: 'I have now become quite skilled in the manipulation of the tape recorder and my last efforts have been masterly.'; though the progress from novice to master had not been without its setbacks: 'I was very much puzzled last week by a small piece of black tubing that was in the box with the other things. I couldn't think where it fitted on, then discovered that it was a "liquorice all-sort" that the young gentleman must have dropped into the box accidentally during one of his private feasts.'

The relationship between Edward – now, like William, eleven – and Richmal was still very close. She noted in April: 'Edward and I still seem to speak the same language. I hope, as one always does, that it will last.' When he had to take an entrance exam in London, some days before his parents could return from their archaeological work in the Scilly Isles, Edward spent a few days with Richmal at Beechworth. That his great-aunt's culinary interest had not developed much beyond the hesitantly proffered tomatoes-on-toast of Toc H canteen days presented no problem: 'Fortunately he adores frozen food and those "paella" things you get in packets, so not much cooking will be needed!'

In April she reported the recent visit of a Swedish William fan and his wife. Richmal was entertained to learn that a Swedish radio programme had broadcast street interviews with passers-by on the subject of William; and was inclined to agree with the programme's conclusion: 'Yes, I think I've worked out all my criminal tendencies on the boy!' The title story of the 1966 collection, *William and the Masked Ranger*, saw the criminal spirit of William briefly revived; though the following extract is the very last echo of William as his older fans knew and loved him. The Outlaws have decided (for very involved reasons) to add, by means of forged postscripts, an historical flavour to a collection of letters written circa 1900:

> 'Yes,' said William. 'We'll put a bit of hist'ry in all of them an' that'll make it a hist'ry mirror in day-by-day life all right.'
>
> They set to work with energy.
>
> An account of a Church Bazaar ended with the words: 'P.S. Christopher Columbus has jus' set off to discover America. I hope he gets there all right.'
>
> An account of the local Point-to-Point ended with the words: 'P.S. I saw in the paper this morning that Charles the First has been executed. We'll have to wait till 1660 for the restoration.'

> Henry, whose energies were chiefly taken up in supervising the spelling of the other three, tried to confine his historical references within certain roughly defined limits. 'Mr. Bell's just invented the telephone. We're going to have one put in next week.'... 'Queen Victoria went up in one of the new balloons this morning. They wanted to reach outer space but the gas began to leak and they had to make a forced landing.'... 'The Black Hole of Calcutta took place yesterday and tomorrow the six hundred are going to ride into the Valley of Death.'
>
> William's references spanned the whole field of history with wild abandon. 'Henry VIII got married to the third of his six wives this morning'... 'I went down to Hastings yesterday to watch the battle. Harold looked as if he'd got an arrow in his eye.'... 'I helped Guy Fawkes carry gunpowder into the House of Commons last night. We nearly got caught by a policeman.'... 'The civil war broke out yesterday. I'm going to enlist in the roundheads.'... 'I went to London in a horse-coach last week. It took hours and hours. I shall be jolly glad when someone invents railways'... 'I was helping to put out the fire of London all yesterday. I feel rotten this morning. I think I must have caught the plague.'

On the eve of her departure at the beginning of September for the Chichester Festival ('... I feel that it isn't worth the uprooting – but will, I know, feel quite differently once I've fought my way through packing, putting off milk and papers and all the rest of it. I'm looking forward to "Macbeth" and "The Cherry Orchard".), Richmal recorded her present 'glorious hodge-podge of books': '*Pride and Prejudice* over my meals, *The Betrothed* in bed, *The Way We Live Now* in the car (for odd moments of waiting for people or things); and Teilhard de Chardin in the evenings... Freddie Bason brought me a little book *The Best Of Hazlitt* and I dip into that, too, every now and then.'

Her April 1967 reading list she described as 'a very odd collection of oddments': 'In bed, *Paradise Lost* and *Villette* (you wouldn't think they'd mix, but they do!). Out of bed, I've just finished Fitzgibbon's *Life of Dylan Thomas* and am now reading *Millais and the Ruskins*... for light reading I've just finished Graham Green's (sic) *The Power and the Glory* and embarked on a novel of Anthony Burgess, just to see what it's like!' By August, she was still with Charlotte Brontë and back with

Henry James: '... reading *Shirley* in bed and *The Europeans* at meals. I got *Lord Dismiss Us* [Michael Campbell] from the library as it has so many good reviews ... All books about boys' boarding schools these days seem to consist solely of adolescent love affairs between the boys! I think it's highly exaggerated ... When I've finished *Shirley* I think I'll re-embark on Proust.'

Having been held responsible, a decade earlier, for the emergence of Britain's Angry Young Men, she was perhaps not too taken aback in September when someone suggested that the creator of William should be hailed as the 'Mother of the Beat Generation'. Her response implies that she shared the view attributed to the chronicler of the movement, Jack Kerouac, that the Beat Generation was basically religious: 'I feel quite gratified ... I don't think they've left the world much worse then they've found it!' On *Enter Patricia* (1927), discovered by a friend in a secondhand-book shop, she was a little vague: 'I think it must have been written about 1920 or so and I think that the bits and pieces of it were published in a now-defunct magazine called *The Humourist* (sic). I hadn't read it since then, but I dug it out when I got your letter and read it again and even laughed once or twice. It carries in it – rather pathetically – something of the atmosphere of care-free innocence that one associates (probably wrongly!) with those days.'

On the 16th November, the day after her seventy-seventh birthday, she reported: 'I was at Richmal's for the day yesterday and when I got back about 10, I found a car waiting by the gate. It was a lorry-driver who comes over from Tooting every year with his girl friend to bring me a birthday card and a box of chocolates! He has all the William books. I provided coffee and cakes and then they set off for Tooting again.'

Three months later, early in February 1968, Richmal tripped over a rug in her hallway and broke her 'good' leg. After it had been set, and encased in non-weight-bearing plaster, she insisted on being returned home. With both legs out of action, however, independence was no longer so easy to maintain. Mrs Watts, her domestic help, remained on weekdays till after lunch, but 'she and the family were terribly worried at the thought of my tottering about on crutches during the rest of the day and evening'. Richmal concluded, noticeably subdued: '... so in the end the doctor got me a bed here [Farnborough Hospital] and I shall be here for a few weeks (I'm not quite sure how many) and when I have this plaster taken off and a weight-bearing plaster put on I gather that I shall return home.' Three days later, her natural optimism yet further reduced, she reported: 'I'm still vegetating here... It's an odd regime – so many pathetic people in the ward that I'm beginning to feel pathetic myself!' It was a distressing period also for those who loved her. Mrs Ashbee vividly recalls the horror she felt on hearing a member of the nursing staff refer indulgently to her patient as 'a funny old thing'. On the 23rd, however, after glumly noting, 'I don't take kindly to hospital life. I think I must lack the human touch that makes the whole world kin...', Richmal brightened sufficiently to respond to news of a friend's writing efforts: 'I don't yet feel that I can settle down to writing proper but (you've) inspired me to pin down a William plot that's been hovering in my mind for some time and refused to settle.'

Further stimulation was provided by the visting friend who lent her a book 'proving that Bacon wrote Shakespeare's plays'. 'The wretch of an author,' Richmal wrote indignantly, 'referred to S. as an "unlettered peasant"... He says that it was common knowledge among contemporaries that Bacon wrote the plays. If so, it's strange that there is no mention in contemporary letters or literature. He points out too that there was no general mourning of S's death; but I don't think that his contemporaries appreciated him at his worth. They preferred the "classical" drama of Jonson... The people who say that Marlowe wrote the plays are more irritating still. There isn't a glimpse of S's poetry or vision in Marlowe's work. (I hate "Tamburlaine"!)' An unashamed 'Shakespeare addict', Richmal had revealed her scorn of the Bacon theory three and a half decades earlier, in the story 'William Holds the Stage':

> 'Now,' continued the headmaster rather maliciously, 'I want one of you to give me a short account of Mr. Welbecker's lecture. Let any one of you who thinks he can do so put up his hand.'
>
> Only one hand went up, and it was William's.
>
> 'Well, Brown?' said the headmaster.
>
> 'Please sir, he told us that he thinks that the plays of Shakespeare were really written by a man called Ham and that Shakespeare poisoned this man called Ham and stole the plays and then pretended he'd written them. And then a man called Bacon pushed a woman into a pond because he wanted to marry his mother. And there's a man called Eggs, but I've forgotten what he did except that–'

Mr. Welbecker's complexion had assumed a greenish hue.
'That will do, Brown,' said the headmaster very quietly.[34]

The Rev. Simon Bannister, then chaplain to Farnborough Hospital (and later, coincidentally, priest to St. Mark's, Bury: the parish in which Richmal spent her childhood), visited her frequently and administered Holy Communion during the remaining three weeks of her stay. Whatever she suffered in pain or worry did not detract from the warmth and animation of her conversation, he recalls; little Miss Lamburn was 'always good to talk to'.

When she returned at last to the blessed privacy of Beechworth, life was inevitably more difficult than before. She recounted with obvious enjoyment one incident that occurred shortly after her return home. Finding crawling more effective than struggling with crutches, she had dragged herself along the floor to answer the doorbell. The visitor, stunned by the door's having opened apparently through some invisible agency, was doubly confused by Richmal's amusement ('There I was, like something out of Doctor Who') at his reaction; and when she crawled away to fetch a pencil and brought it back in her mouth, the flustered caller departed in haste. Waking late one night to see a hand groping for the bedroom window-catch, Richmal switched on the bedside light and settled down to read; in the morning, she had her doors and windows checked and the locks and catches replaced where necessary. One friend believes that in this, as in her refusal to make concessions to ill health and disability, Richmal was 'simply trusting God, and so had no fears'; but that, perhaps, does not do full justice to her courage.

By June, four months after her accident, she was determinedly reporting herself 'now quite fit again'. The continuing thrice-weekly visits to Farnborough Hospital were a necessary bore: 'I still can't walk much (except with a couple of sticks – very warily and uncertainly) but I find now that I can drive the car (already adapted for the unbroken leg driving!), which is a great joy.' A letter early in November, to a friend who had embarked on life as a mature student, brought a reminder of Richmal's schoolmistress past: 'Greek Literature, of course, is quite the world's loveliest . . . I hope you're reading Sophocles and Euripides in translation?' Of her 78th birthday, on the 15th, she reported: 'I had a very happy birthday with Richmal and family and on the Sunday we all gathered at my sister's for a family Celebration . . . the day was well and truly honoured.'

Five days after that birthday, the thirty-seventh volume of William's adventures (*William the Superman*) was published; and on the same day appeared the most accurate and least trite of all the articles ever written about his creator. Those who knew Richmal took issue only with the title of Madeleine Harmsworth's *Daily Mirror* article: 'The Old Lady Of Beechworth'.

It had been, Richmal noted in December, 'a year of upsets' for the whole family: her brother's wife had died, and Edward and Kate had each had a spell in hospital. By Christmas, however, life seemed to have become a little calmer and she was able to report another Christmas Day spent in the bosom of her family: 'We spent the day at Richmal's and had a lovely time. Paul cooked the turkey, Edward made the trifle and Kate made the Christmas cake . . . ' She added, prophetically: 'It may be our last Christmas together, as Paul has been appointed Lecturer in Archaeology at the East Anglian University and they will be living in or near Norwich. I shall miss them very much, of course, but I'm lucky to have had them near me so long.'

An old friend from her teaching days, a former pupil, was due to visit Beechworth on January 11th, a Saturday. Early that morning, however, Richmal rang to postpone the visit; she thought she might be 'coming down with 'flu'. The telephone call to friends nearer at hand, in Chislehurst, was more urgent but still undramatic: she was very sorry to bother them, but could they possibly come round? They drove immediately over to Beechworth, and found her in the middle of another coronary attack. They summoned the doctor, packed a case for her ('Find me a Trollope book . . . ') and notified the family; but not long after her arrival at Farnborough Hospital, Richmal died.

The obituary notices would doubtless have amused Richmal. Several of the daily papers dwelt on the 'unfinished story lying across her desk'. One can almost hear her mild comment to the effect that it would be more startling, in such circumstances, to find a writer's desk clear of work. There is equally little doubt that her amusement would have turned rueful over the percentage of obituary space allotted to her novels – William hogging the limelight yet again. Much of the fortune created principally by him had earlier been directed toward the establishment of a family trust; much of what remained was to go to the continued support of religious charities, and of organizations working for the physically handicapped.

Five stories for the next book were ready. The unfinished story was completed by her niece and literary executor, Richmal Ashbee; and *William the Lawless*, the thirty-eighth and final new volume of his adventures, was published in 1970. The print order was not high, and mint copies of this last William book are therefore much sought after by collectors – even at the current secondhand price of £85. A secondhand copy of one of the forty Richmal Crompton novels, should you be so fortunate as to find one, would cost you only a pound or so.

Obscurity was not to be William's destiny. Each episode of the most recent (1977) television series was awaited as eagerly by parents as by their offspring. Jealous of the pleasure to be derived from dipping in to the best of William, we do not hand down the familiar red volumes; we allow our children to borrow them. The range of devoted William fans has long encompassed all sorts and conditions of men, from luminaries of rock music (Rick Wakeman, the late John Lennon) to at least one Cabinet Minister (Norman Tebbit). Respected novelists are happy to confess their addiction, and often their debt, to William; and at least one literary critic has used him to illustrate a point (Auberon Waugh: 'The only writer I can think of who uses childish vernacular successfully is Richmal Crompton of Just William fame.') Writers as diverse as Georgette Heyer and Alan Coren have admired Richmal's craft; publications as diverse as the *Daily Mail* and the *New Statesman* have reproduced William's image in political caricature. The 'Hello, Cheekie!' radio team, in a sketch entitled 'Bookshelf', invented a 'latest title' (*William and the Perverts*); while a *Guardian* crossword clue immortalized both creator and created: 'Novelist thought of William – or Mr Pat McNichol, possibly (7,8)'.

Dennis the Menace and his mongrel Gnasher, in their weekly *Beano* encounters with Soppy Walter (leader of the polite, maths-loving Softies), frequently and unmistakeably bring to mind early William plots. At a more elevated level, an *Observer* Review article on Peterhouse men attributed to Colin Welch a 'magisterial authority' and a reputation as writer and wit, before stating, no less reverently: 'He is an authority on the "William" books.' Dennis Potter, giving his choice of literary extracts on Radio 4, placed William in the company of the Bible, T. S. Eliot and Hazlitt. Keith Waterhouse, inspired by a report on Marxist influence in education, wrote a skilful pastiche for

Punch: 'William the Marxist', which sees the adult Browns welcoming a National Front speaker and William determined to thwart the 'fashist skum'. Richmal herself would probably most have appreciated Leslie Thomas's account of his devotion to the six William books that comprised all his worldly goods on his arrival at a Dr. Barnardo's Home in the 1940s.

William lives on, indeed. The family that claimed 'throughout our lives, we have quoted William as some people quote Shakespeare' was by no means untypical of the many who, filled with regret that they had never communicated their gratitude to Richmal Crompton, now wrote from all over the world to offer their sympathy to her family. But perhaps the most fitting of all the tributes was a brief eulogy from Spain, which concluded:

> The 'mother' of William will have presented herself before God with her arms full of children's smiles.

References

1. *Matty and the Dearingroydes* (1956).
2. *Anne Morrison.*
3. *The Innermost Room.*
4. *The Bury Times.*
5. *More William.*
6. *Just – William.*
7. *Happy Mag* February 1925 & *Still – William.*
8. For details of this television series, see *William – a Bibliography* by W. Lofts & D. Adley.
9. *Penrod.*
10. *Penrod and Sam.*
11. 'William Leads a Better Life', *William the Conqueror.*
12. 'Not Much', *Home* October 1922 & *William Again.*
13. 'William and the Smuggler', *Home* February 1920 & *More William.*
14. 'William and White Satin', *Home* November 1919 & *Just – William.*
15. 'William Goes to the Pictures', *Home* April 1919 & *Just – William.*
16. 'Jumble', *Home* May 1919 & *Just – William.*
17. 'Georgie and the Outlaws', *Happy Mag* May 1927 & *William – the Outlaw.*
18. 'The Show', *Home* June 1919 & *Just – William.*
19. *William Again.*
20. *William.*
21. *Still – William.*
22. *Female Friends*, Fay Weldon (Heinemann).
23. 'William and the Prize Cat'.
24. 'The Pennymans Hand on the Torch'.
25. 'William, Prime Minister'.
26. 'The Row'.
27. 'William and the Eastern Curse'.
28. Published by John Murray Ltd.
29. *William – the Showman.*
30. Foreword to the Bodley Head Press collection of Leacock's works.
31. *Quartet.*
32. *A Final Burning of Boats, etc.*, Ethel Smyth (Longmans, Green & Co.).
33. *William's Crowded Hours.*
34. *William – the Pirate.*
35. *Sweet William.*
36. *William – the Gangster.*
37. *William – the Fourth.*
38. *Just William's Luck*, based on the 1947 film and published in April 1948.
39. Julian Denham in all but the final episode of this third radio series.
40. 'William and the Haunted Cottage'.
41. 'William's Thoughtful Act'.
42. The Lofts & Adley Bibliography gives details of the different editions published.

Bibliography

NOVELS by Richmal Crompton	first published in
The Innermost Room	1923 (Andrew Melrose)
The Hidden Light	1924 (Hodder & Stoughton)
Anne Morrison	1925 (Jarrolds)
The Wildings	1925 (Hodder & Stoughton)
The House	1926 (Hodder & Stoughton)
David Wilding	1926 (Hodder & Stoughton)
Leadon Hill	1927 (Hodder & Stoughton)
Millicent Dorrington	1927 (Hodder & Stoughton)
The Thorn Bush	1928 (Hodder & Stoughton)
Roofs Off!	1928 (Hodder & Stoughton)
The Four Graces	1929 (Hodder & Stoughton)
Abbots' End	1929 (Hodder & Stoughton)
Blue Flames	1930 (Hodder & Stoughton)
Naomi Godstone	1930 (Hodder & Stoughton)
Portrait Of a Family	1931 (Macmillan)
The Odyssey of Euphemia Tracey	1932 (Macmillan)
Marriage of Hermione	1932 (Macmillan)
The Holiday	1933 (Macmillan)
Chedsy Place	1934 (Macmillan)
The Old Man's Birthday	1934 (Macmillan)
Quartet	1935 (Macmillan)
Caroline	1936 (Macmillan)
There Are Four Seasons	1937 (Macmillan)
Journeying Wave	1938 (Macmillan)
Merlin Bay	1939 (Macmillan)
Steffan Green	1940 (Macmillan)
Narcissa	1941 (Macmillan)
Mrs Frensham Describes a Circle	1942 (Macmillan)
Weatherley Parade	1944 (Macmillan)
Westover	1946 (Hutchinson)
The Ridleys	1947 (Hutchinson)
Family Roundabout	1948 (Hutchinson)
Frost at Morning	1950 (Hutchinson)
Linden Rise	1952 (Hutchinson)
The Gypsy's Baby	1954 (Hutchinson)
Four in Exile	1955 (Hutchinson)
Matty & the Dearingroydes	1956 (Hutchinson)
Blind Man's Buff	1957 (Hutchinson)
Wiseman's Folly	1959 (Hutchinson)
The Inheritor	1960 (Hutchinson)

Volumes of SHORT STORIES/SKETCHES by Richmal Crompton

Kathleen & I and of course Veronica	1926 (Hodder & Stoughton)
Enter – Patricia	1927 (Newnes)
A Monstrous Regiment	1927 (Hutchinson)
Mist & Other Stories	1928 (Hutchinson)
The Middle Things	1928 (Hutchinson)
Felicity Stands By	1928 (Newnes)
Sugar & Spice	1929 (Ward, Lock & Co.)
Ladies First	1929 (Hutchinson)
The Silver Birch	1931 (Hutchinson)
The First Morning	1936 (Hutchinson)

OTHER WORKS by Richmal Crompton

Published by Newnes:

Just – William	1922
More William	1922
William Again	1923
William – the Fourth	1924
Still William	1925
William the Conqueror	1926
William – in Trouble	1927
William – the Outlaw	1927
William – the Good	1928
William	1929
William – the Bad	1930
William's Happy Days	1930
William's Crowded Hours	1931
William – the Pirate	1932
William – the Rebel	1933
William – the Gangster	1934
William – the Detective	1935
Sweet William	1936
William – the Showman	1937
William – the Dictator	1938
William and A.R.P. (William's Bad Resolution)	1939
JUST WILLIAM Book of the Film	1939
William and the Evacuees (William the Film Star)	1940
William Does His Bit	1941
William Carries On	1942
William and the Brains Trust (William – the Hero)	1945
Just William's Luck	1948
Jimmy	1949
William – the Bold	1950
Jimmy Again	1951
William and the Tramp	1952
William and the Moon Rocket	1954
William and the Space Animal	1956
William's Television Show	1958
William – the Explorer	1960
William's Treasure Trove	1962
William and the Witch	1964
William and the Pop Singers	1965
William and the Masked Ranger	1966
William the Superman	1968
William the Lawless	1970

Published by J. Garnett Miller, Ltd.:

William and the Artist's Model (a play)	1956

Photograph Acknowledgements

Plates 1 to 5: Richmal Ashbee collection. Plate 6: Richmal Ashbee collection, Nancy Bowden. Plate 7: Richmal Ashbee collection. Plate 8: Richmal Ashbee collection, Nancy Bowden. Plate 9: *Bury Times*, Richmal Ashbee collection. Plate 10: Richmal Ashbee collection. Plate 11: Roy Williams courtesy of David Schutte, Richmal Ashbee collection. Plate 12: Roy Williams courtesy of David Schutte, Richmal Ashbee collection. Plate 13: Richmal Ashbee collection. Plate 14: Richmal Ashbee collection, Planet News Ltd. Plate 15: Roy Williams courtesy of David Schutte, Richmal Ashbee collection, Roy Williams courtesy of David Schutte, Roy Williams. Plate 16: Roy Williams, Richmal Ashbee collection.

Illustration Acknowledgements

The illustrations by Gordon Grant from *Penrod* by Booth Tarkington (copyright 1913, 1914 by Booth Tarkington) are reprinted by permission of Doubleday & Co. Inc. The illustrations on pp. 66, 92, 94, 97, 111, 112, 113, 114, 117, 122, 125, 130, 156, 162, 166, 169, 178, 181, 187, 208 and 222 and on front and back covers are reprinted by permission of The Hamlyn Publishing Group Limited; cartoon by Nicholas Garland by permission of New Statesman; illustration p. 109 reprinted by permission of Jarrolds Publishers London Ltd.; illustration p. 127 reprinted by permission of Hodder and Stoughton Ltd; illustrations pp. 138 and 141 reprinted by permission of Macmillan and Co. Ltd.; illustrations pp. 168, 175, 189, 195 and 198 by permission of Hutchinson and Co. (Publishers) Ltd., illustration p. 197 reproduced by permission of J. Garnet Miller Ltd., illustrations pp. 11, 17, 19, 37, 39, 49, 57, 60, 103, 121, 129, 154, 206 and 211 by Roy Williams.

Index

Afterword

What a lovely book. How good to find so much goodness. The reassurance that resounds in that name: *Richmal Crompton*! Her naughty boys, William, Douglas, Henry and Ginger, foreshadowed four others: John, George, Paul and Ringo – and had this brave, amused old lady met *them* for afternoon tea (by no means an improbability then) she would assuredly have come to conclusions far removed from those offered on page 211, as Kay Williams and her distinguished illustrator could confirm. Each has served both foursomes well in their time.

Derek Taylor